D0927882

RICHARD PETERS

Richard Peters, 1848.
(Georgia Department of Archives and History)

RICHARD PETERS: CHAMPION OF THE NEW SOUTH

Royce Shingleton

MERCER

ISBN 0-86554-126-4

Richard Peters: Champion of the New South
Copyright ©1985
Mercer University Press, Macon GA 31207
All rights reserved
Printed in the United States of America

All books published by Mercer University Press
are produced on acid-free paper that exceeds
the minimum standards set by the
National Historical Publications and Records Commission.

Library of Congress Cataloging in Publication Data

Shingleton, Royce.
   Richard Peters: champion of the new South

  Bibliography: p. 245.
  Includes index.
    1. Peters, Richard, 1810-1889. 2. Businessmen—
Southern States—Biography. 3. Politicians—Southern
States—Biography. 4. Southern States—Economic
conditions.   I. Title.
HC1025.P44S55   1984   338'.04'0924 [B]   84-22701
ISBN 0-86554-126-4 (alk. paper)

CONTENTS

In memory
of my parents

and to
Dr. John Dixon
Dr. David Hewett
Dr. B. R. Tilley

And there are some who have no memorial. . . .
But these were men of mercy, whose righteous
deeds have not been forgotten; their
posterity will continue forever, and
their glory will not be blotted out.
            Ecclesiasticus 44:9-10, 13

PREFACE

Southern themes have been cultivated by historians with an intensity unparalleled in the study of any other region in America. Yet one of these topics, the New South, lacks precision. The New South is not a place name, nor is it precisely a time period. Rather, the concept has the color of a slogan, and unlike the time-set of the Old South, has often proven useful through several chronological periods as a propaganda device for some phase of Southern development. To Edwin De Leon of South Carolina, who first used the slogan in an article in *Putnam's* in 1870, the New South was a blueprint for the regeneration of the region following the Civil War—an article of faith, a vision of the future. This is how the term is most commonly used and how it applies in this work.

The New South, in this case, identifies the credo of Southern journalists and business leaders who worked for implementation of certain economic proposals. While the Old South consisted of the cotton culture worked by the slave system, coupled with the ambition of all farmers to become plantation owners and be accorded the privileges of that class, the New South saw a change of goals. After the Civil War, farming became a business rather than a way of life. The basic difference was the social goals of the one and the economic goals of the other. But there were other differences. The New South was characterized by an interest in a variety of crops, the application of industry and science to agriculture, development of natural resources and transportation, and notably, emphasis on urban growth.

Today, the New South creed has triumphed. Most Americans are now remarkably alike because regional features have greatly diminished within the South. However, for decades the New South philosophy failed to take root among rural Southerners, as they continued to depend on one staple crop and to resist what they considered the evils of diversification, industrialization, and urbanization. For reasons not entirely their own fault, it was next to impossible to get farmers out of the habit of cotton dependency. Another drawback was the freight rates set by Northern-dominated railroads. Manufactured goods moving southward received preferential rates, as did raw materials en route to the North. The effect was to maintain the South as a colony—a supplier of raw materials to the industrial North. These two major obstacles, Southern farmers and Northern capitalists, stunted the growth of the South's natural economic advantages. Because it was the business-oriented Southern urbanites who reflected the values of the New South, the cities of the region were the keys to the vision of an economically independent South.

After 1880, New South spokesmen multiplied rapidly. Most of the notable voices were well educated for their time and had been too young to serve in the Civil War, thereby attaining maturity during Reconstruction. Although their formative years coincided with the greatest failure of the South, these New South prophets believed the plight of their section was perpetuated by the conditions in the Old South rather than defeat in the war. To them, wealth and power did not flow from fields of white cotton but from machines and factories. They looked to the all-important Northern capital to invest in the South in their attempt to convert Southern poverty into prosperity. Not only did they preach reconciliation between North and South, but also Old South and New, rich and poor, black and white, farmer and businessman.

Quick-witted Henry W. Grady, by far the most important and renowned of the New South prophets, was born in 1850 in Athens, Georgia. After graduating from the University of Georgia in 1868 and editing two newspapers in Rome, Georgia, Grady arrived in Atlanta in 1872 and helped found the *Atlanta Herald*. The paper became a casualty of the depression during the decade and carried down with it the last of Grady's inheritance. But in 1879 he borrowed $20,000 and purchased a fourth interest in the *Atlanta Constitution*.

Although Grady had a boyishness that he never completely outgrew, he was sobered by his budding power as an editor. A born journalist, he gave considerable attention to state politics, but he also began to plead the cause that brought him fame. On the night of 31 August 1886, when the east coast was rocked by its worst recorded earthquake, Grady went to the Charleston, South Carolina, area to report from the center of the disaster. His articles on the damage received favorable attention in the North, resulting in an invitation to speak to the prestigious New England Society at Delmonico's in New York. There he delivered his powerful "New South" speech—the first of several addresses in various parts of the country—and one in which he maintained that holding on to Civil War animosities was more evil than good. It was probably the most famous after-dinner speech in American history, and when Grady sat down, he was a national figure.

In Boston in December 1889, Grady delivered his famous "funeral oration" in which he urged the South to industrialize. This description of the burial of a Confederate veteran became immensely popular with New South ideologues: "They buried him in a New York coat and a Boston pair of shoes and a pair of breeches from Chicago and a shirt from Cincinnati, leaving him with nothing to carry into the next world with him to remind him of the country in which he lived, and for which he fought for four years, but the chill of blood in his veins, and the marrow in his bones." Ironically, Grady himself had only days to live; he died of pneumonia shortly after returning to Atlanta. Grady was not an original thinker, but he was the foremost proselytizer of the dynamic spirit of the South.

While Grady was the greatest symbol of the New South, the leading practitioner of the movement must have been Richard Peters. Well known in his own day, Peters has been virtually lost in time chiefly because Grady—the one man most likely to perpetuate Peters's memory—died prematurely. Yet, the New South historian, by studying the philosophy and contributions of Richard Peters, can reach closer to the truth concerning the source of Grady's inspiration. Such study reveals that Grady's New South ideals attained focus and matured following his formal interviews and informal visits with Peters. Indeed, for a decade prior to his New South speech in New York, Grady learned firsthand the basic tenets of the New South creed as practiced by Peters—transportation, urbanization, diversification, conciliation, and industrialization.

Therefore, the career of Peters, a striking example of enlightened self-interest, is the story of the emergence of the New South. To him, the New

South had its origins in the antebellum era, rather than beginning after the Civil War; he saw no sharp division in goals between the *ancien regime* and the new order. If there was a single Southern business leader of the nineteenth century who promoted New South tenets in as many ways and for so long a time as did Peters, he has escaped my scrutiny. Peters's life, as Grady knew, is a matrix for the New South creed.

ACKNOWLEDGMENTS

It has been said that the introductory pages of a book are the last written and the least read. I hope that is not true in the latter case, because not only do historians draw from the works of earlier writers—many of whom belong to generations past and all of whom receive proper credit in the literary trappings that accompany works such as this—but from librarians, archivists, and others of the present generation who stand ready with material and suggestions that often lead to "pay dirt." In preparing this study, more records administrators helped than can conveniently be named here, but the services of all have been received with most grateful appreciation.

Much of the material for the book came from manuscripts, newspapers, and illustrations maintained by the Atlanta Historical Society. First credit properly goes to the society's eminent historian, Franklin Garrett, whose suggestions have been very much appreciated. The society's archivists, Richard Eltzroth and Grace Sherry, were uniformly cooperative and gracious during the many months that I made use of the resources in the archives division—first in cramped basement quarters and then in the society's splendid modern complex.

The usual prompt and professional reference services were rendered by my friend and former classmate, Jane Adams, Central Research Division archivist, Georgia Department of Archives and History. I would also like to express my gratitude to the staffs of the Atlanta Public Library; Emory University Library; Fulton County Courthouse; Fulton County Administration Building; Georgia Surveyor General's Department; University of Georgia Libraries; Southern Historical Collection, University of North Carolina; and the Military Archives Division, National Archives and Records Service. Of particular value, too, has been the dedicated service of the Albany Junior College Interlibrary Loan personnel and other library staff members—Debbie White, Kay Lowry, and Mary Washington. A special bouquet is accorded Mrs. Ralph Peters Black, Jr., great-granddaughter-in-law of Peters. Mrs. Black supported the project with material from the family holdings, material that was not otherwise obtainable.

Finally, and not merely because it is customary, the list must include my family: Royce, Jr., who has never known a time when his father was not working on a manuscript; young Justin, who has not known such a time as well and who constantly asked when it would end; and my wife, Ruth, who helped in countless ways, including the typing of the manuscript.

CHAPTER ONE

SUNRISE: PENNSYLVANIA HERITAGE

I n July 1864 the northern sky glowed red in the predawn darkness enveloping Atlanta. Suddenly, a pounding on the door shattered the slumber of the Richard Peters household at the corner of Mitchell and Forsyth streets. Peters opened the door. David Mayer of the governor's staff brought news that Confederate General Joseph E. Johnston had crossed the Chattahoochee River and burned the Western and Atlantic Railroad bridge behind him. Over the treetops toward Marietta, smoke was rising in the coming light. Union General William T. Sherman was closing on Atlanta.[1]

Peters, thinking troops from Sherman's invading army of over 100,000 men would enter the city by noon, decided to send his family to Augusta immediately and soon left the house to secure passage on a Georgia Railroad train. Space was at a premium, but as one of the railroad's directors, he was able to take possession of a freight car. He went next to the Georgia

---

Railroad Bank building and gathered the assets of the bank. Finally, he hurried home where his wife had packed some of the family valuables—clothing, bedding, silver, and jewels. He quickly moved his family, the bank money, and his personal goods to the railroad station.

Working their way through a large, excited crowd at the depot, they loaded the bank assets and personal baggage in the freight car. Peters then helped his wife and five children board the car, the children nestling on bags of gold. They were on the Georgia Railroad's last train out of Atlanta before Sherman's troops cut the rail. Hiring a guard to accompany his family to Augusta, Peters remained behind in the hope that he could protect his property.[2]

The locomotive noisily gained traction and pulled away from the depot, heading toward Decatur, where his wife had lived when he first met her. Back then he had been superintendent of the railroad that was now carrying her and their children into the distance. The daughter of a physician-entrepreneur, she had married Peters, a boarder at her father's hotel, while a young girl. Peters was well established prior to the marriage and the couple had enjoyed an affluent life in early Atlanta. Now, as the train rumbled out of sight to the east and the invading army closed in, Peters must have wondered whether he would again see her and the children.

Who was Richard Peters? In the beginning, his education and judgment, along with some family influence in Philadelphia, were his chief assets, for he had no money. Although one arm was crooked at the elbow as a result of a boyhood accident, he radiated excellent health. He was a robust, handsome man with fair hair that surmounted gray, forceful eyes set in a ruddy face of fine features, and this cast of countenance was underpinned by a strong jaw.[3] In maturity, he had the air of a man who successfully managed his affairs, being a quiet-spoken businessman. He led a happy, disciplined life, possessing a ready humor, void of temperamental outbursts. At home with his sons and daughters, he taught quaint, everyday maxims they were not likely to forget, such as "Take both hands to what you do." Yet he was philosophical concerning matters beyond his influence: "If the weather be wet, don't fret, if the weather be cold, don't scold, but, with

---

[2]Richard Peters, "Personal Recollections," *Richard Peters: His Ancestors and Descendants*, comp. Nellie P. Black (Atlanta: Foote and Davies, 1904) 29.

[3]Helen K. Lyon, "Richard Peters: Atlanta Pioneer—Georgia Builder," *Atlanta Historical Bulletin* 38:10 (December 1957): 25.

the weather that's sent, learn to be content."[4] His unerring display of common sense caused young Henry W. Grady, in one of his first Peters interviews, to describe him as a "practical old man."[5]

In his rise from a penniless youth to a public benefactor, Peters reflected the two standard creeds of nineteenth-century America. He first concentrated on promotion within the organization, in his case the railroad industry. As a neophyte engineer, he came of age in the 1830s when America was beginning its love affair with the railroads. During this transitional period of the nation's industrial development, he later added the second creed of success—alertness, judgment, and luck in seizing opportunities in a new town. He was a speculator first and a home-seeker second. Like many others who settled in the new towns across America, Peters was a vigorous man whose canny instinct for trade prospects enabled him to choose one of the best sites. Other men of his ilk include San Francisco's Theodore D. Judah, Seattle's Thomas Burke, Chicago's William B. Ogden, Cincinnati's Daniel Drake, and Denver's William Larimer.

Indeed, Peters could well be the prototype of *Businessman Americanus*, a term Daniel Boorstin applied to this particular type of community leader in the "upstart" cities of the nineteenth century. This businessman, referred to more recently as a "booster,"[6] interfused public and private prosperity; that is, he intermingled his own destiny with that of the community. His two chief commodities were land and transportation, and his most important community service was to attract people to the city. "Not to boost your city showed both a lack of community spirit and lack of business sense," concluded Boorstin.[7]

---

[4]Black, *Richard Peters*, 31-32.

[5]Scrapbook, Henry W. Grady Collection, Special Collections Department, Emory University Library, Atlanta.

[6]"Urban boosterism—dismissed by most historians as supersalesmanship or mindless hoopla—was actually an expression of the urban ethos," wrote Blaine Brownell. He defined urban ethos as a "conception of the city which stressed . . . both urban growth and social order in such a way that they would be mutually reinforcing." Brownell concluded that we should take boosterism seriously; it was "more complex and substantive than most historians have suggested." Blaine A. Brownell, *The Urban Ethos in the South, 1920-1930* (Baton Rouge: Louisiana State University Press, 1975) xix.

[7]Daniel J. Boorstin, *The Americans: The National Experience* (New York: Random House, 1967) 115-23; Thomas C. Cochran, *Business in American Life: A History* (New York: McGraw-Hill, 1972) 146; Glenn C. Quiett, *They Built the West: An Epic of Rails and Cities* (New York: D. Appleton-Century Company, 1934) 180, 194; Blake McKelvey, *The Urbanization of America, 1860-1915* (New Brunswick: Rutgers University Press, 1963) 34.

Most of these upstart cities spawned in the American West, but the South had Atlanta. In terms of actual urban population, the antebellum South lagged behind only the North and Great Britain in the Western Hemisphere. As settlement proceeded inland in the early nineteenth century, large river ports such as Memphis, Natchez, Louisville, and St. Louis grew in response to backcountry commerce and the ever-expanding distance from the seaport cities located on the South's perimeter. Secondary river towns also appeared on navigable streams that connected frontier areas to the coast, including Richmond, Columbia, and Augusta. Finally, a number of smaller towns such as Atlanta developed in the agricultural hinterlands, most of them serving as the collection, storage, and shipment points of the region's agricultural products. In all these cities and towns, someone had to grasp the problems and make hardheaded decisions in tune with the ethics of the day and movement of the era. These were the wise, aggressive, determined men, who, with farsightedness and love of accomplishment, often provided social betterment as well as profit-motivated enterprises in the towns.[8]

Peters stands without equal as a promoter of Atlanta. His hand is evident in almost every urban promotion project in the city during the nineteenth century. He set the city on the path to greatness. With the exception of William B. Ogden of Chicago, Peters's record in city building may not be surpassed in United States urban history. His career is all the more extraordinary when it is remembered that most great cities of America were built around port facilities; he had faith in the future of Atlanta when ports such as Charleston and Savannah were, and seemed likely to remain, the leading cities of the Southeast. Without question, his role as a builder of Atlanta ranks him as one of the most important figures in the urbanization of America.

However, during his lifetime, he was nationally acclaimed as a noted stockman and planter, and not so much as a builder of cities. One of the world's foremost livestock enthusiasts, he conducted "perhaps the most extensive series of experiments in grass and livestock farming to be found anywhere in the antebellum South" at his plantation north of Atlanta. His documented trials are probably also the first, considering the variety of live-

---

[8]Blaine A. Brownell, "Urbanization in the South: A Unique Experience?" *Mississippi Quarterly* 26 (Spring 1973): 108-10.

stock he handled. Peters had a passion for experimentation that was both a hobby and a business. He endeavored to import the best strains from abroad, but so little was known about diseases in the South or animal selection that the beasts died in droves. His records show that he invested some $50,000 in animals that he found to be unsuited for the Southern climate and diseases. Instead of planting cotton, he devoted his tillable land to grain and grasses, and by trial and error discovered the best varieties suited to the South. In the process of generously pouring his financial resources into the improvement of Southern agriculture, he developed a privately owned experiment station and publicized his methods by encouraging agricultural fairs and contributing articles to farm journals. The importance of these pursuits is that he proved certain kinds of grasses and stock would thrive in the South, and that scientific breeding was possible and beneficial.[9]

Peters's contributions to his adopted South are incalculable. The varied interests and activities of his adult life in the region, a period of over half a century (1835-1889), allowed him to develop a wide circle of friends across the nation, and he was regarded as one of the outstanding Southerners of his day. His strong sense of character, suggestive of some of America's founding fathers whom he had known as a boy through his Philadelphia grandfather, made him a model, rather than a typical, nineteenth-century capitalist. Of particular note in establishing his significance in Southern history was his unusual dual role as both urban promoter and agriculturist. Such evidence strongly suggests that Peters was the greatest New South practitioner of all time.

He had a rather distinguished family heritage. His great-grandfather, William Peters, an English lawyer who became the family progenitor in America, ventured from Liverpool sometime before 1739 to forget the death of his first wife. His grief was consoled by his marriage to Mary Brientnall of a respected Philadelphia family. Obtaining a grant of land near Philadelphia on the Schuylkill River from William Penn, Great-grandfather Peters in 1742-1743 built the family home, Belmont, high on the west bank. Landscaped in grand style, including walks lined with pyramid-, obelisk-,

---

[9]Henry W. Grady, "Forty Years All Told Spent in Live Stock Experiments in Georgia," in *Richard Peters*, 34-36; Fletcher M. Green, *The Role of the Yankee in the Old South* (Athens: University of Georgia Press, 1972) 113-14.

and sphere-shaped evergreen hedges, Belmont became a mecca for horti-
culturists. However, William Peters was a loyalist, and he returned to England as the Revolutionary War drew near. He willed his American property
to his son, Judge Richard Peters.

Judge Peters (1744-1828), Peters's grandfather and his most illustrious
ancestor, was graduated from the College of Philadelphia (University of
Pennsylvania) and then studied law—solid preparation for the high positions he later filled with honor in the early days of the republic. In 1776, he
married Sarah Robinson of Naaman's Creek, Delaware. During the war he
served briefly as a soldier, then rendered momentous service to his country
as Secretary of the War Board, where he worked with Robert Morris to raise
money and provisions for George Washington's army. After the conclusive
battle of Yorktown in 1781, he resigned from the War Board and served a
year in the Confederation Congress. Reflecting the influence of an uncle,
Reverend Richard Peters (1704-1776), he traveled to England in 1785 and
obtained the ordination of three bishops for the independent and newly
named Episcopal Church in America. He was a member of the Pennsylvania
Assembly from 1787 to 1792, when President Washington commissioned
him Judge of the United States District Court of Pennsylvania, a post he
filled with distinction for the remainder of his life.[10]

Philadelphia was the national capital from 1790 to 1800, a decade that
included most of the tenure of President Washington.[11] The president knew
the judge well, and "took great delight in his society."

> When a morning of leisure permitted, that great man would drive to Belmont, the
> birthplace and country residence of Judge Peters; it was his constant habit to do
> so. There, sequestered from the world, the torments and cares of business, Wash-
> ington would enjoy a vivacious, recreative, and wholly unceremonious [visit] with
> the Judge, walking for hours side by side in the beautiful gardens of Belmont, be-
> neath the shade of lofty hemlocks placed there by [William Peters]. In those ro-

---

[10]Samuel Breck, "Judge Richard Peters," address before the Blockley and Merrion Agriculture Society, 20 September 1828, in Black, *Richard Peters*, 68-77; Genealogical Notes,
Nellie P. Black Collection; Stevenson W. Fletcher, *Pennsylvania Agriculture and Country
Life, 1640-1840* 2 vols. (Harrisburg: Pennsylvania Historical and Museum Commission,
1950) 1:219, 230; Bennett Nolan, *The Schuylkill* (New Brunswick: Rutgers University Press,
1951) 200; Federal Writers' Project, *Pennsylvania Cavalcade* (Philadelphia: University of
Pennsylvania Press, 1942) 179-80.

[11]E. Digby Baltzell, *Philadelphia Gentlemen: The Making of a National Upper Class*
(New York: The Free Press, 1958) 81.

mantic grounds there stands a chestnut tree, reared from a Spanish nut planted by the hands of Washington. Large, healthy, and fruitful, it is cherished at Belmont as a precious evidence of the intimacy that subsisted between those distinguished men.[12]

Judge Peters's hospitality became a tradition in the land. Thomas Jefferson, John Adams, Baron von Steuben, David Rittenhouse, William Bartram, and many other American and European celebrities of the day journeyed to Belmont to enjoy the company of the judge, for "he could write the best song, tell the best story, and was the greatest wit of his time."

From 1805 to 1828 Judge Peters was president of the Philadelphia Society for the Promotion of Agriculture, founded in 1785 as an outgrowth of Benjamin Franklin's American Philosophical Society. On his estate at Belmont, Judge Peters experimented with new agricultural methods, including the invention of a cultivator known as "Peters's Horse-Hoe Harrow." In 1797, he wrote a pamphlet, which he dedicated to President Washington, urging fertilization with plaster of paris (used in mixing mortar); it was widely influential in promoting the culture of clover and other grasses. Encouraged by this success, in 1816 the judge published a general history of farming that stressed the need for scientific agriculture, urged the use of plaster and other fertilizers, recommended land drainage, favored premiums for excellence in production, and advocated a state system of roads and canals to move produce to market. He had previously proved his point when in 1803, as the head of a private company, he raised $300,000 and built the High Street Bridge across the Schuylkill River. The early nineteenth century was a period of agricultural awakening in Pennsylvania and any valid

---

[12] Breck, "Judge Peters," 78-79. Belmont, with its exterior grounds and ornate ceilings and paneling inside, remained a showplace until after the judge's death. Then four years later in 1832, the state of Pennsylvania built an inclined lift for a railroad that ran through the grounds, which ended all privacy, as passengers entraining for the West were brought up from the river level to enter cars located directly on Belmont's terrace. These impromptu tourists pilfered flowers and trampled shrubbery, while train crews made off with fence rails for engine fuel. In 1876, Belmont was restored to some measure of its grandeur and popularity when the building was converted into a restaurant, and a Hungarian orchestra played Strauss waltzes as diners looked out on the moonlit river. Nolan, *Schuylkill*, 201. Belmont is now a part of Philadelphia's Fairmount Park, which from its origin as a modest reserve for the municipal reservoir, was vastly extended and developed with the advice of, among others, Frederick Law Olmsted. McKelvey, *The Urbanization of America*, 116.

appraisal of this "New Husbandry" must give preeminence to the efforts of Judge Peters.[13]

The life of Ralph Peters, son of the judge, is a study in failure. He trained to become a merchant, having sailed for many years as a cargomaster for the patriotic Philadelphia merchant and banker, Stephen Girard. He went into business for himself, sending a ship to China. In this initial enterprise Peters's cargomaster, through neglect, allowed some unscrupulous Chinese to load a cargo of willow leaves instead of tea. This voyage was so disastrous that Ralph Peters never recovered from the loss and remained poor the balance of his life.

Richard Peters, the second of Ralph Peters's ten children, was born 10 November 1810 in a small house in Germantown, near the famous battlefield. His mother was Catherine Conyngham Peters, the daughter of David Hayfield Conyngham, a merchant from Dublin, Ireland, who had immigrated to Philadelphia, and May West Conyngham of Philadelphia. Soon after Richard was born, Ralph Peters moved into his father's house. In January 1815, as the boy watched an excited crowd on the lawn of Belmont celebrating the end of the War of 1812, he fell from a window and broke his arm. Improperly set by a local physician, the arm remained permanently bent, but apparently resulted in no physical impairment. Young Peters's formal education, which began at age five, was somewhat sporadic, but was better than most boys of his era received because both of his grandfathers encouraged learning. He also absorbed the culture of Belmont as he was a favorite grandson of the judge.

Peters's family subsequently moved to Bull Farm, a tract of two hundred acres that his father rented from the judge. There Ralph Peters started a large milk and butter dairy. Young Richard instinctively took to the outdoor life; he especially enjoyed hunting and developed into a marksman, taking South Carolina rice-fed woodcock and wild pigeons. Another boyhood favorite was ice skating on ponds near Matthias W. Baldwin and Company, a locomotive works near the Schuylkill and one of the most advanced

---

[13]Breck, "Judge Peters," 80, 89; George Washington to Judge Peters, 21 January 1797, in *Pennsylvania Magazine of History and Biography* 44:4 (October 1920): 325; "Membership of the Philadelphia Society for the Promotion of Agriculture, 1788," in *Early American Imprints, 1639-1800*, ed. Clifford K. Shipton (New York: Readex Microprint Corporation, 1954-) n.p.; *Dictionary of American Biography*, s.v. "Peters, Richard" (1744-1828); Fletcher, *Pennsylvania Agriculture*, 1:97, 142, 344-45.

in the world, and at Fairmount Dam, where Philadelphians often congregated in winter to roast oxen and hold a carnival. A grim side to Peters's boyhood was illness. While at Bull Farm, he was sick with scarlet fever; unlike his brother Henry, Richard slowly recovered. This same disease would later claim his brother John and his mother, and render another brother, Edward, a mute.

The dairy proved a failure, to a large extent because of the limited market for milk as it was common for town dwellers to keep one or more cows. Too, transportation facilities were inadequate, and most adults preferred more stimulating beverages. So in 1821 the Peters family moved to Wilkesbarre, where they lived for three years. It is not clear what work Ralph Peters engaged in at this time, but he probably acted as land agent for the judge's frontier lands in Bradford County. Young Peters attended school in Wilkesbarre and discovered math was his favorite subject, an inclination that helped shape his future career.

The family moved into the backwoods of Bradford County and again engaged in farming. Peters's father built a large frame house in the middle of 150 acres of newly cleared ground. "This was the greatest error of his life," recalled Peters. "He bought the land but never paid for it, when he could have settled on my grandfather's land only ten miles distant." The boy became keenly interested in the place and spent his early teens working with the farm hands, breaking oxen, hunting, and fishing.

Refinements such as schools, however, had yet to invade this remote area of Bradford County; the only redeeming social feature was the annual visit of Grandfather Conyngham. On one such visit, a family council took place, where it was agreed that young Peters had a mental capacity worthy of cultivation and should attend school in Philadelphia. Dressed in an uncle's old suit, the boy found himself spirited away to Grandfather Conyngham's house for a two-year stint of learning. Judge Peters paid the tuition and invited him to spend the weekends at Belmont, where the carefree youngster hunted and trapped in the woodlands, and enjoyed the fruits and melons from the orchards.[14]

---

[14]Peters, "Personal Recollections," 7-14, 19; Sam B. Warner, Jr., "Innovation and the Industrialization of Philadelphia 1800-1850," *The Historian and the City*, ed. Oscar Handlin and John Burchard (Cambridge: M.I.T. Press and Harvard University Press, 1963) 66; Fletcher, *Pennsylvania Agriculture*, 1:183; Baltzell, *Philadelphia Gentlemen*, 89.

After two years of school in Philadelphia, the youth, then perhaps seventeen years old, was ready for college. Judge Peters had deeded a thousand acres of land to Peters's father in trust for the young man's college education. But upon returning to the Bradford County farm, Peters learned that "through carelessness and neglect, the deed was not recorded and the land was sold for taxes without having done me the good that was intended." The awareness that he would have to make his own way in the world was less of a blow to the young man than his bitter disappointment in his father.

With the few dollars he earned making maple sugar—the first money he ever made—Peters returned to Philadelphia, where through the influence of an uncle (a Philadelphia lawyer named Richard Peters), he obtained an interview for a position with celebrated engineer and architect William Strickland. When he arrived in Strickland's office, the architect asked for a handwriting sample and queried the youth about drawing and mathematics. Unimpressed with the results, Strickland suggested that he study writing, drawing, and mathematics for one year and then return for a second attempt. After eighteen months at Franklin Institute in Philadelphia, Peters returned and this time gained employment as a draftsman in Strickland's office. The architect was very active during these years; he had recently completed the United States Bank and was supervising the construction of the Arch Street Theatre, the United States Mint, and the Medical College, all in the city. Peters drafted almost all of the blueprints for the mint and the college, but by his own account, he had little architectural talent, and Strickland reworked most of the plans.

After six months as an architect, he faced reality and asked Strickland, who was also in charge of building the Delaware Breakwater, to give him a position on that project as an engineer. His duty consisted of calculating the cargo of rock on each loaded vessel. Unfortunately, Peters's first employment as a civil engineer quickly degenerated into a functionary's role of merely counting the stones thrown from the ships and certifying the bills of lading. Realizing that engineering skills could hardly be learned from that employment, he resigned.[15]

As yet Peters had been unable to give direction to his career. Bad luck also continued to hound his father and Peters made clear his refusal to be reconciled with him.

---

[15]Peters, "Personal Recollections," 15-17.

During my residence at the Breakwater, I received a letter from my father enclosing a ten-dollar bill, saying that he then had plenty of money, having been successful in coal speculations in Pottsville, Pennsylvania. I returned it and wrote him that I had all the money I could use, also that I could get along and take care of myself. This is the first and only money I can ever recollect his giving to me. On returning to Philadelphia, I found him at Grandfather Conyngham's bemoaning his fate. A panic had seized the coal men in Pottsville, and he had lost every dollar he had invested and was in debt besides to the amount of five thousand dollars. This was his last attempt at making money. He had given his notes for this amount, and was in daily fear of the sheriff; twenty years after I paid these notes from the proceeds of his estate.[16]

Again through his uncle's influence, Peters became a rodman for the survey of the Camden and Amboy Railroad and found that the work suited very well. He soon received a better offer and transferred to the Philadelphia and Lancaster Railroad (later a division of the Pennsylvania Central) as an assistant engineer. During the next few years, he gained valuable experience and became a first-rate civil engineer, earning promotion to division assistant. "My rugged constitution," he said, "was formed [on the farm], and I could outwalk and outwork any of the assistant engineers when in the field, and my services were always in demand."

In November 1834, Peters returned to Philadelphia and remained there through the Christmas season. He spent the $350 he had saved the past five years paying for his board and "frolicking with the boys." His next offer of employment came from J. Edgar Thomson, the well-known civil engineer whom Peters had met while surveying the Camden and Amboy Railroad. Thomson offered him a position as an assistant engineer for the construction of the Georgia Railroad. Peters accepted. Before going south, he returned to the Bradford County farm for a short visit, mainly to see his mother. In order to finance the trip to Bradford County, he sold the heavy gold case of a watch he had inherited from the judge. He remained at the farm for one week, and when he departed, it was for the last time.

Bumping along through the Pocono Mountains of northeast Pennsylvania on the return trip, the stagecoach afforded scant protection against the unusually bitter cold. The driver, urging his horses onward through the frozen landscape, was unaware that there was something of a crisis inside the coach, where Peters, his thinly clad body shivering from the frigid air, con-

---

[16]Ibid., 17.

sidered the possibility that he might freeze to death. A fellow passenger, an army officer who had killed several wolves in Ohio, offered him a splendid robe made from their pelts. This and a drink of the officer's whiskey ended the young man's dilemma.

Settling back in his seat amid the newfound warmth, Peters remembered the five-dollar gold piece tucked away in his pocket. It was all that remained of the $25 he had received from selling the watch case. Before departing the Bradford County farm, he had debated at length whether to give the coin as a present to his mother. She died shortly afterward and he always regretted not giving it to her and could not bring himself to spend it. This was the last time he saw his mother because the family then moved to Towanda, where she died. Peters remembered his mother as "a noble, self-sacrificing woman, devoted to her children to whom she gave her entire life."

The snow was nearly six feet deep when the stagecoach pulled into Philadelphia.[17] Peters needed money to finance his trip to Georgia and, since he had spurned his father, he secretly turned to his Aunt Ann in Philadelphia for funds. One hundred dollars safely in hand, he continued on to New York, where he embarked on a "miserable" side-wheel coastal steamer for Charleston, South Carolina. Struggling through a blinding snowstorm that greeted his arrival in the "holy city," he continued his journey over the rudimentary Charleston and Hamburg Railroad to rail's end at Hamburg on the Savannah River opposite Augusta.[18] On a cold day in February 1835, Peters ferried across the river between snow-covered banks and first set foot in Georgia—where from $100 in debt he would rise to personify the successful quest for the American dream.[19]

---

[17]Peters gave considerable insight into the origin of the Peters name in America when he commented that Jake Peters, a German who operated a Philadelphia stagecoach inn and was unrelated to Peters's family, was "married four times and left sixteen stalwart sons to represent him, thus giving a widespread growth to the Peters name from this family." Peters, "Personal Recollections," 12.

[18]Ibid., 15, 18-20.

[19]E. Merton Coulter, *Georgia: A Short History* (Chapel Hill: University of North Carolina Press, 1960) 257; James A. Ward, *J. Edgar Thomson: Master of the Pennsylvania* (Westport: Greenwood Press, 1980) 27.

CHAPTER TWO

GEORGIA YANKEE: RAILROAD, PETERS LAUNCH ATLANTA

Atlanta is in part a by-product of the railroad. Settlers had shown little interest in the Chattahoochee River area of North Georgia, which had been inhabited by Creek Indians until 1821. However, this neglect ended in May 1837 when Abbott H. Brisbane hammered a stake into a ridge upon the instruction of Chief Engineer Stephen H. Long. From the moment Brisbane's blows rang through the forest, the projected state railroad had a southern terminal (zero milepost) from which to build northward and settlers had a reason to venture into this isolated frontier. Unknowingly, these rail men had pegged the center of a future metropolis.

A few months earlier, the Georgia legislature had authorized the state to build a railroad from the Chattahoochee River in North Georgia to the Tennessee River in East Tennessee, a project designed to benefit the southeastern seaboard by tapping the rich trade from Cincinnati and the entire Mid-West. Yet the Chattahoochee River was unnavigable at the terminal point and did not flow to the East coast. Was the southern terminal of the Western and Atlantic, as the state-owned railroad came to be named, to be located in a wilderness with no transportation links to Southern port cities? Private companies provided the answer.

Most railroads were controlled by cities at the time, and already residents of Athens and Savannah, seeking increased trade for their particular city, were promoting railroads designed to connect with the terminal point. As a result, the Georgia Railroad would eventually extend from Augusta (linked to the East coast by river and rail) to the terminal, with a branch, the Atlanta and West Point Railroad, from the terminal to the Alabama state line with a connection to Montgomery. The Central of Georgia Railroad would be built from Savannah to Macon, with a branch, the Macon and Western Railroad, from Macon to the terminal. The resulting railroad network was a grand scheme for regional economic glorification.[1]

It is hardly surprising that the famous explorer, Stephen Long, did not realize he was marking the site of a future city—particularly since the underbrush on the ridge was so dense that the exact location of the terminal point had to be made later by a devotee of the project and former governor of Georgia (1831-1835), Wilson Lumpkin. A few small, isolated settlements dotted the landscape; Whitehall tavern and post office to the southwest was nearest, while twenty miles to the north was Marietta. Individual farms scarcely disturbed the wilderness between the villages. The unsuitability of Atlanta's hinterland for large-scale cotton production seemed to confirm a dismal future for the site where the rails would interlock. Engineer Long believed that the nascent railroad junction would amount to little more than a refueling station. Long's earlier expedition to the Rocky Mountains is credited for developing the myth that the prairie was a "great American desert"; now he refused an offer to buy real estate at the terminal, remarking that at most the site would be "a good location for one tavern, a blacksmith shop, a grocery store, and nothing else."[2]

---

[1]Oliver H. Prince, comp., *Digest of the Laws of Georgia to 1837* (Athens: Privately printed, 1837) 304-14; Walter G. Cooper, *Official History of Fulton County* (Atlanta: Walter W. Brown Publishing Co., 1934) 56-58; E. Merton Coulter, *Georgia: A Short History* (Chapel Hill: University of North Carolina Press, 1960) 225-36, 260.

[2]George Raffalovich, "The Streets and Sidewalks of Atlanta," Railroad Collection, Atlanta Historical Society, typescript; Eugene M. Mitchell, "Atlanta's First Real Estate Subdivision and Other Curious Facts About the Early History of Atlanta," *Atlanta Historical Bulletin* 1:3 (May 1930): 9-12; David R. Goldfield, *Cotton Fields and Skyscrapers: Southern City and Region, 1607-1980* (Baton Rouge: Louisiana State University Press, 1982) 35.

Nonetheless, Terminus, as railworkers called the terminal point, became an important rail junction because it had the necessary combination of geography and local enterprise.[3] Its natural asset of being at an elevation of over one thousand feet above sea level tended to reduce epidemics which were common to other parts of the South. In addition to "altitude," Terminus attracted men with a productive "attitude." Although most settlers were Southerners, a minority of Northern businessmen made their way to the junction and gave added impetus to the spirit of enterprise. Many of these early settlers saw the connection between a prosperous frontier community and an increase in their personal wealth.[4] The citizen most representative of this attitude was the young Pennsylvanian who, two years before Engineer Long staked the terminal point, was leading the Georgia Railroad survey team toward the Chattahoochee River.

When Peters joined the survey team, heavy snow had stalled progress just ten miles beyond Augusta. After persuading Chief Engineer Thomson to advance him $100 on his salary in order to pay the debt to his aunt, he began work surveying the line. Although Thomson at first assigned equal rank to the five assistants, most of them Southerners, Peters soon demonstrated superior ability as an engineer, especially in determining the best route for the road. Therefore, it was with a clear conscience that Thomson designated his fellow Northerner principal assistant, with a substantial raise in salary—from $1,000 to $1,500 a year.

Peters was now in charge of directing the trunk line westward, with a branch line northward to Athens, the city that controlled the railroad. Thomson occasionally visited the survey party in the field and revised the line, a practice Peters found humiliating. As a result, Peters meticulously corrected each ten-mile stretch himself. He carefully charted the course for the road along a ridge and personally rechecked it prior to Thomson's arrival in the field, so that few changes could be made. Peters's task was made somewhat easier by the topography of the region between Augusta and Athens which was favorable for railroad construction. There were few problems

---

[3]Blake McKelvey, *The Urbanization of America, 1860-1915* (New Brunswick: Rutgers University Press, 1963) 34.

[4]Ivan Allen, *The Atlanta Spirit: Attitude and Altitude* (Atlanta: Allen-Marshall Co., 1948) 3-4.

with steep grades and watercourses, which allowed an almost direct survey line.

However, his attempt to provision his survey team from farmers who lived along the route presented a difficult problem. The generally conservative nature of these rural folk, combined with the belief that the railroads represented a conspiracy to disrupt their trade with wagoneers, resulted in hostility toward the railroad men. Peters complained that his engineer corps was "often insulted by the piney-woods people, who looked upon us as adventurers." Not only was it difficult to obtain supplies by this method, the farmers at times threatened the surveyors, compelling them to arm themselves. Peters solved the supply problem by requisitioning rations from the company, a move that prevented further trouble with the locals, although as a precautionary measure his entire party remained conspicuously well armed.[5]

As the terminal stake was being driven by Brisbane, a significant event was occurring at the Augusta depot—the first steam-powered locomotive was tested in Georgia. The results of the test were extremely impressive. The engine, one of seven Thomson had ordered from Matthias W. Baldwin and Company in Philadelphia, "started beautifully and majestically from the depository and, following the impetus given, flew with surprising velocity on the road which hereafter is to be her natural element."[6] The "surprising velocity" was only ten miles an hour, but Peters and his fellow engineers later discussed the subject around their campfire and concluded that the resistance of the air against the engine would prevent much higher speed, which would be impractical for passengers anyway, they reasoned, because moving to different parts of the earth so quickly might destroy a person's health.

Peters's engineer corps had penetrated to the vicinity of Greensboro by October 1837 when Thomson appeared in camp and offered Peters the position of superintendent. After Thomson agreed to a $1,000 raise, Peters ac-

---

[5]Richard Peters, "Personal Recollections," *Richard Peters: His Ancestors and Descendants,* comp. Nellie P. Black (Atlanta: Foote and Davies, 1904) 20-21; *Athens Southern Banner* (8 June 1833); James A. Ward, *J. Edgar Thomson, Master of the Pennsylvania* (Westport: Greenwood Press, 1980) 27.

[6]Mary G. Cumming, *Georgia Railroad and Banking Company, 1833-1945: An Historic Narrative* (Augusta: Walton Printing Co., 1945) 30-31, 93; Ernest C. Hynds, *Antebellum Athens and Clarke County Georgia* (Athens: University of Georgia Press, 1974) 28.

cepted and departed immediately for Augusta as Superintendent and General Agent of the Georgia Railroad. He rented a room at Mrs. Hall's celebrated boardinghouse on Broad Street and assumed his new duties at the depot. Peters was in charge of operations, repairs, car construction, accounts, and road maintenance departments. He quickly became severely overworked, and Thomson appointed one supervisor for each department except road maintenance, which had three—each one responsible for fifty miles of road. Authority went directly from Thomson to Peters to the supervisors.[7]

Since the company was just moving into steam locomotion, one of Peters's chief problems was the frequent accidents caused by the new equipment. The tracks had a pine base with lightwood or oak crossties. On top of the crossties ran stringers, on which rested an iron-plate rail two-and-a-quarter inches wide, and only five-eighths of an inch thick. These lengths of strap rail on wooden stringers caused constant derailment, and when the rail became loose and was caught by a passing wheel, it could be forced upward through the floor of the car to the consternation and sometimes horror of passengers. T-rail, which came into general use before the Civil War, was a welcomed improvement, and this solid iron rail could also accommodate the heavier rolling stock. In spite of numerous accidents, the Georgia Railroad maintained a splendid passenger-safety record.[8]

As superintendent, Peters also had to contend with the fire hazard caused by locomotives. Blazing cinders showered from the smokestacks of these "mechanized pyromaniacs" each time the fireman stoked the fire, which not only inconvenienced passengers in the open coaches, but threatened the cargo and caused fire damage beside the tracks. A farmer sued the Georgia Railroad for damage to his cotton crop burned by sparks from a locomotive, but company officials refused to pay on the ground that the train had a right to operate "over its own road in a manner it was obliged to do" as a carrier of freight, passengers, and United States mail.[9] Peters, however, worked on a solution to the vexing problem of sparks and met with

---

[7]Peters, "Personal Recollections," 21; Cooper, *History of Fulton County*, 61; Ward, *J. Edgar Thomson*, 63.

[8]*Athens Southern Banner* (31 May 1834); Cooper, *History of Fulton County*, 598; Alexander Mackay, *The Western World* 2 vols. (London: R. Bentley, 1849) 2:243-44.

[9]Cumming, *Georgia Railroad*, 96.

some success. He protected passengers, cargo, and surrounding country-side by inventing a "spark arrester," which consisted of a screen hooked over the top of the smokestack.[10]

A particularly demanding duty for Peters was to call on farmers along the line and procure a right-of-way through their property. Railroads were gaining acceptance, although many farmers still believed the roads were planned by the rich to exploit the poor, and some vowed that no spade would turn their ground for the purpose of building a railroad. Peters's calm and businesslike attitude usually won the farmer's confidence, but in letting construction contracts he had to cope with the much more difficult problem of convincing these men to help grade the roadbed. With free labor scarce and disease prevalent in the antebellum South, Northern laborers demanded high wages and were reluctant to expose themselves to the hot climate, so Peters had to persuade the farmers to use their slaves and mules for railroad construction when crops did not need attention. Some farmers agreed, payment being made with stock in the company, plus free rail transportation to one of the biggest events in the area—the annual stockholder's convention.[11] This policy, which caused North Georgians to feel they were part of a local road not controlled by outsiders, made the Georgia Railroad one of the most popular in the state.

Peters returned to the North in 1837, perhaps to check on the delivery of locomotives from Baldwin, although the reason for the trip remains speculative. On his return voyage, the sea began to run heavy under the gathering clouds of a "very severe storm" raging off Cape Hatteras, North Carolina. Giant waves began to break across the deck of the coastal steamer, pushing water into the engine room and extinguishing the fires. Without steam pressure, the vessel was powerless, and for the next forty-eight hours the steamer and all aboard were at the mercy of the angry sea. Under the veil of night, high winds thrust the steamer dangerously close to the beach near Beaufort. When the storm suddenly abated, the captain dropped both anchors "within a stone's throw of the shore" of Wilmington.

---

[10]Peters, "Personal Recollections," 22.

[11]Scrapbook, Nellie P. Black Collection, University of Georgia Libraries, Athens; Robert B. Pegram, "The Railroads: An Example of the Challenge to American Ingenuity," Atlanta Historical Society, typescript; Cumming, *Georgia Railroad*, 33, 93-95.

Once back in Georgia, Peters watched the rails stretch steadily westward. Greensboro had service by 1839, and at that time the eighty-seven-mile main line extended halfway from Augusta to Terminus. The company pushed construction toward Madison, through one of the most densely settled sections of the state, creating a strong passenger demand. As for freight, increasing amounts of cotton and foodstuffs from the West and manufactured goods from the eastern ports created a rush season in fall and winter. Peters realized that the heavy traffic necessitated improving the roadbed, strengthening bridges, and adding better designed and more powerful engines, as well as stronger cars. His pragmatic thinking helped shape a company policy that favored the gradual improvement of rolling stock and fixtures.

Shortly after the rails reached Madison, Peters had another close call. After taking charge of a freight train for an ill conductor, he was standing on top of cotton bales loaded on an open car when the train passed under a bridge. His head struck the bridge and he tumbled unconscious between the cars. His alert engineer saw him fall, stopped the slow-moving train, and ran back to find him sprawled on the edge of the car with his arms caught between the bumpers. He was pulled from the train and carried to the Madison home of one of the road's directors. Peters commented in his memoirs that he was well cared for, "a severe scalp wound being the extent of my injuries."

The most severe economic slump America had yet experienced, together with friction among some of the stockholders, combined by 1840 to slow construction of the Georgia Railroad. Company stock was hard to sell and dividends were irregular. The company's bank (authorized by the Georgia legislature in 1834, only a year after the railroad's original charter) caused another problem for the railroad by successfully competing for company funds as a result of the bank's ability to yield quick profits. To keep construction moving, Peters bought cheap pinelands along the line and set up a sawmill to produce stringers; he also demonstrated his faith in the railroad by investing the savings from his salary in the company's stock as it plunged from $100 to $25 a share. In 1842, after two years of stagnation and complaining of bad management by President William Dearing and the Athens directors, Peters and some Augusta stockholders bought enough stock to take control of the company and reduced Athens to a local branch station. The new president of the company was John P. King of Augusta, one of the most outstanding rail magnates of the nineteenth-century South.[12]

As the trains chugged further westward from Augusta, Peters wanted to operate trains at night. This was an astonishing concept, but a necessary one because daylight runs alone could no longer accommodate the company's increased business that was being generated by the extension of the tracks. Since the most pressing need was for some kind of forward illumination, he had a small wooden platform constructed in front of the smokestack, covered the shelf with sand, and piled a few blazing pineknots on it. This simple innovation worked quite well according to Peters: "We found after a year's experience that we had fewer accidents at night than in the day time." The rudimentary light cast in front of the engine was probably the first locomotive headlight ever devised, and the Georgia Railroad was the first of any length in America to risk night travel.

After trains began to run at night, Peters worked on another innovation—in anticipation of George M. Pullman's sleeping cars. His interest in passenger comfort led him to direct that boards be laid across the seats, with valises, shawls, or bundles available to make improvised pillows. "Thus," said Peters, casting aside his usual modesty, "the first sleeping-car was inaugurated" for America's trains. His crude accommodations were highly practical for children and adaptable for everyone in a country the size of the United States.[13] The subsequent development in the evolution of the sleeping car was inevitable—charging a fare for a berth—and apparently the first to do so was George W. Adair, a native Georgian from Decatur whom Peters had appointed assistant to Conductor William P. Orme. Adair had built a berth in a corner of the express car so he could rest between stations; when passengers began appropriating it, he established a fee for its use in an attempt to stop the annoying practice.[14]

---

[12]Peters, "Personal Recollections," 29-30; Peters to Lemuel Pratt Grant, 21 May 1845 (?), and "Railroad Construction in the United States Before 1845," L. P. Grant Copybook, Grant Papers, Atlanta Historical Society; *Niles Register* 57 (8 February 1840): 377; Ulrich B. Phillips, *A History of Transportation in the Eastern Cotton Belt to 1860* (New York: Columbia University Press, 1908) 238-39.

[13]Peters, "Personal Recollections," 22; *Railway Passenger Travel, 1825-1880*, Railroad Collection, Atlanta Historical Society, pamphlet.

[14]Walter McElreath, "The Builders of Street Transportation in Atlanta," Atlanta Historical Society, typescript; *Atlanta Constitution* (27 July 1873); Cooper, *History of Fulton County*, 60-62; James B. Adair, ed., *Adair: History and Genealogy* (Los Angeles: Privately printed, 1924) 213-14.

Peters first visited the village at the terminal in 1844, which by that time was formally called Marthasville. He drove through in a two-horse company vehicle en route to Newnan to inspect the supervision of a stagecoach line that his company operated as an extension of its railroad to the west. Peters immediately saw the potential of Marthasville. The place was rough-hewn, but unlike other Southern towns, it bustled. He realized that Stephen H. Long had made a good choice for the terminal point because the ridge from the north converged with ridges from the east and south. This topography was well suited for the entrance of the rail lines from Augusta and Macon. Peters was so impressed with Marthasville that he began buying lots in the hamlet—his first connection with the great inland city of the New South.

As the rails extended beyond Madison to Stone Mountain (New Gibraltar) and approached the town of Decatur, Peters encountered a final pocket of resistance to the company. The moralistic and conservative inhabitants of Decatur believed "snorting, screeching, hissing engines" could cause horses to run away; cows to produce poor quality milk and butter; chickens to lay inferior eggs; and the nuisance would disturb the sleep of the people. Interested in trains only as a novelty, Decaturites refused to allow the rails within a mile of the town. When Peters and Lemuel P. Grant, Maine-born assistant engineer under Thomson, visited a sawmill south of Decatur to buy lumber, they ran into hostile locals in the log yard who were holding a protest meeting against James Moore, owner of the mill. Moore's angry neighbors demonstrated their strong antipathy to the Georgia Railroad by resolving that "every man who has the good of his country at heart and wishes to avert the ruin of its citizens, should protest anyone sawing stringers for the railroad." Peters informed the protesters that the road would be completed and as he departed suggested that they would be wise to invest in real estate in Marthasville.

What was noise to the inhabitants of Decatur was music to those in Marthasville. Pioneer merchant Jonathan Norcross set up a sawmill to provide stringers and other timbers for the road, and on 14 September 1845 the first Georgia Railroad train puffed into the village with ten carloads of railroad iron. The historic arrival of this freight train was overshadowed the next day, however, when the first passenger train made its way from Augusta. As the train approached Decatur, the curious walked the mile out to the tracks to wait, some placing their ears to the tracks to hear the first sounds of the engine. Rolling past at twelve miles an hour, the train ended its 170-mile trip that night at Marthasville where Peters, King, Thomson,

Orme, and Adair stepped from the train to be greeted as celebrities. There was general rejoicing at both ends of the line; an Augusta newspaper called the opening of the road "a source of unfeigned pleasure."

The Georgia Railroad was the first line to connect Marthasville to the outside world.[15] Since the village lacked hotel space, the rail men slept that first night on the office floor of the chief engineer of the Western and Atlantic Railroad, Charles F. M. Garnett, who had succeeded Long. Walking in the darkness to Garnett's office, King plunged ten feet into an open well and had to be rescued by the others. This unpleasant encounter soured King's opinion of the town from the beginning and his attitude reinforced a company policy that awarded Augusta lower freight rates at the expense of Marthasville.

As a rail junction in the southern Appalachian foothills, Marthasville was similar to the frontier towns (and roaring gold camps at times) of the Old West. The town consisted of four main roads—Marietta, Peachtree, Decatur, and Whitehall—all of which joined at the "cross-roads" where leading retailers Thomas Kile, Washington Collier, and Jonathan Norcross operated grocery and general merchandise stores. Railroad depots and machine shops completed the central business district. Spreading out from the crossroads were other business houses, mostly saloons, and new buildings were being erected at a rapid rate. The stump-dotted woodlands were full of shanties where merchants, many of them Northerners, lived until they could find time to build permanent residences.[16]

---

[15]Three years earlier in 1842 the Western and Atlantic track-laying crew had reached Marietta, the "gem of north Georgia," but at that time the nearest locomotive was a Georgia Railroad engine at Madison—over sixty miles distance from Terminus with no intervening track. This problem was surmounted when a huge wagon pulled by sixteen mules bore the engine, named the "Florida," cross country to the Western and Atlantic tracks. The excited villagers turned out to see the "Florida," with its large balloon smokestack, polished brass, and bright colors of the day. The first train out of Terminus pulled away on Christmas Eve and carried a happy throng (including a young girl who later became Peters's wife) on an overnight trip to Marietta. Sarah Huff, "Trail of the Pioneers," Huff Collection, Atlanta Historical Society, handwritten ledger; Franklin M. Garrett, "The City the Railroads Built," Atlanta Historical Society, typescript.

[16]Peters, "Personal Recollections," 21-22, 25, 29-30; Thomson to Grant, 12 September 1845, Railroad Collection, Atlanta Historical Society; *Athens Banner* (18 September 1845) quoting *Augusta Chronicle*; *Atlanta Journal* (18 July 1915, 6 December 1936); Thomas Moore, "Recollections," *Atlanta Historical Bulletin* 14:2 (June 1969): 45-47, 59; Cooper,

Shortly after the completion of the Georgia Railroad, Peters became increasingly interested in promoting transportation facilities westward and devoted more and more of his attention to the line of stagecoaches that he operated for the company. Because rail service was now available from the east to Marthasville, he moved the headquarters of the stage line from Madison to the frontier village and continued his daily supervision of the stagecoach service into Alabama. This move gave the village its greatest booster; with his input, it was destined to become a flourishing economic complex. Apart from an ideal port situation, two factors explain why a town grows: first, the site must be usable by the railroad (then by bus, truck, and plane); and second, "it is as well to look for the role of accident, of personal decision, . . . taste, or loyalties of an inventor or entrepreneur."[17] Peters's decision gave the future capital of the New South something of an accidental origin.

Peters immediately began to influence events in the village, and one of the first things he did was to change the town's name. From 1837 until the end of 1843, the informal name of Terminus had been used by common consent. However, Samuel Mitchell, a wealthy Zebulon planter who owned the site [Land Lot 77] and had encouraged growth by donating lots to the railroads for depots and machine shops, thought that Terminus was an inappropriate name. Chief Engineer Garnett was also interested in a formal name, so he and Mitchell decided to honor former Governor Wilson Lumpkin by naming the village after him. But when consulted, Lumpkin, somewhat too modest at this point, suggested that the village should be named after Mitchell. They reached a compromise, honoring Lumpkin's young daughter, Martha. The Georgia legislature on 23 December 1843 incorporated the village, appointed a governing commission, and specified the name of Marthasville. Not only did Peters consider this name unsuitable for a future major city, it was too long to write conveniently on his freight orders as well.

History of Fulton County, 313; Phillips, *History of Transportation*, 244; Thomas H. Martin, *Atlanta and Its Builders: A Comprehensive History of the Gate City of the South* 2 vols. (Atlanta: Century Memorial Publishing Co., 1902) 1:32; Franklin M. Garrett, *Atlanta and Environs: A Chronicle of Its People and Events* 2 vols. (Athens: University of Georgia Press, 1969) 1:218-19.

[17]Denis W. Brogan, "Implications of Modern City Growth," *The Historian and the City*, ed. Oscar Handlin and John Burchard (Cambridge: M.I.T. Press and Harvard University Press, 1963) 152-53.

As superintendent of the Georgia Railroad, it was his duty to announce the completion of the road, and in a letter to Chief Engineer Thomson, then residing in Madison, Peters asked him to suggest a better name. Thomson replied that since Atlantic (from Western and Atlantic Railroad) was masculine, perhaps the feminine form, Atlanta, would be acceptable. He correctly pointed out that Atlanta was a coined word. Peters heartily approved the suggestion, and a few days later published a company circular giving freight and passenger rates that was headlined: "Completion of the Georgia Railroad from Augusta to Atlanta." This was the first use of the name Atlanta.

The circular, distributed by the thousands in Georgia and Tennessee, created a sensation. Peters's high-handed act brought charges that he illegally altered a name granted by legislative charter. He argued that he did not intend for his railroad circular to represent an action by the town commission, and that company officials could choose the names of their depots. After Peters explained the origin of the name, it was generally accepted in Marthasville. However, realizing the legislature must act on the matter, he led a movement to request state lawmakers in Milledgeville to affirm the change. His efforts met with success on 26 December 1845: "Be it enacted . . . that from and after passage of this act, the name of Marthasville, in DeKalb County [Fulton County after 1853], shall be changed to that of Atlanta."

The name change resulted in considerable confusion and controversy outside Atlanta. First of all, many newspaper editors ("addicts of classical mythology," according to Peters) believed the word Atlanta was a misprint which should have been Atalanta—Greek goddess of fleetness. Others incorrectly believed the name was derived from the "lost continent" Atlantis. Garnett and Mitchell, who had selected the name Marthasville, were displeased with the change. Lumpkin was outraged. He had earned the right to voice his opinion when he, as governor, had promoted the state railroad, and as a private citizen had left the comfort of his Athens home to ride into the thickets of west Georgia and determine the final location of the terminal. Never reconciled, he regarded the change an affront to the family name and accused Peters of representing the "low voice of envy." However, Lumpkin's daughter Martha, Atlanta's godmother, later accepted the name change and complimented Peters for his efforts in promoting the city.[18]

––––––––––

[18]Peters, "Personal Recollections," 23; *Acts and Resolutions of the General Assembly*

That part of Peters's life that had been devoted to climbing the organizational ladder was now coming to completion. He resigned as superintendent of the Georgia Railroad, but continued to serve the company as a member of the board of directors for decades. Peters had been superintendent during the years of construction, when trackage and rolling stock were increasing so rapidly that the company had 213 miles of track and twenty-one locomotives by 1845. The building of the road was a remarkable success story—it had continued to expand during the heart of the depression, and when completed, it was the longest railway under one management in the world. Peters, a true company man who refused to exact commissions from those who supplied materials for the road, had been "quite successful in keeping down expenses and was highly complimented."[19] Now, as he cast off the role of technocrat, he would deal more with people and intangibles, endeavors for which he was eminently qualified by inner nature and personality.

of the State of Georgia (Georgia Laws), comp. William H. Hotchkiss (Savannah: J. M. Cooper, 1845) 91; Martha Lumpkin Compton, Scrapbook, Atlanta Historical Society; Edward Y. Clarke, Illustrated History of Atlanta (Atlanta: n.p., 1877) 31-32; Paul W. Miller, ed., Atlanta: Capital of the South (New York: O. Durrell, 1949) 11.

[19]Peters, "Personal Recollections," 21-22; Phillips, History of Transportation, 244; Ward, J. Edgar Thomson, 44,

CHAPTER THREE

ADOPTED SON: PROPRIETOR, BOOSTER, AGRARIAN

J oseph Thompson was a well-known antebellum personality. He was a semi-retired physician, a planter, and a brusque, loud-talking wit, as well as the proprietor of a restaurant on the lower floor of Garnett's office in Atlanta. (True to his nature, Thompson's wedding to a sixteen-year-old widow, Mary Ann Young, on 15 October 1829 climaxed a dinner party. After the meal, Thompson and Mary Ann simply rose and a minister performed the marriage ceremony to the surprise and delight of the other guests.) Thompson claimed that he had suggested the name Atlanta to Engineer Thomson and, as if to substantiate the honor, named his daughter born in July 1846 Atlanta Thompson. The jovial Thompson was from Decatur, where he operated a hotel in addition to his restaurant in Atlanta.

There was only one structure devoted entirely to public lodging in Atlanta—a four-room boardinghouse owned by the Georgia Railroad, located on Pryor Street conveniently near the depot. When its rooms could no longer accommodate Atlanta's visitors after the advent of the railroad, the Georgia Railroad Company removed it and built a hotel on the site. Peters and other company officials persuaded Thompson to operate the hotel, which Thompson leased and later bought from the company. The two-story, brick Atlanta Hotel was the city's first hotel worthy of the name. In accommodating rail passengers who were beginning to appear in large numbers, the Atlanta Hotel became a Southern landmark.[1]

Peters boarded at the Atlanta Hotel and developed a close relationship with the Thompson family. Of particular interest to him was Thompson's eldest daughter, Mary Jane, who was "one of the prettiest young women in Georgia." Born in Decatur on 31 December 1830, Mary Jane Thompson was, like her father, a staunch Presbyterian, and her life became an example of "religion practically applied." She was usually the first to know of illness in her vicinity and to offer aid and comfort. Peters approved this public-mindedness on the part of his host's daughter. In short, the thirty-five-year-old bachelor was smitten. But she was quite young, only fifteen years old, and he kept his sentiments to himself.[2]

When he resigned as superintendent of the Georgia Railroad, Peters purchased the company's stagecoach subsidiary and worked hard to make the line one of the best in the South. The stagecoach was "a very primitive, rough sort of conveyance . . . calculated to meet the very severe shocks" to which the roads subjected it; when a wheel struck a tree stump "the centrifugal effect was sublime."[3] Although less desirable than journeying by train or steamboat, stage travel must have been more pleasant via Peters's company than most stage lines; unresponsive management was widespread according to the unending list of complaints preserved in the accounts of antebellum travelers.

Peters's stagecoaches ran from Atlanta through the Georgia towns of Griffin, LaGrange, and West Point, connecting with the Montgomery and West Point Railroad, which was under construction in Alabama. From Montgomery, travelers could continue by steamboat down the winding Al-

[1]*Atlanta City Directory* (1859) Atlanta Historical Society; Scrapbook, Nellie P. Black Collection, University of Georgia Libraries, Athens; Samuel P. Richards, Diary, Atlanta Historical Society; *Atlanta Constitution* (5 September 1883); Wallace P. Reed, *History of Atlanta, Georgia, with Illustrations and Biographical Sketches of Some of Its Prominent Men and Pioneers* (Syracuse: D. Mason Co., 1889) 38-39.

[2]Richard Peters, "Personal Recollections," *Richard Peters: His Ancestors and Descendants*, comp. Nellie P. Black (Atlanta: Foote and Davies, 1904) 26; Scrapbook, Black Collection; Louise Black MacDougald, "My Seventh Move," *Atlanta Historical Bulletin* 32:8 (December 1947): 31-41.

[3]John Palliser, *Solitary Rambles and Adventures of a Hunter in the Prairies* (London: J. Murray, 1853) 14.

abama River to Mobile. The route allowed Peters to capture some of the tourist business of travelers making the "grand tour" of the South. For the convenience of his passengers, he entered into an agreement with the railroads whereby travelers could purchase a $26.50 through-ticket via rail and stage from Charleston, South Carolina, to Montgomery, Alabama. Peters charged ten cents per passenger-mile for the stage portion of the route and spared "no pains nor expense" to satisfy those who patronized his line. He bought a stable and lot on Forsyth Street in Atlanta and filled it with the best horses, hired competent and courteous drivers, and purchased new coaches of superior quality—keeping three or four at each end of the line in order to meet any unexpected passenger demands that might arise.

In a letter to L. P. Grant, then superintendent of the Montgomery and West Point Railroad, Peters was very explicit concerning passenger grumblings against company workers: "Let me hear any complaints made against our stage folks so that an investigation may in all cases be gone into." Peters's efforts to satisfy the public were generally successful, but he could do little about bad road conditions. In the fall of 1845 rain mired the road between Atlanta and LaGrange, and for weeks it was almost impassable. Again writing to Grant, Peters lamented: "Our only consolation now is, that it cannot get worse." He could only wait for a week of dry weather to reduce passenger dissatisfaction.

Lady Luck, however, proved as fickle as ever. Peters's difficulty with bad weather was more than offset the following spring when an unforeseen turn of events worked in his favor. In May 1846, as he was beginning to think that he had reinvested his profits in his business too quickly, the war with Mexico began, touching off a period of heavy westward travel that brought in high company profits. In addition to profits, Peters received his first tribute from the town. The stages arrived in Atlanta on a dirt street that was part of the original road to Whitehall tavern. Above the rattle of the coach and the din of hooves, the townspeople could hear the driver's bugle, as he entered with the customary flourish. This mixture of function and ceremony prompted town officials to name the road Peters Street.[4]

----

[4]Peters to L. P. Grant, 9 August, 9 September 1845, Grant Papers, Atlanta Historical Society; *Atlanta Constitution* (20 October 1885); *Atlanta Journal* (22 January 1933); Mary G. Cumming, *Georgia Railroad and Banking Company, 1833-1945: An Historic Narrative* (Augusta: Walton Printing Co., 1945) 62; Franklin M. Garrett, *Atlanta and Environs: A Chronicle of Its People and Events* 2 vols. (Athens: University of Georgia Press, 1969) 1:219; Allen D. Candler and Clement A. Evans, eds., *Cyclopedia of Georgia* 4 vols. (Atlanta: State Historical Association, 1906) 3:89.

But a tinge of doubt had crept into Peters's thinking that even this recognition could not dispell—he began to wonder whether Atlanta had much of a future. He wrote Grant and urged him to sell his real estate in Atlanta because "the place can never be much of a trading *city*, yet may be of some importance in a small way." Some of Peters's friends agreed. Thomson acknowledged that Atlanta "seems to be looking up a little, but unfortunately no person of capital has located here to commence business," and he predicted slow progress for the town. For years, John P. King refused to invest in Atlanta real estate because he considered the site merely a backcountry wood station. Many of the inhabitants were transient railroad laborers who frequented the dramshops and gambling rooms, and their ranks were swelled in 1846 by the arrival of the track-laying crews of the Macon and Western Railroad. The resulting lawlessness during these early days blunted Atlanta's social and political progress.[5] However, Peters's reservations concerning the city's growth and prosperity amounted to only a passing moment of doubt.

In order to boost the moral tone of the city and alleviate the rowdiness, which in turn could increase the influx of population, and because he adhered to the Episcopal tradition of his forebears, Peters was interested in establishing organized religion in Atlanta. Prior to the construction of church buildings, interdenominational services were held in a dirt-floor warehouse with pine-slabbed seats, under which pigs slept at night. By the mid-1840s, however, when various denominations began building churches and attracting resident ministers, Peters joined a small group of Episcopalians under the spiritual guidance of a missionary from Athens, John J. Hunt. At their first meeting, held on 1 November 1846 in the residence of Macon and Western Engineer Samuel G. Jones, Atlanta's Episcopalians began to plan for the future.[6]

In April 1847, the group decided it was time to organize a parish. Peters and Thomson of the Georgia Railroad, Garnett of the Western and Atlantic, and Jones of the Macon and Western drew up a charter, elected officers, and began plans for a church building. As a vestryman and member of the build-

---

[5]Peters, "Personal Recollections," 25; Peters to L. P. Grant, 26 July 1846, Thomson to Grant, 12 September 1845, Grant Papers.

[6]Alex M. Hitz, *A History of the Cathedral of St. Philip* (Atlanta: Conger Printing Co., 1947) 1-7; Garrett, *Atlanta and Environs*, 1:239-40.

ing committee, Peters helped raise funds for the structure. He purchased a lot from the Georgia Railroad for the Episcopal group, but when Samuel Mitchell unexpectedly donated a lot, Peters exchanged his for one adjoining the Mitchell lot. The two fronted three hundred feet on Hunter Street at the Georgia Railroad.

When this organizational work for a local church began, there were only a dozen parishes in the state, most of them in eastern Georgia. The Diocese of Georgia, organized in 1828 in Augusta, had grown slowly because the Revolutionary War had made the British and their religion unpopular in America. This prejudice hampered efforts by Atlantans to build a strong church and helped shape the thinking of the distinguished Bishop of Georgia, Stephen Elliott, concerning expansion into the state's frontier. Elliott reasoned that there was little need for a substantial outlay of funds to erect ornate buildings for small congregations, and he applied this "cheap church" policy to Atlanta. Under these circumstances, the small group of founders in Atlanta proceeded with plans for construction of a building, with Hunt, who had moved to Marietta, as itinerant rector. The parish seemed ready for growth. Peters was elected warden and a delegate to the Twenty-fifth Diocesan Convention held in May 1847 in St. John's Church, Savannah. There Hunt reported only five members (communicants) in Atlanta, but praised their zeal and said he expected the construction of the building to take only a few months.[7]

Peters also worked for improvement in Atlanta's government. Religion had its place, but Peters knew more was needed to improve the town's moral tone, especially since he was thinking of becoming a family man. By 1847, the population numbered around two thousand, many of whom were unemployed laborers. Because the town government was an ineffective commission appointed by the state legislature, the disorder went unabated. Peters understood that Atlanta's reputation as a lawless frontier town would frighten away prospective settlers, so he began a movement to petition the Georgia general assembly—much as he had done to change the town's name two years earlier. But now his objective was a city charter with an ef-

---

[7]St. Philip's Episcopal Church Parish Minutes, 1847-1859, 1870-1884, Georgia Department of Archives and History, Atlanta; Hitz, *History of St. Philip*, 8-15; Virgil Sim Davis, "Stephen Elliott: A Southern Bishop in Peace and War" (Ph.D. dissertation, University of Georgia, 1964) passim; Audria B. Gray, "History of the Cathedral of St. Philip's in the City and Diocese of Atlanta," *Atlanta Historical Bulletin* 4:1 (December 1930): 5-6.

fective form of government. For months, less ambitious citizens hampered Peters's efforts by retaining a lawyer to disrupt the movement, but Peters fought back, lobbying in meetings and door to door, with the result that the petition requesting a new charter with a mayor-and-council form of government went forward, and on 29 December 1847 Georgia lawmakers altered the status of Atlanta from a town to a city with substantial powers residing in a mayor and council.

Yet Peters's victory seemed empty. Atlanta's first city election, held January 1848, thrust the reform movement upon a snag when the Rowdy party candidate won the top office. Evidently elected by the railroad laborers, the first mayor was Moses W. Formwalt. Charged with disorderly conduct in his own saloon, Formwalt seemed uninterested in taming the city. In spite of Peters's fight for good government, frontier Atlanta remained wide open.[8]

During Peters's struggle for social and political reform, he got the opportunity to revive his fondness for the outdoors, joining some friends for a deer hunt near Calhoun in North Georgia. It was a fateful decision. The hills of the upcountry reminded him of Chester County, Pennsylvania, where he had worked on the Philadelphia and Lancaster Railroad. Like thousands of other migrants, Peters was attracted to land much like that of his native area. This part of northwest Georgia, west of the mountains and north of the piedmont tablelands, is known as the Great Valley, as distinguished from the Piedmont Plateau across the middle of the state, and the Coastal Plain of South Georgia with its central core of wiregrass and pines.[9]

Calhoun, some eighty miles north of Atlanta on the Western and Atlantic Railroad, is situated in the small Oothcaloga Creek Valley, a picturesque part of former Cherokee Indian lands. The limestone soil of the region is drained by the Oostanaula River, and the pleasant but often unpredictable

---

[8]*Atlanta Southern Miscellany and Upper Georgia Whig*, 4 December 1847; *Georgia Laws 1847*, n.p.; Martha Lumpkin Compton, Scrapbook, Atlanta Historical Society; George Raffalovich, "The Streets and Sidewalks of Atlanta," Railroad Collection, Atlanta Historical Society, typescript; "Diary and Letters of Dr. William N. White," *Atlanta Historical Bulletin* 10:2 (July 1937): 36, 39, 47; James M. Russell, "Atlanta, Gate City of the South 1847 to 1885" (Ph.D. dissertation, Princeton University, 1971) 249.

[9]Henry W. Grady, "Forty Years All Told Spent in Live Stock Experiments in Georgia," Black, *Richard Peters*, 35-37; James C. Bonner, *A History of Georgia Agriculture, 1732-1860* (Athens: University of Georgia Press, 1964) 69; Willard Range, *A Century of Georgia Agriculture, 1850-1950* (Athens: University of Georgia Press, 1954) 65.

climate produces a six-and-a-half month growing season. Cotton was grown in the Coosa Valley near Rome to the west, but the principal farm products of the Georgia upcountry were corn, small grains, and livestock.[10]

In much of the South, especially the cotton belt from central Georgia to Texas, farmers concentrated on special money crops. Nonetheless, slovenly farming methods abounded, along with general disrespect for grasses and livestock. Unable to recognize grass as part of livestock production and crop rotation, most farmers were intent on destroying grass, not cultivating it. Then, too, it was difficult to disseminate information about grasses because a single variety usually had a multitude of names. A few farmers did use commercial fertilizers imported from Peru as early as 1845. Livestock, while fairly plentiful, consisted of "ragged starvelings" that often roamed the open range much as they did in the West. The average farmer learned by experience to grow enough food for his family and to use the corn crib as insurance against low cotton prices, but he failed to diversify, lacked self-sufficiency, and resisted "book farming."[11]

Peters significantly broadened his activities and took a major step toward his long-term efforts to reform Southern agriculture on 1 January 1847 by paying a mixed-blood Cherokee $4,000 for 745 acres of creek bottom and upland in the Oothcaloga Valley near Calhoun. Peters began modestly, renting out his land on shares of the corn crop the first year, and otherwise investing in only a corn sheller and some fencing.[12] At the end of 1847 his share of the corn crop was one thousand bushels, which he sold at thirty cents a bushel for $300. But his seven-percent interest rate was $280, so for

---

[10]Burton J. Bell, ed. and comp., *1976 Bicentennial History of Gordon County, Georgia* (Calhoun: The Gordon County Historical Society, Inc., 1976) 69-71, 261, 410.

[11]Some cotton planters, such as Farish Carter, David Dickson, William Terrell, and Martin W. Philips were noted for balanced practices, and there were a few editors or nurserymen, such as Edmund Ruffin, Robert Nelson, Jarvis Van Buren, and Louis and Jules Berckman, father and son, who called for agricultural reform. Many of the latter group lived in towns and cities. Weymouth T. Jordan, *The United States From Revolution to Civil War, 1783-1861* (New York: Pageant Press, Inc., 1964) 160-61; Bonner, *History of Georgia Agriculture*, 43-45, 76-77, 87-89, 111-12, 129-31; Range, *Century of Georgia Agriculture*, 6, 10, 18; Fletcher M. Green, *The Role of the Yankee in the Old South* (Athens: University of Georgia Press, 1972) 113-14.

[12]Jewell R. Alverson (Gordon County historian) to Royce G. Shingleton, 3 March 1975; Farm Book, Peters Estate Collection, Atlanta Historical Society; Bell, *History of Gordon County*, 106, 260.

the 1847 farming year, Peters netted only $20. He was quite displeased with the results of this initial year—not so much by the financial outcome, but with the work of the farmers. The tracts under cultivation yielded from twenty to thirty bushels per acre, which was near the national average of twenty-five bushels, but Peters complained in his farm record book that the land was "badly cultivated," and he made a decision: "Whole farm and fences in very bad order—decided not to rent land again."[13]

Peters's main interest at the moment, however, centered on the Thompson family. Mary Jane Thompson was now seventeen years old. She found Peters successful, handsome, well-dressed, responsible, informed, and above all, eligible. Peters considered her of age, believed himself fortunate to receive her attention, and waited no longer. As he explained in his memoir:

> When business brought me to Atlanta I boarded with Dr. Joseph Thompson, who occupied the brick hotel which had been built by the Georgia Railroad Company. Here I met his eldest daughter, Mary Jane, and fortunately, for me, fell in love with her. We were married on Friday, the 18th day of February, 1848, and I have never had any reason to regret my choice, as she has proved the most faithful and loving wife, devoted to me and our children, all of whom I have reason to be proud.[14]

Reverend John S. Wilson married them that rainy February day at the Thompson home in Decatur. After a honeymoon of six weeks in Philadelphia, New York, and Boston, Peters returned with his young bride to a house he had purchased at 99 South Forsyth Street. It was the same house where the Episcopalians had held their initial meeting, for which he paid $1,500 to its owner, Samuel G. Jones. The L-shaped, two-story, weatherboarded structure was a departure from the Greek influence of the period. Light lattice supports, a then recent Victorian modification, substituted for the usual columns. One of Atlanta's most prominent residences, it was situated on Forsyth at Mitchell on two acres of beautiful grounds with a fruit orchard and garden in the rear. He owned several nearby lots on which he planted various grasses, and also purchased ten acres on Mitchell Street to pasture his cows. The house and grounds, admired by travelers in the rustic

---

[13]Farm Book, Peters Estate Collection.

[14]Peters, "Personal Recollections," 26.

little community, gave tangible evidence that the new owner was one of Atlanta's most influential citizens.[15]

Wash Houston, agent of the Atlanta and West Point Railroad, in commenting on Peters's marriage to Mary Jane, also noted Peters's significance in Atlanta history:

> My first impressions of him were coupled with high appreciation of his good judgement, and the indignation of the small Presbyterian congregation, when he removed from it one of its most amiable, honored and charitable members in the person of Miss Mary J. Thompson, who was its main dependence in dispensing charity, so much needed in the early history of Atlanta, by reason of exposure caused by insufficient shelter, and privations incident to rapid increase of population. In this connection permit me to say, that our indignation at her loss was fully reconciled by his endorsement of her noble spirit, and contributing bountifully to all worthy objects, and every institution or cause having in view the elevation of our then cosmopolitan population.[16]

On 18 May 1848, a few months after Peters's wedding, Bishop Elliott consecrated St. Philip's Church. The small frame structure cost less than $1,000, was painted white inside and out, and contained grained pews and pulpit. The plain architecture of St. Philip's reflected Elliott's pragmatic cheap-church policy as did the small size of the building. The bishop was of the opinion that the edifice would be large enough for years to come; he had sufficient reason to think so since there were still only five members. He believed the parish would remain weak until a new generation, that lacked prejudice against the British stigma, required a more suitable building.

The following year St. Philip's parish suffered a crisis that, at least for the moment, made Elliott's cheap-church policy seem all the more prudent. Hunt resigned, causing irregular services, and two of the five members left Atlanta. Disappointed at this turn of events, Peters wrote the missionary board in Macon pledging parish support for a regular minister, a move that proved successful, resulting in a period of growth that set the church on a self-sustaining course. Reverend William J. Zimmer became the new rector and soon the church boasted nine members, including Peters's wife Mary

---

[15]Ibid.; Harold Bush-Brown, "Architecture in Atlanta," *Atlanta Historical Bulletin* 23:5 (October 1940): 281; Reed, *History of Atlanta*, 42-43.

[16]Washington J. Houston to Nellie P. Black, 23 December 1901, in Black, *Richard Peters*, 48-49.

Jane, with between forty and sixty others attending services. As a result of this growth, Zimmer, who suffered some illness from sleeping in the cold church, collected over $1,300 and built a rectory. With growing enthusiasm, the parishioners next added a small schoolhouse and enclosed the entire physical establishment with a wooden fence.[17]

Early in 1849 Peters was at work on another venture—a telegraph line. This important adjunct to the railroads began in 1845 when Amos Kendall, former United States Postmaster General who had become Samuel F. B. Morse's agent, encouraged private companies to construct lines. Part of the resulting network, the first in the South, was a line built by the Washington and New Orleans Telegraph Company. The wire swung southward from Washington to Macon, then westward to New Orleans. The Mexican War gave a sense of urgency to the project, and the company built segments of the system simultaneously. The Macon and Western Branch Telegraph Company proposed a branch line designed to tie into the system; its line would stretch northwestward from Macon through Griffin to Atlanta.

Peters, a stockholder in the Macon and Western Branch Telegraph Company, attended a meeting in Griffin in February 1849 where he became one of the four directors of the company. With some of the poles already in place, the directors pushed for an early completion date and Atlanta was connected to the outside world by telegraph in May, seven years before the organization of the famous Western Union Company, with which the branch was ultimately merged.[18] By pushing for the branch, Peters rendered an important service to his adopted city because the wire enhanced the system of railroads connecting in Atlanta. Fast, accurate communication improved the quality of business in Atlanta and decreased reliance upon agents in coastal cities. A particular advantage to farmers, merchants, and bankers was that shipments of produce from the west could be regulated to take ad-

---

[17]St. Philip's Episcopal Church Parish Minutes; Stephen Elliott, Diary, Georgia Department of Archives and History, Atlanta; Hitz, *History of St. Philip*, 8-15. One of the original members to leave Atlanta was Thomson, who returned to Pennsylvania and became president of the Pennsylvania Railroad.

[18]Robert L. Thompson, *Wiring a Continent: The History of the Telegraph Industry in the United States 1832-1866* (Princeton: The University Press, 1947) 44, 140, 240, 289, 422; Robert S. Cotterill, "The Telegraph in the South, 1845-50," *South Atlantic Quarterly* 16 (April 1917): 149-54; Garrett, *Atlanta and Environs*, 1:277-78; Elma S. Kurtz, "War Diary of Cornelius R. Hanleiter," *Atlanta Historical Bulletin* 14:3 (September 1969): 10.

vantage of the highest prices. This was especially applicable after completion of the General Depot in Atlanta, where grain could be stored until prices in Southern ports reached favorable levels. In turn, the storage depot gave Atlanta the advantage of being a breaking point, a development that increased the city's business activity.[19]

Peters's efforts to reform Atlanta's government also began to show results. Jonathan Norcross, a reform-minded citizen, won the 1850 mayoralty election and became the first mayor to represent the Moral party. But the Rowdy party then renounced elections as the way to decide issues in Atlanta. As a result, the two factions had a showdown during Mayor Norcross's term of office. Following a drama in mayor's court where a Rowdy defendant drew a knife and escaped, an armed clash developed on the streets between the two groups. The Moral party won this miniature civil war and the Rowdy party disintegrated as a leading force in Atlanta. Peters's unique contribution to the establishment of public order in Atlanta was the successful appeal to the legislature for an act of reincorporation that had provided the reform movement with a solid foundation.

As a result of the reform movement, city officials were able to confine bawdiness and brawling to a restricted area within the city. That area, ironically, was a section of Peters Street. "Snake Nation," the junction of Peters Street and the Macon and Western Railroad crossing, was the meeting place of the city's disorderly element, full of reprobates and "low female characters." Further east on Peters Street, toward Fair Street, a more respectable community spirit prevailed. It was best reflected in meetings, usually in a merchant's store, of the street's residents and businessmen, gathering to consider some local question. All of Peters Street was full of activity. Street auctions, medicine shows, wagonyards, and boardinghouses attracted farmers who came from Atlanta's hinterland for supplies.[20]

---

[19]Roger L. Ransom and Richard Sutch, *One Kind of Freedom: The Economic Consequences of Emancipation* (Cambridge: The University Press, 1977) 116; David R. Goldfield, *Cotton Fields and Skyscrapers: Southern City and Region, 1607-1980* (Baton Rouge: Louisiana State University Press, 1982) 58.

[20]Helen K. Lyon, "Richard Peters: Atlanta Pioneer—Georgia Builder," *Atlanta Historical Bulletin* 38:10 (December 1957): 22-23; *Atlanta Constitution* (20 October 1885); Walter G. Cooper, *Official History of Fulton County* (Atlanta: Walter W. Brown Publishing Co., 1934) 58-59, 313; Paul W. Miller, ed., *Atlanta: Capital of the South* (New York: O. Durrell, 1949) 15-16.

Peters's dual role of urban builder and Southern planter was beginning to come into clear focus in these years. He added 160 acres to his farm lands, hired an overseer and three laborers, and bought two slaves. His purchase of farm equipment included ten plows, ten cultivators, a harrow, a small mill, a thrasher and separator, a two-horse wagon and harness, a four-horse wagon and harness, and four work horses. In addition, he bought some Chester County swine and Durham, or "short-horn," cattle to begin livestock breeding and sales. Peters also began using a variety of fertilizers, including wood ash and land plaster. He sowed forty acres of wheat, one hundred acres of corn (three different varieties), and began some limited experimentation with clover. At the end of his second year, according to his figures, income—including livestock born during the year and grain in the crib—was $1,595; outlays, mainly interest and labor, amounted to $1,449, or a $146 profit.[21]

In 1849 he improved his plantation by adding a house two miles southeast of Calhoun. This made it convenient for Mary Jane, who could ride the Western and Atlantic train up with him (a trip of some four hours), and for him to provide what was the chief extravagance of most planters—hospitality to guests. Intended mainly for summer and weekend living, the house was constructed of hand-cut internal supports and had eight plastered rooms and a fireplace. A covered passage stretched from the rear of the main house to a two-room servant house. Across the road, Peters raised a barn and thrasher house. He also added another tract of land to his holdings, bringing the total to some 1,200 acres, of which about 300 were under the plow and a like amount in woodland pasture with the remainder forested. He expanded his experiments with grains and grasses to include wheat, rye, clover, oats, millet, and corn, and recorded the results of the different varieties. He increased his stock of choice animals, so that the amount of money invested in livestock almost equaled that invested in land; interest on livestock and land purchased to this date amounted to $775 a year, a factor that sometimes caused Peters a loss on his operation.[22]

However, his livestock was beginning to attract attention. "Mr. Peters has gone into this matter 'con amore,' " commented one farm editor. "He

---

[21]Farm Book, Peters Estate Collection.

[22]Jewell R. Alverson to Royce G. Shingleton, 3 March 1975; Farm Book, Peters Estate Collection.

has made his selections from good stock, and with the proper care and treatment bestowed, we are sure he will sweep off a goodly number of premiums at every exhibition" of the 1849 Stone Mountain Fair. The Stone Mountain fairs were sponsored by the new agricultural society in Georgia. John W. Graves, who wanted more guests for his hotel at Stone Mountain Depot, interested Mark A. Cooper and David W. Lewis, who wanted to improve agricultural techniques, in organizing the Southern Central Agricultural Society. The group prospered, and since no adjoining state had as yet a large agricultural society to compete for the few members from outside Georgia, it was to some extent regional in nature, as the name suggests. At the society's first fair at Stone Mountain, a "jubilee" held in August 1846, Graves had improvised some stands on his property south of the Georgia Railroad where the only exhibit was his own "jack and ginnett." Yet from this inauspicious beginning sprang a series of increasingly successful fairs at Stone Mountain.[23]

Peters, a member of the society's board of directors, displayed his contribution to the improvement of Southern agriculture at the August 1849 fair. Among his livestock exhibits were a pair of Devon yearling cattle, Cotswold, South Down, and Leicester sheep, Chester County and Barrow swine (called "aristocratic porkers"), and Malay and Poland fowls. Among the field products he displayed were Imperial oats and "very fine corn of the White Flint species." Peters took six cash premiums.

The 1849 fair had its flaws. First of all, some fair-goers tormented P. T. Barnum's elephant, "Sultan," until the big animal became unmanageable, "winding up in the falling of the seats, then a scramble for the exit, followed by the collapse of the canvas, resulting in painful bruises." The greatest problem, however, was overcrowding. There were five hundred exhibits, double the number of the preceding year, and some exhibitors, including Peters, were forced to display their stock in pens and boxes amid tree trunks, roots, and rocks. Several thousand homespun country folk from surrounding counties created "din and confusion, thirst and dust." Complaints became vigorous about the lack of "fixings" such as tents, signs, booths, hotels, and restaurants. "Hundreds roamed about the woods, sitting over camp fires, snoring in wagons and making the night hideous with

---

[23]*Atlanta Constitution* (18 September 1900); *Southern Cultivator* 7:9 (September 1849): 137; Bonner, *History of Georgia Agriculture*, 111-13.

all sorts of unearthly sounds." Many left daily by rail for want of sleeping quarters. "The good people at Stone Mountain ought to manage these things better," concluded the editor of the *Southern Cultivator*.

The growing pains of this "most successful of all previous fairs" gave Peters an opportunity to move the fair to Atlanta. As a director and major exhibitor, it was not difficult to arrange for a seat on a five-member committee appointed to select a new site for the fair. But the issue itself was hotly contested. Peters, the only member from Atlanta, pointed out that the city had better rail connections,[24] and as an additional impetus, secured from his friend L. P. Grant a donation of ten acres of open ground on the south side where a clear spring provided an ample supply of water. The committee finally agreed that this land would be a good location for the 1850 fair—hence the name Fair Street (Memorial Avenue).[25]

To insure the success of the fair, Peters took a seat on the local arrangements committee with David W. Lewis, secretary of the association, Mark A. Cooper of North Georgia, and Peters's fellow Atlantans William Ezzard and James M. Calhoun (cousin of John C. Calhoun). By August, all was in readiness. Since Atlanta lacked adequate hotel space, they made arrangements for the three railroads in Atlanta to carry visitors in special cars to and from hotels in Griffin, Decatur, Stone Mountain, and Marietta. Many farmers brought tents and met under canvas on the enclosed grounds at the site. All exhibits were registered and, if for sale, prices recorded. Doorkeepers and clerks protected the grounds and buildings, and arranged and labeled articles for judging. Peters exhibited and sold liberally, taking cash premiums for his Devon bull, "Boston," and heifers, "Beauty" and "Jenny Lind"; his half-Durham and half-Devon bull calf, "DeKalb"; Lincolnshire and Medley boars; Cotswold, Oxforshire, and South Down sheep; as well as silver cups for White Flint corn and Imperial oats.[26]

---

[24]Peters's reference to Atlanta's rail connections received dramatic emphasis on 1 November 1849 when a crowd inside a mountain at Tunnel Hill north of his plantation celebrated the completion of the Western and Atlantic Railroad. After regular service began the following year, Atlanta entered the national railroad system and stood preeminently at the center of Southern transportation. Georgia Department of Archives and History, *Newsletter* 4:4 (February 1982): 4.

[25]*Southern Cultivator* 7:9 (September 1849): 137, 7:10 (October 1849): 145-57; *Atlanta Constitution* (18 September 1900).

[26]Farm Book, Peters Estate Collection; *Southern Cultivator* 8:6 (June 1850): 108, 8:9 (September 1850): 136, 141; Scrapbook, Black Collection.

Atlanta's first agricultural fair surpassed by far any previous fair in Georgia. Its success, a symbol of Atlanta's growing importance, was due in large measure to Peters.[27] Atlantans valued him as a townsman, and many Georgians admired him for his stockraising and diversified agriculture. He was now an adopted son of the South.

---

[27]*Atlanta Constitution* (18 September 1900).

CHAPTER FOUR

ANTEBELLUM YEARS:
MAN OF VISION,
CITY PROMOTER

Peters's next venture was to form a company and build the largest flour mill in the cotton states. With associates L. P. Grant, John F. Mims, and William G. Peters (a younger brother who was an Atlanta merchant in the firm of High, Peters Company), and a $50,000 capital investment, Peters erected the plant on a four-acre lot.[1] (The exact date and location remain unknown since several sources are in conflict on these points. There seems little doubt that the mill was in operation by 1850 and was near the Georgia Railroad freight depot, probably bounded by Piedmont Avenue, Butler and Hunter streets, and the Georgia Railroad.) Starting with a rock foundation, he constructed a well-built, three-story frame building and equipped it with a powerful 130-horsepower steam engine that had two cylinders, five boilers, and a flywheel weighing fourteen tons that drove four stones for wheat and one for corn. To provide firewood for the steam engine, Peters bought some four hundred acres of pine land just north of the Atlanta city limits,

---

[1]Richard Peters, "Personal Recollections," *Richard Peters: His Ancestors and Descendants*, comp. Nellie P. Black (Atlanta: Foote and Davies, 1904) 27.

paying $900 for Land Lot 49 and $1,200 for adjoining Land Lot 80 (a land lot consisted of 202.5 acres), with Peachtree Street—later West Peachtree—being the Lot line that divided the two tracts. The land cost less than five dollars an acre.

The Atlanta Steam Mills—or as it was better known, Peters Flour Mill—took its place as one of Atlanta's premier industries. Other important antebellum industries in Atlanta consisted of a few foundries, the machine shops of the Western and Atlantic and Georgia Railroads, and the Rolling Mill, which produced mostly railroad iron. As Peters's was the only flour mill in the city, business was often brisk; local farmers sometimes waited all day to have their wheat and corn ground. Women brought their knitting and settled under shade trees where they could keep an eye on the children. Men gathered into groups and discussed politics or crops while waiting their turn at one of the stones.

Peters soon discovered, however, that although his mill was the largest flour mill south of the great grain-processing city of Richmond, he had strong competition in selling flour. Just north of Atlanta, beyond Kennesaw on the Etowah River near the Western and Atlantic Railroad, was situated the Mark A. Cooper Iron Works (later the Etowah Mining and Manufacturing Company). This large operation included blast furnaces, a rolling mill, dams, a branch railroad, and twelve thousand acres of iron-ore fields. Cooper also operated a flour mill and, in order to raise money for his iron business, he sold flour at cost (or less) in Atlanta. Since Cooper consistently undersold Peters in the Atlanta market, the latter had difficulty making a profit. Peters also found that freight rates in and out of Atlanta worked against the flour mill.[2] He continued operation, however, and his persistence as a grain processor, combined with the large size of his mill, reflected his maxim: "Take both hands to what you do."[3]

As Atlanta grew, Peters Flour Mill seemed to prosper, and at times during the twilight of the antebellum South it operated day and night, grinding out 280 barrels of flour every twenty-four hours. And when Peters, com-

---

[2]Atlanta City Council Minute Books, 15 November 1850, 20 June 1851, 21 April 1852, 1 April 1853, Atlanta Historical Society; Sarah Huff, *My 80 Years in Atlanta* (Privately printed, 1937 [?]) 65, Huff Collection, Atlanta Historical Society; Paul W. Miller, ed., *Atlanta: Capital of the South* (New York: O. Durrell, 1949) 63; Walter G. Cooper, *Official History of Fulton County* (Atlanta: Walter W. Brown Publishing Co., 1934) 313.

[3]Peters, "Personal Recollections," 31.

bining business acumen with his genuine friendliness, presented a sack of flour to a local newspaper editor, the latter touted the flour as a "very superior, super-excellent article" that would compare favorably with the best American or English brands. Because the flour made splendid light-bread and biscuits, the editor predicted that Peters's mill would become world-famous.

Yet the milling operation continued to represent a blotch of red ink, caused not only by the railroad's refusal to lower freight tariffs on wheat shipped to Atlanta and the success of Cooper's mill, which was closer to the grain districts of North Georgia, but also by city property taxes, a problem he brought before city council. After this first mill venture proved unprofitable, he reorganized with William P. Orme and Dr. W. P. Harden as partners. This second effort was a financial failure as well and, at the end of the decade, Peters returned his associates' investments by buying their shares in the mill. In making good his partners' shares in a failing enterprise, his friends showed increased confidence in him and considered his paper gilt-edged.

Although the flour mill failed to turn a profit, it was nonetheless an important industry in the history of Atlanta and the South. The mill helped diversify Atlanta industry for a decade, played a role in winning tax concessions for industry in the city, and demonstrated to Southerners that machinery was no longer dependent on water power. For Peters personally, the business venture was also very important. Land Lots 49 and 80 became the nucleus of his wealth as Atlanta grew northward. As the years passed, he realized that his purchases were fortuitous: "Few make fortunes by good judgment or hard work," commented Peters. "Something they never foresaw takes place in their favor. Now here am I. I bought 400 acres of land merely to get wood from it, and it is in the heart of Atlanta."[4]

In these years, good citizens were called upon for necessary public service and on one occasion Peters saw duty as a police captain. On 21 April 1852, the city council's Committee on Patrol appointed him Captain of Pa-

[4]Ibid., 27; Atlanta Assessors Book (1861) Atlanta Historical Society; *Atlanta Intelligencer* (18 August 1857, 13 January 1858); *Atlanta National American* (24 March 1859); Atlanta *Southern Confederacy* (5 July 1862); Wallace P. Reed, *History of Atlanta, Georgia, with Illustrations and Biographical Sketches of Some of Its Prominent Men and Pioneers* (Syracuse: D. Mason Co., 1889) 457; Allen D. Candler and Clement A. Evans, eds., *The Cyclopedia of Georgia* 4 vols. (Atlanta: State Historical Association, 1906) 3:89.

trol for the Third District. Police organization was in its infancy at the time and citizens found themselves appointed by the committee to serve approximately one month's duty under the supervision of the city marshal. Atlanta was divided into three districts with a patrol captain and three patrolmen in each district. Peters probably doubled as patrolman as well since the Committee on Patrol appointed a total of only three men in his district.

Duty consisted of guarding the city from the time a bell rang at dusk until sunrise and reporting any ordinance violations to the marshal, who in turn reported to the mayor and council. This system seems to have been essentially a police force, although in some respects it was like the antebellum rural patrols whose express purpose was to insure that slaves remained in their cabins at night.

Within a few months of Peters's duty, the police force became more professional. On 4 June, a deputy was selected to aid the marshal and the following August the council appointed two salaried night watchmen to serve under the deputy marshal. Shortly thereafter the council designated a new title for the deputy marshal, that of Chief of Night Police—a step toward solving the problem of night watch.[5]

As Atlanta prospered, the city's modest banking institutions seemed to lag. In 1852, sentiment began to stir for a full-fledged banking institution and Peters joined a group of citizens to incorporate the Atlanta Bank. However, he quickly assumed a wait-and-see attitude and refused to subscribe to stock in the company, especially after George Smith of Chicago visited Atlanta and purchased most of the shares. After two years of controversial banking operations that included a state legislative investigation and a paper-money policy that caused a run, Smith closed the bank.

Perhaps another reason Peters decided against the Atlanta Bank was that the agency branch of the Georgia Railroad and Banking Company was located in Atlanta (corner of Peachtree and Wall streets) and Peters was a director of the company. Under his guidance, the agency bank kept pace with Atlanta's growth and became one of the largest and most respected banks in the city. The city council selected it as the source of borrowed funds on behalf of the city and Peters in turn invested in city bonds. Peters's

---

[5]Atlanta City Council Minute Books, 21 April, 9 August 1852; David R. Goldfield, "Pursuing the American Urban Dream: Cities in the Old South," *The City in Southern History: The Growth of Urban Civilization in the South*, ed. Blaine A. Brownell and David R. Goldfield (Port Washington: Kennikat Press, 1977) 65.

financial ties to the city government increased his interest in municipal affairs and linked more closely his career with the growth of Atlanta.[6]

On 4 February 1853, Mayor John F. Mims, one of Peters's partners in the flour mill venture, appointed him to the Atlanta Board of Health. According to Atlanta's enabling laws, the board consisted of up to nine people, at least one of whom should be a physician, although most members were physicians; a term was one year and members served without pay. The duty of the board was to examine causes of ill health in the city and report to the council, which would then proceed to remedy or remove the causes of concern. The incoming board had an organizational meeting and divided into two committees: one group served the south side of the city and one the north. Peters was a member of the committee serving the south side, his area of residence. Typical of the issues that came to the attention of the board was the existence of slaughter pens in Atlanta. Peters helped draft the report to the council: "We believe these pens to be nuisances, equally injurious to the comfort and health of the City, and they should therefore be immediately abated." The council acted swiftly, directing the marshal to notify the owners to have them removed within ten days.

The major problem, however, was the prevention and treatment of smallpox. In the 1850s, most boards of health were emergency bodies whose activities increased significantly during epidemics. However, such diseases were not just health problems, they were also bad for business since the comings and goings of planters, merchants, and others were often determined by the presence of epidemics. The Atlanta Board of Health usually advocated smallpox vaccination to all willing citizens (an outbreak in 1882 resulted in a city ordinance that required vaccination), but stringent measures were sometimes taken to contain the menace. It was common practice for the city council to hire a guard to insure the quarantine of a stricken person or group, and occasionally a house and its furnishings would be burned. The latter usually affected the poor, whose crowded conditions often encouraged epidemics.

Atlanta promoters liked to boast that their city was healthful because of its altitude, which they thought must have been a deterrent because one

---

[6]Atlanta City Council Minute Books, 6 January 1857; Franklin M. Garrett, *Atlanta and Environs: A Chronicle of Its People and Events* 2 vols. (Athens: University of Georgia Press, 1969) 1:346.

source of smallpox was the local hotels, where visitors presumably introduced the disease. During one epidemic, the board requested the transfer of all exposed persons from one of the hotels to the hospital where they were quickly quarantined under guard. The action highlighted the need for a new hospital; Atlanta's first hospital, built in 1848, was meant to be temporary and the board obviously considered it inadequate. At a special meeting, the board admonished that "too great attention cannot be paid to this subject." As a result, the council immediately secured a lot and began a hospital, adding an almshouse with a smallpox room on the same tract, all to be erected at the fairgrounds.[7]

Urban life for Peters was, of course, more than public duty. A good example of how the city's growth rewarded him personally with a quick profit was the case of "Peters's Reserve"—a four-acre block at Mitchell and Washington streets that Peters had purchased for $225. City fathers had grown weary of conducting public business in various makeshift quarters and requested Mayor Mims to learn the price of "Peters's Reserve" as a possible site for a city hall. Peters informed Mims that the price was $5,000 and, when the mayor reported back to the council, the group directed him to close the deal. Such an increase was tremendous, even for Atlanta real estate during the six years Peters owned the lot, but his close business ties with the city leaders may well have facilitated the transaction. Whereas the figure was high for the municipal budget, the city was growing by one thousand people a year, which would directly, positively affect the budget.

The council's Committee of Public Works soon reported plans for a $15,000 building. The committee noted that most citizens favored the project and many thought a $20,000 structure would be more suitable for Atlanta's growing importance among the cities of the South, a figure which, after cost overruns, was nearer the mark. The evening of 17 October 1854 was a grand moment for Atlantans. They celebrated the completion of Atlanta City Hall with a gala dress-ball inside the building, which after a one-year construction period stood proudly on "Peters's Reserve." The two-story brick City Hall served not only the city, but also the county and state ex-

---

[7]Atlanta City Council Minute Books, February, April, June, August, November, December 1853; David R. Goldfield, *Cotton Fields and Skyscrapers: Southern City and Region, 1607-1980* (Baton Rouge: Louisiana State University Press, 1982) 40; Blake McKelvey, *The Urbanization of America, 1860-1915* (New Brunswick: Rutgers University Press, 1963) 89.

tremely well for three decades. It was often the scene of spirited public meetings and was a favorite place for corporate meetings, religious meetings, social gatherings, and lectures. Peters himself was to accomplish some of his most important work as city builder in the multipurpose building constructed on his former property.[8]

In 1854, the last link of Atlanta's four antebellum railroads was in place as the Atlanta and West Point Railroad now stretched southwestward from Atlanta and connected with the Montgomery and West Point Railroad, providing an all-rail route to Montgomery, Alabama. (Subsequently, Peters transferred his stagecoaches to a line between Montgomery and Mobile that ran until the Civil War.) The railroad industry was the primary impetus of Atlanta's growth and while Peters was a director of two of them—the Georgia Railroad and the Atlanta and West Point Railroad—none of the four companies was controlled by Atlanta. This lack of control posed a dilemma for Atlantans because rail officials in Georgia favored the city whose citizens owned a majority of the stock and where the company was headquartered. Furthermore, these rail officials assigned low freight rates to cities like Augusta in order to compete with their water transportation and high rates to cities like Atlanta that had no competition. The same freight discrimination that hampered Peters Flour Mill also irked Atlanta's merchants.

Peters realized that Atlanta needed a railroad controlled within the city and he favored transportation links to the west, as evidenced by his stagecoach line. Expecting therefore to build a direct line to the west, Peters and other Atlantans obtained a legislative charter in 1854 and incorporated the Georgia Western Railroad. The line was to extend westward from Atlanta through Carrollton to the state line, where it would connect with railroads projected in Alabama. A factor of growing importance was that the road would provide access to Alabama's coal and iron-ore region. Because minimal grading would be needed, approximately $1,000,000 would be needed to construct the Georgia Western.

On the other hand, Jonathan Norcross, who was northern-trade oriented, had long favored a direct route through North Georgia. Failing repeatedly to have the city finance a plank road to Dahlonega, he led a movement that resulted in a legislative charter for the Air Line Railroad (a

---

[8]Atlanta City Council Minute Books, 9, 16 February, 29 July, 9, 24 September, 11 November 1853, 9 January 1854; Garrett, *Atlanta and Environs*, 1:355-56, 380.

direct route was called an "air line") to extend from Atlanta northward through Charlotte, North Carolina, to Richmond, Virginia, forming a link in a trunk line from New York to New Orleans. Curiously, the incorporators included Peters and Grant, who later opposed the route. The total cost of the Air Line was difficult to project, but it was agreed that construction would not begin until $750,000 had been raised by "good and responsible subscribers."

Unfortunately, Atlantans became divided on the merits of the two routes and two highly partisan groups quickly developed. Peters and L. P. Grant, both trained engineers, led the Georgia Western company, and Norcross and E. M. Seago, both merchants, led the Air Line company. When the opposing forces canvassed Atlanta for funds, they found the confused merchants reluctant to subscribe. Needing additional funds, both companies sent representatives into the countryside, holding railroad meetings in small villages along the proposed routes. Large crowds would gather to hear glowing speeches and consume a barbeque dinner, after which the subscription books were opened. But the several thousand dollars raised in this manner represented only a small fraction of the total amounts needed. In addition, many people subscribed only if the company promised to build through their town, which would add unnecessary mileage and expense as well as reduce the advantage of a direct line.

Relations between the rival companies grew increasingly caustic: Peters accused Norcross of poor management in "running the road hither and thither after driblets of conditional subscriptions"; Norcross charged that Peters helped obtain the Air Line charter in order to defeat another proposed charter that would be in direct competition to the Georgia Railroad.[9] Whatever the merit of Norcross's charge, there is no question that Peters and his associates fought the Air Line proposal and succeeded in delaying its construction. But in checkmate fashion, lack of subscriptions also stalled progress on the Georgia Western. Atlanta still did not control a railroad.

By 1855 Peters's irrepressible business and public improvement instincts were again exerted when he and Dr. William Harden purchased Wil-

---

[9]Atlanta City Council Minute Books, 22 July 1853, 17 November 1856; Atlanta Ordinance Book, 1851-1860, Atlanta Historical Society; James M. Russell, "Atlanta, Gate City of the South 1847 to 1885" (Ph.D. dissertation, Princeton University, 1971) 81-86.

liam H. Thurmond's Downing Hill Nursery in Atlanta.[10] The headquarters for the new Peters, Harden Company, located on Fair Street, contained the salesrooms and plots for small shrubs and plants, while the trees were grown in a fifty-acre orchard just south of present-day Grant Park. Determined to learn the fruit business thoroughly and develop the best trees, Peters divided the orchard into a grid, with each square planted with a single tree. Every tree was closely observed until it bore fruit. If the fruit was satisfactory, Peters propagated new scions from it. But if the fruit was undesirable, the tree was discarded. His painstaking experiments in the orchard cost $8,000 or $9,000 a year and resulted in the production of fruits of superior beauty and quality.

To supervise the new business on a day-to-day basis, Peters hired a highly regarded nurseryman from Cincinnati, William P. Robinson, who described the scope of Peters's horticultural work:

> Mr. Peters made importations of 40,000 plants a year from France, Japan and any place where they could be obtained; this included nursery stock, shrubs, evergreens, roses, every kind of plant that might suit our climate. We found trees from France more adapted to our section than those from any other country. The plants came in small pots packed in large cases. It took three months for them to come, but we never lost more than a dozen in a thousand, except when there was a delay caused by their being missent, then we would sometimes lose one-half the entire lot. From these importations Mr. Peters secured and distributed the best varieties of fruits known, and the fact should be recorded that his close attention, his experiments and the generous amounts of money he spent in the business brought about results, the value of which it is impossible now at this day to compute in dollars and cents.[11]

---

[10]For some time, Peters had noticed that Southern fruit was often of poor quality. The antebellum South lagged behind the North in horticulture both because of better transportation in the North as well as the Southern emphasis on cotton. There was also a great deal of confusion about the names of fruit, in spite of the publication of Andrew J. Downing's *Fruit Trees in America* (1845), because "every individual cultivator seemed to have a special name for his own." Ulysses P. Hedrick, *A History of Agriculture in the State of New York* (Albany: New York State Agricultural Society, 1933) 277, 283; James C. Bonner, *A History of Georgia Agriculture, 1732-1860* (Athens: University of Georgia Press, 1964) 149-55, 167; James C. Bonner, "Peach Industry in Antebellum Georgia," *Georgia Historical Quarterly* 31:4 (December 1947): 246-47. A notable Georgia horticulturist (and a predecessor to Peters's agricultural experiments) was John Couper (d. 1850) of St. Simons Island. Burnett Vanstory, *Georgia's Land of the Golden Isles* (Athens: University of Georgia Press, 1966) 122-23.

[11]William P. Robinson as told to Nellie P. Black in *Richard Peters*, 46-47.

Shipping trees far and wide in a thriving business, Peters sent the first peach trees to California, including one order of four thousand sent by sea around Cape Horn. These trees, from his best varieties, became the nucleus of California's fruit industry as large orchards were planted from the scions of the original shipment. From his nursery went the first ornamental shrubs and fruit trees planted by white settlers in New Zealand. He had to ship them via London, apparently because of the British mercantile system, and from there around Cape Horn to their destination. The plants and trees were en route for ten months, but arrived in good condition and grew well in the favorable climate. The result was New Zealand's fruit industry.[12]

Peters's reputation in fruit culture was recognized by the American Pomological Society, which named him their perennial vice-president from Georgia. He was also a director of the Pomological Society of Georgia, which originated in August 1856 in Athens. At a fruit display during the Athens meeting, Peters, Harden Company exhibited twenty-one varieties of pears, twelve of grapes, twelve of plums, twenty-one of peaches, six of nectarines, and twelve of apples—eighty-four varieties of fruit "making a very attractive show of itself." Peters contributed greatly to the Southern pomological boom of the 1850s, introducing varieties that today make the section noted for its fruit.[13]

In the semirural setting of antebellum Atlanta (a thriving but relatively small city—population six thousand in the mid-1850s), Peters's neighborhood was a lively place. Mary Jane's sister, Joan, and her husband, Thomas M. Clarke, an Atlanta hardware dealer, lived across from the Peters's home on Mitchell Street. The children of both families came in quick succession, and Richard, Jr., Nellie (baptized Mary Ellen), and the youngest, Ralph, would run across the street to "Aunt Jo's" for tea cakes. On Sunday, the families took a usually dusty walk to St. Philip's.[14]

---

[12]Ibid.; Lewis C. Gray, *History of Agriculture in the Southern United States to 1860* 2 vols. (Gloucester: Peter Smith, 1958) 2:825.

[13]*Southern Cultivator*, 12:11 (November 1854): 358, 14:1 (January 1856): 39, 14:9 (September 1856): 283-84, 14:10 (October 1856): 325; *Atlanta Journal* (18 July 1915); Bonner, *History of Georgia Agriculture*, 156-66.

[14]Nita Rucker, Notes on Nellie Peters Black, Nellie P. Black Collection, University of Georgia Libraries, Athens; *Atlanta Journal Constitution* (15 February 1981). Peters eventually had nine children, most of whom received family names, although two were named

St. Philip's slid into decline in 1854 when ill health forced the resignation of Reverend Zimmer. It was only after Peters, senior warden at the time, gave his personal pledge to pay the rector's salary for three years, quarterly in advance, that a new rector arrived. Peters had recently started breeding rabbits with a gray Madagascar buck and a black-and-white doe, both imported from England, and he befriended the new rector, Reverend Richard Johnson, by sending him some of the rabbits to breed on shares.[15]

A problem developed, however, when Peters led an effort to construct a new church building. He developed an intense distrust of Johnson's fundraising motives and wrote to Bishop Elliott, complaining that the rector was "the most troublesome 'Confidence Man' to be found in America." Johnson, according to both Peters and Mary Jane, was turning the rectory basement into a hybrid church, and in the process he was using the building fund for rectory alterations. Peters believed the congregation would reach two hundred if they ousted the Johnsons, "who amused themselves by abusing all who opposed them." Elliott expressed surprise at the rector's behavior and said Johnson had no right to initiate a new church without his consent. To harmonize the troubled parish, the bishop appointed a five-member mediation panel that held hearings in Atlanta and resulted in Johnson and the vestry resigning. The bishop then appointed a new rector, Reverend Andrew F. Freeman.

Elliott's response to the complaints of the Peterses restored harmony and flush times returned for the people of St. Philip's. The membership, which had fallen during the crises, soon rose to a new high of seventy and there was an even larger attendance. Fund-raising benefits became popular

after Southern Episcopal bishops. Richard, Jr., moved to Philadelphia and assumed the old family position as capitalist; Mary Ellen (Nellie) became known throughout Georgia because of her benevolent and organizational activities. Ralph became president of the Long Island Railroad; and Edward C. succeeded Peters as an Atlanta capitalist. Much sorrow surrounded those born during the era of the Civil War. Catherine was probably mentally retarded. Joseph Thompson and Stephen Elliott died as infants during the war and Quintard died as a young adult. The youngest child, beautiful Anna May (born circa 1868), survived to marry the founder of the Georgia Power Company. Peters, "Personal Recollections," 26; Scrapbook, Black Collection; Louise Black MacDougald, "My Seventh Move," *Atlanta Historical Bulletin* 32:8 (December 1947) 31-41.

[15]St. Philip's Episcopal Church Parish Minutes 1847-1859, 1870-1884, Georgia Department of Archives and History, Atlanta; Stephen Elliott, Diary, Georgia Department of Archives and History, Atlanta; Farm Book, Peters Estate Collection, Atlanta Historical Society.

and helped pour $4,000 into the building fund, although the onset of sectional hostilities caused plans for a larger church to be indefinitely postponed. One of the church's activities during the late antebellum period, a concert and dinner, drew an evening audience of townspeople who were unusually well-behaved, if not outright refined. Episcopalianism, already firmly established among the Southern planter aristocracy, had become an important factor in the cultural and religious life of Atlanta.[16]

---

[16]St. Philip's Episcopal Church Parish Minutes; Elliott, Diary; Peters to Stephen Elliott, 1859 (?); Stephen Elliott to Mary Jane Peters, 22 July 1859, Black Collection.

CHAPTER FIVE

DEVON HALL: AGRICULTURE'S GOLDEN AGE—1850s

T he city stimulated, the country fulfilled."[1] This Old World thought applied to Richard Peters, who found physical and aesthetic refreshment in Gordon County. However, he was not solely interested in its
providing him with pleasure, as he was determined to improve the quality
of livestock and contribute to agricultural diversification in the South.
These practices would help make the South independent of the North.

The plantation's close proximity to the Western and Atlantic Railroad
allowed Peters to ship livestock and produce easily and was convenient for
visitors. Dennis Redmond had a habit of traveling from his *Southern Cultivator* editorial office in Augusta to the plantation for a firsthand look. The
coeditor described Peters as "a gentleman of great enterprise, taste and liberality," noting that since retiring from railroad building, the Pennsylvania
native had fortunately possessed both the time and inclination to devote his

---

[1]Carl E. Schorske, "The Idea of the City in European Thought: Voltaire to Spengler,"
The Historian and The City, ed. Oscar Handlin and John Burchard (Cambridge: M.I.T.
Press and Harvard University Press, 1963) 99.

fortune and energy to the general improvement of Southern agriculture.[2] "Few people," wrote Redmond, "out of the immediate range of his acquaintance, are, perhaps, aware of the many industrial and progressive enterprises in which Mr. Peters has been and is now engaged (and mostly with that certain success which follows well-directed effort)."[3]

With a few small additions in the early 1850s, the plantation consisted of 1,360 acres, of which 700 were divided between cultivation and woodland pasture, with the remainder covered in native forest. While it did not have the finish of an old homestead, the plantation was well laid out with orchards, garden, and barns, "all showing the master hand." Peters maintained an extensive array of tools and equipment, some of which were made in his workshop and the others purchased from Philadelphia and Baltimore. As a scientific farmer who believed in deep plowing, Peters acquired extensive practical experience with improved plows and other agricultural implements. His favorite plow was the self-sharpening Subsoil Plow. A new horse-powered mill, the Daniel's Patent Cutter, astonished visitors by grinding enough hay, oats, and corn stalks or shucks in two hours to feed seventy head of stock for a day.

Peters generally planted 150 acres of wheat, 75 acres of corn, and about 100 acres of oats. To make the South independent of the North for seed potatoes, he grew samples of Irish potatoes to find a variety that would keep through the winter and then made them available to Southern farmers. Conducting a variety of experiments with grasses, Peters put in Herds grass (30 acres of which adjoined the Western and Atlantic Railroad tracks below Calhoun), Orchard grass, Velvet grass, and Timothy, White, and Red clovers. He especially liked the Red clover because it could be grazed rather than cut for hay, grown on average land, and it fit his rotation system well. Peters also cleared much of his woodlands of undergrowth and made wood pastures, the shade and moisture supporting Kentucky bluegrass. In all his

---

[2]Peters's farming methods were beginning to attract favorable notice in the agricultural press outside the South. For example, the editor of the *Western Horticultural Review* in Cincinnati, John A. Warder, a naturalist and former schoolmate of Peters in Pennsylvania, noted "the brilliant career as a southern farmer, which has been marked out by my early friend, R. Peters of Atlanta." Cited in *Southern Cultivator* 11:7 (July 1853): 210.

[3]*Southern Cultivator* 10:8 (August 1852): 253, 11:5 (May 1853): 146-47, 12:1 (January 1854): 26.

planting, he took advantage of the use of guano, lime, and other portable and concentrated fertilizers.[4]

In his quest for new plants, Peters introduced Chinese sugar cane to Georgia and became a leader in promoting its growth in the South. A variety of sugar cane had been grown throughout the Gulf coastal plain and along the South Atlantic coast during the early nineteenth century, including experiments by John Couper on St. Simons Island, but the plant failed to achieve notable commercial importance. In the upcountry, where sugar and molasses were expensive, attempts had been made to make sugar from Indian corn and other products, but high-carbohydrate foods remained scarce. During the early 1850s, a variety of cane had been sent from China to France by the French consul at Shanghai and a Boston firm soon imported some of the seed for trial in America. Dennis Redmond and Daniel Lee, who had established an agricultural room in their *Southern Cultivator* editorial office to collect farm products, books, and seed, became interested in the Chinese sugar cane, or sorghum (also known by its French name *Sorgho Sucre*), and forwarded seed samples to a few friends. Since Peters had sent many items to the editors (including two pair of white Fantail pigeons, samples of Guinea grass, a trio of Jersey Blue hens, rolls of Devon butter, popcorn seed, sacks of corn, barley, and oats, plus an assortment of garden vegetables), he received samples of the Chinese sugar cane seed. At first Peters considered the seed "humbug" because of its similarity to millet. He ate a handful and forgot the remainder for a time. Then while browsing in his garden in Atlanta one Sunday afternoon, he discovered some of the seed in his pocket and decided to plant a few. The results were dramatic. The luxuriant stalks, with crisp sweet inner piths, were relished by his children as ready-made candy and convinced him the variety was unlike others in the corn family.

In 1856, Peters hired a new manager, Major Aaron Roff. A New York City native, Roff had grown up in Augusta, Georgia, and had served in the Seminole Indian War and the Mexican War before settling down in Calhoun. The Southern overseer has been stereotyped in history as being brutal and unscrupulous, but Roff was, in fact, a gracious and congenial companion. He shared Peters's belief in progressive agriculture and his long record

---

[4]Ibid., 10:9 (September 1852): 274, 10:11 (November 1852): 343, 11:5 (May 1853): 148-49, 11:10 (October 1853): 314, 12:8 (August 1854): 258, 17:11 (November 1859): 14.

of service on the plantation complemented Peters's efforts.[5] In the spring, Peters planted several acres of sugar cane on his plantation, cultivating it the same as corn—plowing twice and hoeing once. During harvest time that fall, Rebecca Roff, the new overseer's wife, boiled the produce of twenty canes in an iron pot and produced just over a quart of "thick, sweet syrup, equal in all respects to the New Orleans 'Sugar House,' but of a racier and more agreeable flavor."

Encouraged, Peters began producing cane in commercial quantities. He purchased a mill consisting of two vertical iron rollers worked by two mules hitched to a long shaft and prodded around in a circle by a boy, while a man fed the cane through the cylinders. The mill crushed the stalks and in one hour produced enough juice for eight gallons of syrup. To process the juice, Peters designed an elaborate brick furnace; using his engineering skills, he developed specifications, sketches, and instructions. He then hired three masons tended by five of his slaves to construct the furnace on the plantation. It was over twenty-three feet long and had four kettles set in a row at different levels in the brickwork, with a flue running from the fire chamber underneath the kettles to a chimney on the opposite end. The furnace was probably one of the first and one of the largest in Georgia for making syrup from Chinese sugar cane.

Peters's methods and results, among the first reported in the United States on manufacturing syrup from sorghum, were published in the *Southern Cultivator*. He included a report of tests performed on his syrup by friend and chemist Robert Battey of Rome, Georgia. Peters reported that the cost of making syrup in North Georgia would amount to ten to fifteen cents per gallon. "I am satisfied that this plant will enable every farmer and planter in the Southern States, to make at home, all the syrup required for family use." He also expressed the hope that "our chemists will soon teach us how to convert the syrup into sugar for exports, as one of the staples of our favored clime."

Many exaggerated claims were made by the agricultural press, including the United States Patent Office, concerning the Chinese sugar cane. The

[5]James C. Bonner, "Plantation and Farm," *Writing Southern History: Essays in Historiography in Honor of Fletcher M. Green*, ed. Arthur S. Link and Rembert W. Patrick (Baton Rouge: Louisiana State University Press, 1965) 159; Burton J. Bell, comp., *1976 Bicentennial History of Gordon County, Georgia* (Calhoun: The Gordon County Historical Society, Inc., 1976) 356-57.

plant, aside from syrup and sugar, produced alcohol, cider, rum, and dye. The fodder became feed for livestock; the crushed stem could be manufactured into paper; the stubble could produce a second crop in a season without replanting; and the brush at the top when emptied of seed could be made into brooms. The seed itself could be ground into meal for human consumption. Indeed, the "Sorgho" was deemed "a sort of vegetable sheep, every part and constituent of which is valuable."

In order to promote production of the cane, Peters formed a partnership with William P. Orme and advertised small packages of the seed for sale. The editor of the *American Agriculturist*, Orange Judd, in an effort to boost circulation, bought four hundred bushels of seed from Peters and sent a package to each new subscriber. Yet in spite of a pamphlet by Redmond on syrup production, many farmers were ignorant of proper, proven methods of manufacture and the result was "an inevitable glutting of the market with thousands of gallons of overcooked, unpalatable syrup, or else a thin product [from] insufficient boiling . . . which quickly soured." Then, too, overfeeding the green cane to livestock caused some of the animals to die. Furthermore, pure cane seed was ruined if it was raised in too close proximity to "broom corn" or other varieties of millet, plus coastal region cane growers complained that it was potential competition to their own product. While Chinese sugar cane (replaced by the African, or Imphee, variety just prior to the Civil War) did not prove "the greatest boon to the South since the introduction of the Cotton plant," Peters's latest effort at diversification was nonetheless an important addition to the growing list of Southern products—the cane as feed for livestock and "sorghum sirip" as a welcomed addition to the diet of slaves and many whites.[6]

---

[6]Farm Book, Peters Estate Collection, Atlanta Historical Society; *Seventh Census of the United States, Population, Agriculture, 1850*; Aaron Roff as told to Nellie P. Black in *Richard Peters: His Ancestors and Descendants* (Atlanta: Foote and Davies, 1904) 52-53; *Southern Cultivator* 10:3 (March 1852): 93, 11:5 (May 1853): 149, 13:5 (May 1855): 162, 14:4 (April 1856): 119, 14:9 (September 1856): 298-300, 14:10 (October 1856): 313, 332-33, 357, 373; *Atlanta Constitution* (19 October 1884); E. Merton Coulter, *Daniel Lee, Agriculturist: His Life North and South* (Athens: University of Georgia Press, 1972) 11; James C. Bonner, *A History of Georgia Agriculture, 1732-1860* (Athens: University of Georgia Press, 1964) 49, 83-86, 215; Fletcher M. Green, *The Role of the Yankee in the Old South* (Athens: University of Georgia Press, 1972) 113-15; Burnett Vanstory, *Georgia's Land of the Golden Isles* (Athens: University of Georgia Press, 1966) 123; Lewis C. Gray, *History of Agriculture in the Southern United States to 1860* 2 vols. (Gloucester: Peter Smith, 1958) 2:741, 748, 829.

The first cattle Peters bred were Durhams. He purchased them from noted breeder A. B. Allen of New York. But Peters found the Durhams unsuited to the climate of the Deep South as they "ran to bone" in summer and ninety percent of them died of murrain (Texas fever). Peters also found that Durhams retrogressed with each breeding. He had seen none south of Tennessee that did not mature inferior to its parents. Finally, while large and beefy, the Durhams were poor milkers and he concluded that the breed seemed more suited to the bluegrass of Kentucky.

In the fall of 1850, Peters inspected a shipload of Devon cattle in New York imported by the breeder Ambrose Stevens. Although Peters already owned two Devons purchased a few years earlier—"Boston" and "Beauty"—this northern trip was a prelude to his building the largest herd of pure Devons in the South. Named after their native English shire, the Devons were deer-like in color, with long horns and white tails. Northern Devonshire was celebrated for its cattle, which were reputedly beautiful, made fine oxen, and were unrivaled in their ability to fatten. However, breeders had been slow to make careful selections that would develop the breed's milk production. Peters decided to concentrate on the breed and amassed 126 head, spending over $9,000 to purchase animals from such breeders as George Patterson of Maryland, R. H. Van Rensselaer and Lewis G. Morris of New York, and R. C. Gapper of Canada. Later, Peters imported from England with the help of British expert J. Tanner Davy, editor of the *Devon Herd Book*. The Gordon County herd was making Georgia the "Devonshire of America" and Devons became the most favored of the breeds imported into the lower South and in many border states during the antebellum period.

Peters kept his own records on each animal, measuring its growth and studying its condition. He became convinced of the superior value and adaptation of the Devons to the Southern climate. Being as meticulous in his breeding as he was in his purchases, he sold only the best stock in order to upgrade Southern cattle. Inferior calves were sent to the butcher. "There is not a more jealous breeder in any country," wrote one visitor. "A white foot or black nose is death by the law of Devon Farm." Peters considered the purebred male as the key to selective breeding and owned some of the best bulls in the world. "There he stands," one visitor wrote of "Baltimore," one of the most noted bulls of the breed, "with his nostrils dilated, his full round eyes glistening and flashing like convex mirrors, his clean jaws, curved neck, wide bosom, full chin, hoop ribs, straight back, wide and flat loin, all in view at once."

The master of Devon Hall—as his plantation was often called at the time—was interested in breeding good milkers because there were few dairies in the South. Butter from the North sold at the high price of fifty cents a pound, and much of that was a "villainous, greasy, and rancid compound." Peters, therefore, set up a dairy at Devon Hall and hired John Hawks and his family of Otsego County, New York (in the center of the state's dairy district), as manager. A veteran dairyman, Hawks had high praise for Peters's cattle, saying he had never seen such a herd; the cows, "in symmetry of form, style, color [invariably red], and milking points, can hardly be excelled." Many of them gave over twenty quarts of milk a day while suckling their calves. In the milking barn (the "Milky Way"), Hawks sat on a wooden stool that had only one round leg in the middle and extracted the buttery fluid. In a separate building, he churned an average of seventy pounds of high quality butter a week during the spring. Peters marketed much of the butter in Augusta. He was pleased with the butter-making qualities of the Devons and expected to expand his dairy operation.[7]

The editors of the *Southern Cultivator* lauded Peters's herd as "the most valuable collection of milking Devons in America."

> We speak advisedly in claiming this high merit for our model Georgia herd, being fully cognizant of the rigorous taste which has governed all the purchases of Mr. Peters for the last five or six years. Acting upon the true principles that *beef* and *milk* do not go together, he has in all cases given the latter the preference, and the result is, unquestionably, such as we have stated, vis: that he has succeeded in building up a herd of the purest North Devons, *superior in point of uniform milking properties* to any on this side of the Atlantic. For this service he deserves well of his country, and of the South especially, and should receive the thanks and generous support of all lovers of improvement.[8]

The cattle show at the 1851 fair of the Southern Central Agricultural Society was "unquestionably the very best ever made in Georgia or the

---

[7]Farm Book, Peters Estate Collection; *Southern Cultivator* 9:6 (June 1851): 82, 9:11 (November 1851): 62-63, 10:2 (February 1852): 60, 10:5 (May 1852): 257, 10:7 (July 1852): 211, 215, 10:8 (August 1852): 253, 11:5 (May 1853): 148, 11:8 (August 1853): 233-35, 13:2 (February 1855): 58, 13:8 (August 1855): 261, 13:9 (September 1855): 278, 40:11 (November 1882): 2-3; Gray, *History of Agriculture in the Southern United States to 1860*, 2:850; Bonner, *History of Georgia Agriculture*, 136-37.

[8]*Southern Cultivator* 13:2 (February 1855): 58.

South." As a member of the executive committee, Peters helped plan the fair, which drew its largest crowd ever. Held during October in Macon, Peters exhibited nine pure Devons, each of which had a printed statement of its age, food, and individual qualities. Dennis Redmond, after extolling Peters's purebred Devons in his journal, was then critical of some crossbreeds of other exhibitors; whereas some of their stock had good qualities, the animals could not be depended upon "for transmitting those qualities to its progeny." Peters also exhibited a large Georgia-raised mule, pure Suffolk swine, Oxfordshire sheep, self-sharpening plows, a wheat drill, and three bales of hay from clover, crabgrass, and peavine. In addition he displayed, apparently for the first time, flour and meal from Peters Flour Mill, and it was of "very superior quality." For added emphasis, he exhibited the products in special "varnished barrels of excellent workmanship." At the close of the fair, the prizes—silver cups, goblets, and pitchers—were on display in a covered case on the speakers' platform. "This glittering array was opened to the gaze of the multitude as soon as the reading of the reports of the Committees began; and, as often as a prize was awarded, it was handed, amid a flourish of trumpets from the Band, to the successful competitor."[9]

Peters carried away so many premiums that Daniel Lee, co-editor with Redmond and an advocate of cotton, charged that the executive committee of the society might be using the fair for selfish purposes. Stung by his criticism, Peters exhibited without competing for prizes at the annual fall event the following year, again held in Macon. His chief display was two bulls and seven cows from his herd of Devons. The report of the prize committee as read from the stand complimented Peters's Devons and "regretted that they had not been offered for premium, in which case, it was more than hinted that they would have been compelled to award them most of the prizes." Peters's refusal of premiums did open the competition to the smaller, younger herds and some premiums went to the owners of descendants of his Devon bull, "Boston." There was a total of 513 exhibits, up thirty-five percent over the year before, an indication that the fair enjoyed widespread popularity in spite of signs of discontent within the agricultural society.[10]

---

[9]Ibid., 9:5 (May 1851): 78, 9:11 (November 1851): 161-63.

[10]Ibid., 10:2 (February 1852): 60, 10:11 (November 1852): 322, 344, 11:8 (August 1853): 235; Weymouth T. Jordan, *The United States From Revolution to Civil War, 1783-1861* (New York: Pageant Press, Inc., 1964) 176.

When Peters's mahogany-red Devons began to contract murrain, his naturalist friend John Bachman suggested he add the strain of the larger Brahmin, the sacred cattle of India. According to Peters, the Zebus of India were the basis of all cattle, "a type of the original Adam and Eve creation." He paid $3,505 for a herd of twenty, and another $1,000, all in gold, for an imported bull. They were creamy white in color with large pendant ears and the big shoulder hump peculiar to the breed. "The animals did excellently," wrote Peters, "and I thought I had solved the problem." By his own account, he developed "a superior attack of Brahmin monomania. They made fine beef cattle, wonderful, and some of them were extraordinary milkers." One cow, "Ganges," gave over twenty-four quarts of milk a day.

Yet the Brahmins had two faults—the milk lacked butter-making qualities and the animals had a vicious temper. Peters called them "the most malevolent animals in the world with a distinctive aversion to women." Peters bred the Brahmins to Devons, Alderneys, and Guernseys, but the thin milk and viciousness remained. The cross was quite healthy (only one died of murrain) and they made the best working oxen Peters ever raised since they could pull heavy loads through the soft soil in the fields; he abandoned the breed reluctantly.[11]

Chickens also received Peters's attention. "These fowls are a mixture of the Shanghai and Dorking, raised expressly for the table, and combining the size and vigor of the first with the excellent flesh of the latter fowl in a remarkable degree. We commend this 'cross' to all lovers of 'chicken fixens' with perfect confidence." So wrote Dennis Redmond of the poultry set before him at mealtime on Peters's plantation. Peters admired fine poultry, and after experiments with various breeds, he gradually came to favor the Plymouth Rock as ideal for the Southern farmer.[12]

In the fall of 1853 Peters journeyed to Augusta to help with arrangements for the agricultural fair, where he once again entered his livestock in competition. He won several silver cups for his Devon, Ayrshire, and Alderney cattle (the latter from the famous Nicholas Biddle importation), and

[11]Peters to Albert Montgomery, 9, 12, 14, 21 January 1884, Nellie P. Black Collection, University of Georgia Libraries, Athens; *New Orleans Times Democrat* (5 November 1886); *Southern Confederacy* (28 May 1862).

[12]*Southern Cultivator* 10:9 (September 1852): 274; Bonner, *History of Georgia Agriculture*, 148.

a few other prizes, but he completely dominated the swine competition—taking fifteen of the twenty-one cups. Peters thought he had found the best breed for the South in the Suffolk, a pure white hog of medium size and small bones that fattened early. In 1853, however, he discovered that white breeds were not suited to a hot climate because they were susceptible to the mange. He then experimented with the Berkshire, Middlesex, Grazier, Essex and others, some of them of "rare excellence." His pigs came from Robert Marrow, an agent in Albany, Georgia, and from South Carolina and Tennessee; he imported the best males from England.

Finally, Peters decided on a favorite: "I have found the Essex the most profitable of any of the improved breeds; they are free from diseases, are easy keepers, and mature early." He found they produced meat at less cost per pound (two or three cents) and were "ready for the knife" in eighteen to twenty months, weighing 250 to 300 pounds. The Essex was particularly valuable for crossing on the common hog of the South—the "long-legged, lank, razor-backed 'land pikes.' " To be sure, Peters could count on hogs to make a profit. In swine production, as in his other experiments, he became an authority. Redmond began referring swine-related questions that were sent to his journal to Peters, "who had the most complete stock of improved Hogs . . . of any man in the cotton-growing states."[13]

The Southern livestock industry ranged from commercial herding, to haphazard herding and incidental animal husbandry as part of mixed farming, to what Peters practiced—highly specialized and intensive methods of animal husbandry.[14] A case in point was his experiments with Angoras. In 1854, Peters visited the plantation of James B. Davis near Columbia, South Carolina. Davis had served during the James K. Polk administration as consul to Turkey and upon his return introduced the Angora goat into America. From Turkey's Angora province, this goat was an odorless, high-strung animal with long ears and spiral horns. The Georgia stockman admired the "genteel deportment" of the Davis flock and bought all of his purebreds and several grades.

---

[13]Farm Book, Peters Estate Collection; *Southern Cultivator*, 10:9 (September 1852): 274, 11:1 (January 1853): 26, 11:5 (May 1853): 148-49, 11:11 (November 1853): 322-23, 12:2 (February 1854): 47; Bonner, *History of Georgia Agriculture*, 220.

[14]Gray, *History of Agriculture in the Southern United States to 1860*, 2:833.

This initial interest increased as Peters carried on the work begun by Davis. One of the earliest and largest breeders in the Western Hemisphere, Peters ultimately owned goats from six distinct importations from Asia Minor. After two large importations of his own, he realized there was great difficulty in obtaining the best strains. In Asia Minor, some owners mated the animals in the "haphazard manner of range animals," while others protected their monopoly by rendering the bucks sterile with a hot iron before shipping. The Cashmere goat from Kashmir in India was often confused with the Angora. Peters explained that the white Cashmere bore wool by the ounce, while the multicolored Angora produced mohair by the pound.[15]

Peters's chief aim in upgrading Angoras was to provide growers with quality breeding stock. As with other animals, he found that the characteristics of the female were recessive, and since only the male improved the stock, he relied on the finest imported, purebred bucks and not the "full blood" bucks, the progeny of which varied greatly. The fifth cross of imported bucks on native ewes (he preferred the terms "buck" and "ewe," believing that "billy" and "nanny" referred to common goats) came to full blood and produced mohair comparable to that of animals imported from Asia Minor and flesh "superior to most mutton." To keep track of the various stages of breeding, Peters developed a system of markings: the half-breeds were not marked; the three-quarter breeds were marked by a round hole in the left ear; the fifteen-sixteenth animals were marked by a round hole in each ear; and the full, or pure, breeds had a number burned on their

---

[15]After the United States Patent Office, which reported on agricultural matters, certified Peters's flock as "probably of the true Thibet or Cashmere variety," the Southern Central Agricultural Society established a committee chaired by John Bachman to report on Peters's flock. Bachman, whose work foreshadowed Charles Darwin, was a famous minister and natural scientist from New York who had moved to Charleston, South Carolina. Peters, who thought highly of Bachman, was glad to select a young grade buck for testing when the committee visited Gordon County. Studying a hair of the goat under a microscope, Bachman's committee concluded the Cashmere was quite closely related to the Angora.

At the request of Bachman's committee, Peters attempted to cross a male sheep on female goats. Since goats had not been regarded as valuable animals in America, the idea was to elevate the goat to the prestige of the sheep. Peters must have known this had been previously attempted in the United States without success and he could only report that the animals "copulated readily, but not a single young was produced." To this Bachman commented: "We learn here that God only is the creator of species." Farm Book, Peters Estate Collection; *Southern Cultivator* 13:11 (November 1855): 332, 14:9 (September 1856): 294, 14:10 (October 1856): 334-35, 16:2 (February 1858): 45-49. (Scientists using modern laboratory methods recently produced a cross in England.)

horns. At the head of the flock, with the number "1" on his horns, stood a buck from the original Davis importation, "Old Billy Hitchcock."

Unlike sheep, the Angora was a hearty, self-sustaining animal that ranged far and ate vegetation refused by other animals. This munching machine also improved woods pastures by cleaning undergrowth. Peters lauded the Angora's ability to fatten at double the distance from water than sheep because the goat traveled faster and endured the heat. According to Peters's record book, Angoras were also more prolific than sheep, increasing in number approximately one hundred percent annually. The goats required little attention—they were generally exempt from disease, and the bucks in the herd successfully fought off dog attacks. Peters kept a liberal supply of bells on his flock and trained a few goats to be guides, or bellwethers, so that the herd came home at night without a herdsman. He thought that his Angoras "succeeded admirably." Although Peters was chiefly interested in breeding, he did sell some mohair. Each Angora usually yielded three pounds, which in the 1850s fetched about sixty cents a pound. One of the few animals that turned a profit for Peters, he understandably considered the Angora one of the "most valuable acquisitions to the resources of our husbandry."[16]

In 1855, the Atlanta city council donated additional acreage to the Southern Central Agricultural Society provided the fair would locate permanently in Atlanta. The executive committee (under Peters's influence) accepted and the annual event returned to the city during four hot days in September. Peters took the usual premiums for his Devon cattle, Berkshire and Essex swine, and South Down sheep. But it was his exhibition of Angora and Cashmere goats, apparently the first showing by Peters, that attracted great attention and was a redeeming feature of the livestock department, which had deficiencies in several categories. To demonstrate the usefulness of the goats, Peters displayed samples of cloth and knit socks of varying degrees of fineness that had been woven from the fleece. Dennis Redmond regarded the animals as "by far the most important addition to our domestic animals that has been made within our recollection."[17]

---

[16]Peters to John L. Hayes, 1 January 1878, Black Collection; Farm Book, Peters Estate Collection; *Southern Cultivator*, 7:10 (October 1849): 155, 9:2 (18 February 1851): 23-24, 13:5 (November 1855): 344, 16:2 (February 1858): 45-59; John L. Hayes, *The Angora Goat: Its Origin, Culture, and Products* (Cambridge: The University Press, 1882) 68-86.

[17]*Southern Cultivator* 13:1 (January 1855): 26-27, 13:10 (October 1855): 312, 13:11 (November 1855): 332; Green, *Yankee in the Old South*, 101-104.

Peters's plantation became the nucleus for Angora breeders in various parts of America. In the late antebellum period he pastured between five and six hundred head, of which fifty were purebreds. In 1861, he shipped two young Angora bucks to William M. Landrum of California's San Joaquin Valley. Landrum had moved there from Forsyth, Georgia, over ten years earlier and was probably one of the first American settlers to recognize the agricultural possibilities in California. Peters loaded the two bucks on the last through-train from Atlanta to St. Louis. A steamboat carried them from St. Louis to Fort Levenworth, and from there the goats traveled on foot with a wagon train, foraging off the land. They arrived in good condition on the West coast and won a cup at the California State Fair in September. One of the bucks died of snake bite after siring some thirty kids, but the other, widely known on the Pacific coast as "Billy Atlanta," lived to the ripe old age of ten years (when he was accidently killed) and sired about two thousand kids. "This buck," wrote Peters, "won the sweepstake prize, against all competition, at every fair down to that preceding his death; his numerous descendants are scattered all along the Pacific Coast, and his blood courses in the veins of over one-half the Angora flocks, pure-bred and grades, in that part of the Union." Not only were Angoras now raised in thirteen states east of the Mississippi, but later acquisitions from the Peters flock also helped lay the basis for the industry in the West. Landrum shipped some of his goats to Oregon and some went to Brigham Young, who started the breed in Utah. But Peters sent most of his Angoras to the southwest, beginning with eight shipped to William Haupt in western Texas, and others to New Mexico and Arizona.[18]

One of the few scientific breeders of sheep in the antebellum South, Peters paid over $2,000 for imported animals alone, buying South Down, Cotswold, Oxfordshire, Leicester, and finally French and Spanish Merinos. He favored Cotswold for a time. From the bleak Cotswold hills of England, they were a very old, hearty breed that gave a great amount of wool and mutton at an early age. But he eventually decided the sheep for the South was the Spanish Merino because its cross on native sheep resulted in the best weight and fineness of fleece.

---

[18]Farm Book, Peters Estate Collection; Peters to John L. Hayes, 1 January 1878, Black Collection; *Southern Cultivator* 18:2 (February 1860): 69; James C. Bonner, "The Angora Goat: A Footnote in Southern Agricultural History," *Agricultural History* 21 (January 1947): 44-45; Hayes, *Angora Goat,* 84-85; Bonner, *History of Georgia Agriculture*, 224.

Sheep raising had its problems: they were susceptible to diseases and were easily killed by predatory dogs. One day's entry in Peters's Sheep Registry Book reveals ten killed by dogs and eleven dead of unknown causes. Then, too, the market for mutton was weak because Southerners had little taste for it. However, Peters found a market for his fleece in England and retained a large flock of Spanish Merino, believing the sheep industry could flourish in certain areas of the South such as the wiregrass section of South Georgia.[19]

In horse breeding, Peters experimented with blooded Messengers and Morgans. He had some beautiful colts and breeding stock, including a fine trotting stallion, a muscular Messenger sixteen hands high that was a fast, all-day traveler with perfect docility, "equally reliable under the saddle or in harness." Peters was inclined to a "judicious mixture" of the Messenger with the Morgan, combining the strength of the former with the beauty of the latter. Good horses were expensive, costing up to seven hundred dollars for a good carriage horse by the eve of the war, but Peters found horse breeding on a commercial scale infeasible. There was a demand in Tennessee for mares with which to produce mules (a hybrid cross between a mare and a jack that was well suited for field work because the animal worked hard with poor treatment). There was less impetus for breeding for speed in the South than in the racing centers of Kentucky and the North, mainly because many Southerners disapproved of organized racing at the fairs. All in all, the poor condition of Southern horseflesh caused one horse lover to complain that fine stallions were "poorly patronized" and the best mares were "basely prostituted to the forced and ignoble embrace of the assinine ravisher."[20]

Peters and other diversifiers met with considerable success during periods of financial stringency, but in the late 1850s even the specialty-crop farmers prospered when cotton prices soared to ten and eleven cents a

---

[19]Farm Book, Peters Estate Collection; *Southern Cultivator*, 20:11 and 12 (November, December 1862): 198; Gray, *History of Agriculture in the Southern United States to 1860*, 2:832; Bonner, *History of Georgia Agriculture*, 141-42, 223.

[20]*Southern Cultivator* 19:7 (July 1861): 216; *Southern Confederacy* (5 July 1862); Ulrich B. Phillips, *The Course of the South to Secession*, ed. E. Merton Coulter (New York: D. Appleton-Century Co., 1939) 4; Bonner, *History of Georgia Agriculture*, 138-39. Gray explained that there was little attempt to improve the quality of livestock other than by a few enterprising planters. He did note, however, that by the time of the Civil War there were distinct signs of improvement—an indication that Peters was making some progress. Gray, *History of Agriculture in the Southern United States to 1860*, 2:835, 856.

pound; production doubled to supply manufacturers of dresses, shirts, trousers, wagon tops, sails of ships, and other items. Commercial fertilizer, widely advertised and accepted now, added to the Southern boom: "Cotton is everywhere—a great king. . . . The farmers of middle and southwest Georgia . . . were clearing more land, opening new farms to grow more cotton. They were buying more slaves, horses, and mules—to grow cotton."[21]

The cotton mania caused bitter infighting within the Southern Central Agricultural Society that ended in a schism. The majority of the leaders, including Peters, David W. Lewis, Charles W. Howard, Mark A. Cooper, William Terrell, William Schley, and Dennis Redmond, favored diversification. They held the fair as usual in Atlanta with Peters, who was now showing livestock nationally, well represented on the premium list. These diversifiers adopted a new name, the Georgia State Agricultural Society, by now composed strictly of Georgians. Another group, including Robert Toombs, Howell Cobb, Thomas Butler King, and Daniel Lee, chafed at the society's emphasis on livestock and insisted on emphasizing cotton. This faction had more political leaders; they organized the Georgia Cotton Planters Convention with Howell Cobb as president and demonstrated their intransigence by holding a fair in the cotton-planting territory in Macon.[22]

In spite of this agitation, Peters enjoyed life during the 1850s—a golden age for Southern agriculture, a time when animal husbandry in the South, in numbers at least, was as important as the combined total of the North and West.[23] Peters's plantation was in its heyday. On the eve of the Civil War, it

---

[21]Bonner, *History of Georgia Agriculture*, 92, 188-89; Willard Range, *A Century of Georgia Agriculture, 1850-1950* (Athens: University of Georgia Press, 1954) 14.

[22]*Atlanta Daily Examiner* (28 August 1857); *Southern Cultivator* 16:1 (January 1858): 16, 16:9 (September 1858): 286-88, 16:12 (December 1858): 364-65, 17:12 (December 1859): 356; *Atlanta Medical and Literary Weekly* (15 October 1859); Range, *Century of Georgia Agriculture*, 25-26, 290n. The Georgia State Agricultural Society, in an effort to placate cotton growers, installed eight vice-presidents from the state's congressional districts, and its president, David W. Lewis, appointed additional members to the executive committee selected from across the state for their "high character, public spirit, business capacity, and personal influence." The increased management gave more representation to all portions of the state and was apparently designed to remove domination of the society by men such as Peters, although he was both a vice-president and a member of the executive committee. *Southern Cultivator* 18:5 (May 1860): 136, 18:12 (December 1860): 388. The schism extended to the *Southern Cultivator* when cotton advocate Daniel Lee resigned as co-editor and the vacancy was filled by a stock-and-grass man, Charles W. Howard.

[23]Gray, *History of Agriculture in the Southern United States to 1860*, 2:781, 831.

was among the largest in North Georgia, consisting of almost 1,950 acres, of which some 1,100 acres were improved; the entire plantation was a mixture of moderately undulating land, both cleared and wooded. Peters was planting 300 acres of carefully selected grasses in woodland pastures and meadows to accommodate the increase in his improved stock. He had on hand almost 700 head of livestock, 280 bushels of wheat, 4,000 bushels of corn, 200 pounds of wool, 200 bushels of Irish potatoes, 400 bushels of sweet potatoes, 700 pounds of butter, 60 tons of hay, and inexplicably, 6 bales of cotton.

To work his plantation, he used a mixture of free and slave labor. He owned sixteen slaves—all over twenty-four years of age, except for two small children, consisting of twelve males and four females. (This was more than the 11.2 average for Georgia planters in 1860—462,198 slaves owned by 41,084 masters.) Devon Hall, with all it contained, including slaves, had a $40,000 cash value.[24] "The average slaveowner was more than five times as wealthy as the average Northerner, more than ten times as wealthy as the average nonslaveholding Southern farmer. A man who owned two slaves, and nothing else, was as rich as the average man in the North."[25] Peters's Atlanta property and other investments aside, he was a wealthy man for his day.

Occasionally, critics attacked Peters's efforts to improve livestock as mere profit-seeking on his part. Editor Redmond came to Peters's defense, calling him "a true public benefactor," who with little hope of gain had for years devoted himself to the introduction and improvement of domestic animals for the South. This was often done at a sacrifice of time, money, and comfort to himself, and "always at the penalty of annoyance from such as are ever too ready to attribute false motives to those who are endeavoring to benefit them."[26] This was attested to by Martin W. Philips, the noted agricultural commentator who practiced mixed husbandry near Edwards, Mis-

---

[24]*Eighth Census of the United States, 1860: Agriculture and Slave Inhabitants*; Gordon County Tax Digest, 1861, Georgia Department of Archives and History; Jordan, *The United States From Revolution to Civil War*, 167; Bonner, *History of Georgia Agriculture*, 203; T. Conn Bryan, *Confederate Georgia* (Athens: University of Georgia Press, 1953) 260n.

[25]Gavin Wright, *The Political Economy of the Cotton South: Households, Markets, and Wealth in the Nineteenth Century* (New York: W. W. Norton and Company, 1978) 35.

[26]*Southern Cultivator* 19:7 (July 1861): 217.

sissippi. After a visit to Devon Hall, Philips was convinced that Southerners could make a living without cotton. His conclusion: "R. Peters is doing more for the South than any man in it."[27]

[27]Ibid., 14:10 (October 1856): 322.

CHAPTER SIX

WAR CLOUDS
ON THE HORIZON:
SECESSION CRISIS

Peters and men like him urged Southerners to concentrate on industry and agriculture and withdraw from strife and contention as talk of disunion spread across the South during the late 1850s. Dennis Redmond struck the upbeat note: "The course of the South is onward; and if she will be true to herself and sedulously labor for the development of her own un-rivaled resources, the waves of fanaticism will rave harmlessly around her, and finally sink into the calm of impotency and despair."[1] As sectional tensions mounted, Peters continued to pursue his many interests in the hope that reason would prevail.[2]

---

[1]*Southern Cultivator* 14:12 (December 1856): 370, 373.

[2]Of increasing importance as the war approached was Peters's production of fruits and vegetables in an early type of truck farming. In a plantation orchard of ten or twelve acres, he maintained trees that were models of symmetry, and in summer were heavily laden with peaches, apples, pears, and other fruit. "Old Solomon," one of Peters's slaves, managed the extensive market garden. Solomon provided an abundant supply of quality vegetables for everyone on the plantation, white and black, and a considerable surplus for market. *Southern Cultivator* 19:7 (July 1861): 217.

On a more cheerful note for Peters and the city, Atlanta was emerging from a "city in the woods" to a "city among the hills." In the intellectual oasis of his home library, he could contemplate with pride Atlanta's brief history. The city that had been a small frontier town in 1845 had grown to include 9,691 inhabitants (7,751 white, 1,917 slaves, and 23 free blacks) as the antebellum period drew to a close. It was one of 141 cities in the nation with a population over 8,000 and the third largest city in Georgia—surpassed only by Savannah and Augusta. Atlanta was also something of a Southern melting pot prior to the Civil War. The rail center attracted primarily Southerners, Northerners, and Irishmen who fused traditions as they built a better life, causing the city to be more akin the Northern urban centers than at any other time. Most Atlantans had a Southern outlook, but because of the nature of their young city, they did not develop the aristocratic aura found in the older seaport cities of the South. Boosters such as Peters, ubiquitous in government, business, and society, articulated their cities' needs. These city boosters "were cosmopolitan men, well aware of what was occurring in other cities and what should occur in theirs," according to David Goldfield. They were a hard-working elite, who, much like their counterparts in the North, set the tone for their city and created its image, but few Southern urban leaders cut so wide a swath as did Peters.

In 1860, Atlanta's main business section covered several blocks and contained over two hundred stores and offices. Among the fifteen manufacturing establishments were four large railroad machine shops that were clustered along the railroad lines, as were most of the city's warehouses. The screech and puff of locomotives could be heard on every hand. Some forty-four passenger and freight trains arrived and departed daily.[3]

Railroad control continued to haunt Atlanta's economic life, and in 1860 Peters again made a determined effort to push the dormant Georgia Western Railroad project to completion. City council subscribed $300,000 and the Georgia Railroad Company $250,000, providing the fledgling company with half the amount needed to construct the road from Atlanta to the

---

[3]*Atlanta City Directory* (1859); Ralph B. Singer, "Confederate Atlanta" (Ph.D. dissertation, University of Georgia, 1973) 19, 25; David R. Goldfield, "Pursuing the American Urban Dream: Cities in the Old South," *The City in Southern History: The Growth of Urban Civilization in the South*, ed. Blaine A. Brownell and David R. Goldfield (Port Washington: Kennikat Press, 1977) 53, 59, 63; Helen K. Lyon, "Richard Peters: Atlanta Pioneer—Georgia Builder," *Atlanta Historical Bulletin* 38:10 (December 1957): 22-23.

Alabama line. City council subscribed $300,000 to the Air Line Railroad project as well, with the expectation that both railroads would be controlled from within the city. However, when members of the two lines again canvassed Atlanta for additional funds, the merchants were still divided on the merits of each and the resulting polarization stalled the progress of both companies once more.

Peters became convinced that the city could not afford to finance both railroads at the same time, so he urged L. P. Grant, engineer of the Georgia Western, to publicize in the city press a detailed survey of the route into Alabama. In lengthy articles Grant obliged with a passion, pointing out the road's proposed distance of only ninety-six miles across terrain that would allow a relatively low construction cost of $14,900 per mile. He listed the benefits to Atlanta merchants in opening the fresh agricultural and mineral-rich lands in northern Alabama and perhaps forming a direct link to the Mississippi River; the road would bring more shops, depots, managers, and other employees to Atlanta, and the value of stock held in the Georgia, Central, and South Carolina railroads would increase.

While Grant bombarded the public with facts and figures, Peters moved against the Air Line directly. On 15 June, he petitioned the city council for a staying order against the company. To support his petition, which he thought necessary for the completion of the Georgia Western, he pointed out the difficulty of city bond sales and maintained that the resulting taxes would be oppressive. He reasoned that the city's public and private resources should be applied to only one road at the time. According to Peters, the annual interest of seven percent on $600,000 ($42,000) was excessive, especially since Atlanta had never raised in one year over $40,000 from all sources. Peters also pointed out that many Air Line stockholders were unhappy because the road's management had been calling in stock and approving construction contracts in violation of the company's charter. The council acted favorably on Peters's petition by recommending that President Norcross and the directors of the Air Line suspend operations until after the next annual meeting of the road's stockholders.

Having struck a major blow at the opposition, Peters next pushed the construction of the Georgia Western. On 23 July, Georgia Western stockholders met in City Hall and, after Peters as chairman read the minutes of different meetings to demonstrate that the company had met the provisions of their charter, they elected him president of the company. In accepting the office, Peters made a few remarks, saying that since it was easier to make promises than fulfill them, he would make few, but would promise to give his "constant and unremitting care and attention" to the railroad. He said it was important for the road to be built as quickly as possible. And he had a specific plan in mind: current subscriptions amounted to about $750,000, and as soon as $50,000 more was subscribed, fifty miles of the road would be constructed. He wanted to pay for construction as it was completed, so that the cost of the road would be cut by half. The stockholders had confidence in Peters, in part because he had experience in railroading. The Georgia Western directors met a week later and made plans to begin construction. Unfortunately, however, the uncertainty created by national civil strife quashed the project even before work was begun.

The Air Line fared no better. During a 17 August meeting, the stockholders were unable to enjoin the management from letting construction contracts or collecting installments of stock and the city council repealed its $300,000 subscription. The council charged the management with violating a company resolution against beginning construction prior to attaining a specified amount of stock subscription, disregarding a resolution of council to stop grading, and the dissatisfaction of company stockholders. Public sentiment in Atlanta approved the repeal by council, as reflected in a two-to-one vote by a citizens group 4 September at City Hall. The Air Line had definitely lost support. Norcross, dispirited and out of favor, resigned as president and the directors suspended operations, citing as its reason the "unsettled state of public affairs and the depression." Thus, the road that promoters had said would make Atlanta the state capital, center of learning, and foremost tourist resort in the South, also faltered.

Norcross's plan for a direct route to the North was commendable. The state of Georgia had 1,404 miles of rails in 1860, second in the South only to Virginia's 1,771 (West Virginia had not yet become a state). Noteworthy, too, is the fact that of the five major trunk lines in the South at the start of the war, three made connections in Atlanta. Yet the city had no standardized rail connection with the North, much less a direct route which the Air Line Railroad would have provided. But Peters had backed a worthy project as well. The Georgia Western could have been built with relative ease to the coal and iron-ore fields in nearby Alabama, aiding in the industrialization of Atlanta which lacked, among other things, sources of raw materials, and ultimately providing a link in an all-weather line to the West. Under local control, both railroads would have been of great benefit to Atlanta and both should have been built, but the Georgia Western deserved priority because rival cities were pushing their own rail projects toward the West, giving an urgency to the Georgia Western that the Air Line lacked. After the Civil War, cities generally could not afford the higher construction costs so Atlanta never controlled a railroad. Otherwise, the city's growth probably would have been more remarkable than it was.[4]

Peters's world was soon threatened by civil war, to which the presidential election of 1860 was a prelude. Southerners particularly wanted to defeat the Republican candidate, Abraham Lincoln of Illinois, because he held the Union to be constitutionally indivisible. Lincoln also spoke against slavery on moral grounds and opposed its extension into the territories. But "as historians have pointed out," wrote David Goldfield, "the Republicans were less an antislavery party than an antisouthern party—and openly so" in their pledge of support for legislation favoring Northern industrial and agricultural interests. The Northern Democratic candidate, U.S. Senator Stephen A. Douglas, also of Illinois, had some Southern support. Embarking on an early edition of a modern day "whistle stop" campaign, he swung through Atlanta, probably because his vice-presidential running mate was prominent Georgian Herschel V. Johnson. "Little Giant" Douglas was coolly received in Atlanta when he spoke on 30 October 1860, and especially after his response the following day to a question by Jared I. Whitaker. A local newspaperman and political activist, Whitaker supported the Southern Democratic candidate, John C. Breckinridge of Kentucky. When he queried Douglas on secession, the "Little Giant" stated flatly that he would consider secessionists as traitors. This was enough to cause Breckinridge men to organize a military unit immediately—the Minute Men of Fulton County.

With a "patrician's quietude," Peters expressed moderate views. In politics he was a Whig. The Whig party was virtually defunct, having split

---

[4]Atlanta City Council Minute Books, 21, 25 May, 20 July 1860, Atlanta Ordinance Book, 1851-1860; *Atlanta Intelligencer* (17, 29 July, 9, 29 October 1857; 23 January, 3, 4 February 1858; 6 February, 28 March, 5, 23 April, 21 May, 4, 7, 21, 28 June, 5, 12, 19, 26 July, 9, 16 August, 13 September 1860); John F. Stover, *The Railroads of the South, 1865-1900* (Chapel Hill: University of North Carolina Press, 1955) 5, 11-12; Franklin M. Garrett, *Atlanta and Environs: A Chronicle of Its People and Events* 2 vols. (Athens: University of Georgia Press, 1969) 1:383; Walter G. Cooper, *Official History of Fulton County* (Atlanta: Walter W. Brown Publishing Co., 1934) 599-600; Ulrich B. Phillips, *A History of Transportation in the Eastern Cotton Belt to 1860* (New York: Columbia University Press, 1908) 384-85.

on the slavery issue, but for some time it had attracted upper-class planters, merchants, and professional men. Whigs most likely became Constitutional Unionists, and Peters undoubtedly supported John Bell, that party's candidate from Tennessee. As a moderate, Bell called for upholding the Constitution and the Union, which was an attractive policy in Atlanta. The extreme state rights position of the Breckinridge faction excited notice in the city, but the local vote showed Bell the victor with a plurality of 1,070 votes to 825 for Breckinridge, and 335 for Douglas. (Breckinridge carried Georgia, however, with 51,893 votes to Bell's 42,855, while only 11,580 Georgians voted for Douglas. There was no Republican party organization in Georgia and Lincoln's name did not appear on the ballot, nor did he win a single popular vote in ten of the fifteen slave states.) The result of the election in Atlanta—with combined votes for Bell and Douglas constituting an impressive majority for the moderates—makes clear that the city resisted the extremism sweeping most of Georgia and the South, but Lincoln's victory created a crisis atmosphere that allowed talk of state rights and civil war by frenzied secessionists to convert some of the moderates.[5]

In Georgia, the governor, both United States senators, six of the eight congressmen, two of the three members of the Georgia Supreme Court, the Federal circuit judge, and four of five former governors still living in 1860 favored secession. Governor Joseph E. Brown, who bitterly criticized the North for profiting on slave sales to the South earlier and now calling for emancipation, called the legislature into session on 7 November 1860 and pushed for secession. At the same time, events in Atlanta reflected the growing trend of grass-roots support. At a large public meeting in City Hall on 12 November, Atlantans brushed aside the remarks of moderate Mayor William Ezzard and adopted overwhelmingly a petition to the state legislature calling for a state convention. On 21 November, the legislature called for the men of Georgia to vote on 2 January 1861 for delegates to attend a state convention at the capital in Milledgeville to decide on secession.

In the intervening six weeks, secessionists were highly visible in Atlanta. Emotional mass meetings were held almost weekly by the Minute Men, who wore blue cockades to symbolize their desire for independence

---

[5]James L. Roark, *Masters Without Slaves: Southern Planters in the Civil War and Reconstruction* (New York: W. W. Norton and Company, 1977) 8; David R. Goldfield, *Cotton Fields and Skyscrapers: Southern City and Region, 1607-1980* (Baton Rouge: Louisiana State University Press, 1982) 75.

from the oppressive North; more and more Atlantans rallied to the cause of secession. Among the most impassioned speeches—a gargantuan effort of four hours—was one by Thomas R. R. Cobb of Athens, later a Confederate general, who told Atlantans to rise *en masse* and support secession. The Minute Men appointed a Committee of Safety to check the attitude of the citizenry in an effort to brand moderates as less than one hundred percent Southern and to rid Atlanta of dangerous suspects known as "submissionists," or Unionists. Men of property were likely to have been Unionists, while secessionists were chiefly professional men or young men who had little to lose, or politicians who aspired to office in a Southern Confederacy. In addition, some merchant "Southrons" favored secession as a way to free Atlanta's business institutions from Northern creditors and freight laws.[6]

Three delegates would represent Fulton County in the Milledgeville convention. The moderate, or "cooperation," ticket was made up of George W. Adair, Thomas Moore, and James M. Calhoun (cousin of John C. Calhoun), all of whom opposed secession by individual states and pledged to support any compromise that would protect Southern rights. The secession candidates, who had helped organize military units, were Dr. James P. Logan, Dr. James F. Alexander, and Luther J. Glenn. Peters supported the "cooperation" ticket, but on 2 January 1861, the day of the election, news that South Carolina had seceded, together with a fiery call for secession in a speech to the city by Howell Cobb, destroyed the moderate position in Atlanta. The announcement that the three secession candidates won—by an average vote of 953 to 487—highlighted a day of public celebration. (Statewide, secession delegates won by approximately 50,000 to 37,000 votes; it would only be a matter of time before Georgia seceded.) The day after the election of delegates, a small earthquake that lasted some ten seconds shook Atlanta. Ominously, nature seemed to be warning of the coming fury.[7]

Peters opposed the secession movement because he thought it would ultimately flounder upon the shoals of Southern economic insufficiency. An avid reader, industrially minded with access to some of the best minds of

---

[6]T. Conn Bryan, *Confederate Georgia* (Athens: University of Georgia Press, 1953) 5; Singer, "Confederate Atlanta," 44-50.

[7]Richard Peters, "Personal Recollections," *Richard Peters: His Ancestors and Descendants*, comp. Nellie P. Black (Atlanta: Foote and Davies, 1904) 27; *Atlanta Intelligencer* (22 November 1860); Singer, "Confederate Atlanta," 53-57.

the day, and a former Northerner who continued to visit that region, he had an appreciation of Northern strengths that was uncommon in the South. "Very few of the Southern people were conscious of the power of the North," he explained. "They had been kept in perfect ignorance by politicians and were not aware that the whole civilized world opposed slavery, more especially the English nation."[8] Here Peters touched upon an important point, because intervention by England was integral to Southern hopes. To a large extent that intervention never came because the English working class felt that slavery demeaned all labor. Had England intervened for the South, the action might have triggered a revolt by the workers against the British government.

Peters expressed his concern about the future of the South in a letter to former United States Congressman from Georgia Alexander H. Stephens. One of the best constitutional minds in the South, Stephens hoped Southern leaders would allow Lincoln an opportunity to demonstrate that as president he would not violate Southern rights. Above all, he believed Southern states should not act individually, but meet instead in a sectional convention to decide on a course of collective action. Stephens replied to Peters on 9 January 1861 expressing a fear of "evils not yet dreamed of by the people" and promised to work to prevent additional secession and war. He added, however, that "my hopes of resisting them are not strong."[9]

Ten days after writing to Peters, Stephens voted against secession at the Milledgeville convention, but his opposition proved futile. Sweeping aside "little Alex's" vision of a war of terrible magnitude and duration, Georgia seceded from the Union on 19 January 1861 by a vote of 208 to 89, the fifth state to declare independence from "Lincolndom." Atlantans celebrated with torchlight processions, firework displays, firing of guns, ringing of bells, toasts, speeches, bonfires, burnings of Lincoln in effigy, and a balloon ascension from the roof of the Atlanta Hotel. The earlier political moderation, evident in the November presidential election, had given way in January to the flood tide of secession.[10]

---

[8]Peters, "Personal Recollections," 27.

[9]Alexander H. Stephens to Peters, 9 January 1861, in Black, *Richard Peters*, 32.

[10]Paul W. Miller, ed., *Atlanta: Capital of the South* (New York: O. Durrell, 1949) 15-30; James M. Russell, "Atlanta, Gate City of the South 1847-1885" (Ph.D. dissertation, Princeton University, 1971) 98-100.

On 16 February 1861, Atlantans welcomed Jefferson Davis to the city for a brief visit. Recently selected as president of the Confederacy, he was taking a circuitous route of 750 miles from Jackson, Mississippi, to his inauguration in Montgomery, Alabama, because an incomplete stretch in the railroad line between Meridian, Mississippi, and Selma, Alabama, deprived him of a direct route over the 250 miles to Montgomery. A welcoming committee of Atlantans escorted Davis from Resaca in North Georgia via the Western and Atlantic to Atlanta, where another committee saw him to the Trout House. After military units marched by and fired salutes, Davis addressed a throng in excess of five thousand people in front of the hotel. He highlighted the necessity for secession and the formation of a new nation. Less than a month later, on 12 March, Stephens, who had cast his lot with the South and was selected vice-president, arrived in Atlanta amid much the same enthusiasm and celebration. Speaking in front of the Atlanta Hotel, he inaccurately predicted the Federals would evacuate Fort Sumter. Stephens's strong stand on state rights within the Confederacy would eventually help undermine the Southern cause. He should have resigned early in the war because, as Bell I. Wiley wrote, "for him to denounce and obstruct the team of which he was a leading member cannot be justified on any reasonable grounds."[11]

Peters offered his services to the Confederate government, saying he felt unable to "take up arms" at age fifty, but would serve as a civilian transportation agent. In addition, he sold the steam engine from his flour mill to the government for $12,000 in Confederate bonds. The Confederacy derived enormous benefit from the transaction. The powerful engine was moved to Augusta and used in the Augusta Powder Works, the principal

[11]Singer, "Confederate Atlanta," 67-69, 107-108; Bell I. Wiley and Hirst D. Milhollen, *Embattled Confederates: An Illustrated History of Southerners at War* (New York: Bonanza Books, 1964) 17, 128-29. Early in 1861 Atlanta attempted to become the seat of the Confederacy. First the city council offered accommodations and facilities in Atlanta in an effort to attract the Constitutional Convention of the seceded states. The offer, which was sent to all Southern governors with the request that each present it to his state's convention, pointed out Atlanta's central location, accessibility by rail, seven hotels, and abundance of fresh meat and vegetables, including peanuts, or "goobers." The effort failed when the decision favored Montgomery, Alabama. Taking the next obvious step, which also proved unsuccessful, the council then created a committee that journeyed to Montgomery and tried to persuade the members of the Confederate Convention to make Atlanta the Southern capital. Atlanta City Council Minute Books, 31 January, 15 February 1861; Singer, "Confederate Atlanta," 65-67.

powder factory in the South and one of the largest in the world. For three years, until 18 April 1865, the engine drove a massive underground shaft nearly three hundred feet long, which powered twelve independent spurs in the individual factory buildings. The Confederacy manufactured 2,750,000 pounds of high-quality powder here. The Augusta Powder Works is credited with "the remarkable fact that the Confederates never lost a battle for lack of powder."[12]

Why did Peters remain in the South? He was one of some 360,000 former Northerners living in the region at the beginning of the Civil War. Some returned to the North while some remained in the South and attempted to aid the Union. Others, like Peters ("galvanized Yankees"), stayed and were loyal to the Confederacy. When separation or subjugation appeared the only alternatives, he made his decision. It must have been rather painful, but it is doubtful that he seriously considered returning to his native state. He had lived in Georgia for a quarter of a century; his wife Mary Jane had Southern roots; and his brother William was in the ranks of the Fulton County Minute Men. Further, he had considerable economic interests in Georgia that he could not abandon by going back to Pennsylvania—he had built, directed, and invested in Georgia industry, owned Atlanta real estate, and was a slaveholding planter. In summary, while Peters's New South practices exerted influence on his adopted region, he was in turn affected by the environment of the Old South.[13]

---

[12]Bill of Sale, 31 August 1861, Record Group 109, Papers Relating to Citizens and Firms, War Department Collection of Confederate Records, Military Archives Division, National Archives and Records Service, Washington, D.C.; George W. Rains, *History of the Confederate Powder Works* (Augusta: Chronicle and Constitutionalist Print, 1882) 8-9; Lyon, "Richard Peters," 33; Wiley and Milhollen, *Embattled Confederates*, 109.

[13]Ulrich B. Phillips, *The Course of the South to Secession*, ed. E. Merton Coulter (New York: D. Appleton-Century Co., 1939) 152; Fletcher M. Green, *The Role of the Yankee in the Old South* (Athens: University of Georgia Press, 1972) vii-viii; Bryan, *Confederate Georgia*, 137; Roark, *Masters Without Slaves*, 7.

CHAPTER SEVEN

STRATEGIC ATLANTA: PETERS SERVES THE CONFEDERACY

E dmund Ruffin, one of the South's premier scientific agriculturists (and ardent Rebels), touched off the first shot of the Civil War on that fateful day of 12 April 1861, firing against Fort Sumter, located on an island in Charleston Harbor. With patriotism at fever pitch, Atlantans responded with the city's greatest public demonstration yet. There were the usual church bells creating a din, cannon salutes, bonfires, fireworks, pistols discharging, and musical processions through the streets. The city's volunteer fire departments enlisted in local military units *en masse*, most having to furnish their own uniforms, equipment, arms, and horses. Parades and drilling became commonplace, as did public farewells.[1]

Ironically, among the parting words prompted by Ruffin's cannon blast were those of the executive committee of the Georgia State Agricultural Society, which met in Atlanta's City Hall on 29 April and cancelled the annual fair. Peters assisted in drawing up an explanation to the friends and patrons

---

[1]Ralph B. Singer, "Confederate Atlanta" (Ph.D. dissertation, University of Georgia, 1973) 70-73.

of the society. The committee then donated all the society's funds, silver-plate, and large canvas tents to the war effort: "The offering, we know, is small compared to the great cause in which it is to be expended," they explained, "but it is for our all, and is given more as an expression of our warm sympathy, than for its intrinsic value."[2] Sensing dark days ahead, Peters invited a few of his fellow planters to an informal meeting that evening at the Atlanta Hotel and treated them to a number of domestic wines, several of them his own manufacture.[3]

Atlanta, nestled in the heart of the Confederacy, seemed a safe distance from the war, although its strategic location and rail connections made it an ideal site for a military complex. In 1861, Richmond authorized offices of the Commissary Department to be located in the city, and headquarters for both Confederate and Georgia agencies were established in a frame building at Houston, Pryor, and Peachtree streets. The Commissary Department opened a large depot and began to collect, store, and distribute meat, flour, lard, and other foodstuffs for the army. At the same time, Atlanta became the center for the Confederate and state Quartermaster departments, which built shoe and garment shops and let contracts to other shops and factories. Indeed, Atlanta became a "veritable hive of industry" as the Quartermaster Department began producing supplies and munitions, often with machinery brought in through the blockade. Under a wide range of government contracts, city firms produced spurs, bridles, saddles, and harnesses. Other companies made tents, uniforms, haversacks, accouterments, wool hats, rifles, belt buckles, swords, and the famous "Joe Brown Pike." The city quickly became the main base of supply for the Confederacy's western army, the Army of Tennessee.[4]

During the summer, electrifying news reached Atlanta that a great clash of arms had occurred in Virginia. This first real battle of the war took place 21 July 1861 at Manassas (Bull Run) and was, on paper at least, a Confederate victory. Peters attempted to discern its significance. He communicated with his estimable friend and associate in Augusta, John P. King, a Union man who responded that the Southern victory was unfortunate. King

---

[2]*Southern Cultivator* 19:6 (June 1861): 171-73, 197.

[3]*Southern Confederacy* (3 May 1861).

[4]T. Conn Bryan, *Confederate Georgia* (Athens: University of Georgia Press, 1953) 102; Singer, "Confederate Atlanta," 101-10.

thought, and evidently hoped, that if the Northern army had captured Richmond, the new Confederate capital, and with it President Jefferson Davis and other Southern leaders, the war would have ended with this initial battle. Under the circumstances, Union forces could not have captured Richmond immediately after Manassas, but King's view offers an interesting contrast to the usual speculation that the South at that time could have won by capturing Washington.[5]

Peters also requested the opinion of his former Georgia Railroad supervisor, J. Edgar Thomson. In his reply, written from Pennsylvania, Thomson expressed complete confidence that the Northern cause would prevail; the Union rout at Manassas simply demonstrated to the Lincoln administration that more troops and a better commander were necessary. Then, in a remarkable comment, Thomson touched briefly on the economic relationship between the North and South, and perhaps set forth the reason the Union had to be preserved: "As to South Carolina we have doubts as to taking her back at all. We may close her ports and abandon her to her own reflections. There is one thing to be said, however, in their favor and that is they pay their debts to the people of this section more punctually than those of any other state except North Carolina." The Southern cause was weak, continued Thomson, as evidenced by the use of "all the strongest adjectives and the hardest names that our language affords." Peters himself, because of stories that had reached Atlanta of alleged Union atrocities during the battle, had referred to Federal troops as "Hessians," and "Cowardly Yankees," and "Wolves and Reptiles." Thomson concluded that Peters should turn his attention to ending the bloodshed: "You had better go to work at once among your heretical [secession] friends and get them to propose a national assembly to settle our troubles."[6]

Thomson's suggestion of a national convention probably offered the best hope for a settlement, but the effort had failed earlier in the year because important leaders of both sections ignored those assembled in Rich-

---

[5]Richard Peters, "Personal Recollections," *Richard Peters: His Ancestors and Descendants*, comp. Nellie P. Black (Atlanta: Foote and Davies, 1904) 27-28.

[6]J. Edgar Thomson to Peters, 12 September 1861, Nellie P. Black Collection, University of Georgia Libraries, Athens.

mond for that purpose, and after Manassas it was too late. Unyielding politicians on both sides had carried their point, but Peters could now look to the future. After obtaining the views of King and Thomson, he made up his mind as to the final outcome of the war: "From this time to the end," he wrote, "I never again altered my opinion of the ultimate result, but tried to shape my course so as to save our property when the crash came."[7] This statement is lucid testimony as to what was significant in Peters's life. As with most Southern elites, he was not an ideologue: "Only a few consciously adopted the role of defender of their region or class, and most thought primarily in terms of the defense of their own domains."[8]

For the moment, however, Peters turned to his duties as civilian transportation agent. He made his way to crucial railroad junctions to speed trains to the army in the West, giving priority to military freight such as food, clothing, and munitions—and troop transportation. Large numbers of Confederate servicemen traveled northward from Camp McDonald, Big Shanty, and Camp Stephens near Atlanta. Many new recruits reported to a training camp three miles from Calhoun, while the more seasoned troops continued northward to Chattanooga. At times the Western and Atlantic trains between Atlanta and Marietta ran so close together that they created a continuous line of boxcars and locomotives. The crowded conditions in the boxcars made the trip unpleasant for the soldiers. A young lieutenant, Charles C. Jones, wrote: "You cannot imagine the terrible character of the atmosphere in these cars at night. It is enough to make a well man sick. Coming up here [Calhoun] I spent the night on the platform to take advantage of the outside air." Soldiers "thought nothing of knocking holes in the walls of boxcars to improve ventilation or wave at pretty girls." Peters encountered other problems, such as weak rails, poorly constructed roadbeds, flimsy trestles, overworked equipment, deficient maintenance, and a diversity of gauges. Accidents were frequent, cordwood for fuel was scarce, and he constantly struggled with conscript agents for control of the dwindling

---

[7]Peters, "Personal Recollections," 28.

[8]James L. Roark, *Masters Without Slaves: Southern Planters in the Civil War and Reconstruction* (New York: W. W. Norton and Company, 1977) viii.

labor supply.[9] Worst of all for Peters was the confusion and delay caused by inadequate regulation of railroads by the Confederacy.[10]

In February 1862, Peters took part in an effort to mobilize the farming interest in support of the war. He journeyed to Memphis as a delegate from Georgia to the Southern Planters Convention. Since the South was already experiencing pork shortages, the purpose of the convention was to develop an agricultural strategy. Peters favored curtailing cotton production in favor of foodstuffs, but the planters (and Confederate officials) were more enthusiastic in their support of a second point of strategy—to force England to come to their aid by withholding cotton from export. King Cotton diplomacy failed because the world's cotton famine never quite became unbearable for England, mostly because of the huge surplus in England from the South's 1859 bumper crop, and the opening of cotton markets from such countries as China, India, and Brazil. Confederates came to realize that they were more dependent on the outside world than the outside world was dependent on the South.

The food provision of the strategy worked better, especially in Georgia, where Governor Brown, who had farmed in the northern part of the state, joined newspapers, journals, and societies in urging that twice the amount of corn and sweet potatoes be planted, along with three times the usual crop of beets, peas, and other vegetables. "With plenty of grain and vegetables," wrote Brown, "we can raise all the meat we need, and we can raise the grain if we drop the cotton crop." He was successful in prodding the legislature to limit cotton planting to three acres per hand, with a $500 fine for violation of the law; Georgia's cotton production during 1862 plummeted from the usual 700,000-bale crop to 60,000 bales, less than one-tenth the previous year's crop. Declines for the entire South were not as sharp, but

---

[9]Charles C. Jones, Jr., to C. C. Jones, 14, 19 July 1862 in Robert M. Myers, ed., *The Children of Pride: A True Story of Georgia and the Civil War* (New Haven: Yale University Press, 1972) 930-31, 933; Bell I. Wiley and Hirst D. Milhollen, *Embattled Confederates: An Illustrated History of Southerners At War* (New York: Bonanza Books, 1964) 133; Singer, "Confederate Atlanta," 143-45.

[10]Richard D. Goff, *Confederate Supply* (Durham: Duke University Press, 1969) 17; E. Merton Coulter, *The Confederate States of America, 1861-65*, vol. 7 of *A History of the South*, ed. Wendell H. Stephenson and E. Merton Coulter, 10 vols. (Baton Rouge: Louisiana State University Press, 1950) 286-87.

production fell from 4.5 million to 1.5 million bales during the first year of the war.[11]

As the food strategy began to take shape, it was becoming clear to most people that the Confederacy could not quickly win the war. The South's concern over its ability to hold the rivers of the western front turned to grim reality with the Northern victories early in 1862 at Fort Donelson, Fort Henry, and New Orleans, prompting James R. Crew, a Union sympathizer on Atlanta's city council, to write that "the Anaconda is drawing in his coil."[12] At this, Peters decided to liquidate one of his holdings. In April, he and Harden sold their nursery at the corner of Hill and Fair streets for $10,000 to buyers from Richmond. Peters sold the property for several reasons: the increasing scarcity of nursery stock; ornamental shrubs and young fruit trees were unsuited to the food strategy; his service to the Confederacy gave him less time to attend to personal business; and the disruption of war could result in its complete loss.[13]

The Federals now controlled central Tennessee, causing the Confederate government to relocate its Nashville arsenal to the ostensibly secure city of Atlanta, a move that increased the latter's importance as a supply center.

---

[11]*Southern Cultivator* 20:1 (January 1862): 24, 20:3 and 4 (March and April 1862): 68, 20:5 and 6 (May and June 1862): 104-105; Willard Range, *A Century of Georgia Agriculture, 1850-1950* (Athens: University of Georgia Press, 1954) 37-38, 45-57; Bryan, *Confederate Georgia*, 121-22; Roark, *Masters Without Slaves*, 40. Peters advocated cotton spinning in the South and direct trade with Europe because he knew that otherwise the region could not be independent of the North or England. During 1861 he was active in organizing the Manufacturing and Direct Trade Association of the Confederate States in Atlanta. Plans were made to import cotton spinning machinery and an agent was sent to Europe to obtain credit and oversee the sale of the first yarn shipment, but the Confederate strategy of withholding cotton from sale abroad and then the ever-tightening Union blockade gave the organization little chance for success. Atlanta City Council Minute Books, 1, 8 February, 15 March 1861; *Atlanta Intelligencer* (13, 20 February, 20, 27 March, 5, 19, 26 June, 6 November 1861); Walter G. Cooper, *Official History of Fulton County* (Atlanta: Walter W. Brown Publishing Co., 1934) 321. During normal times, the major deterrent to direct trade was the lack of a large Southern market for European manufactures. "The problem was that ships returned home with ballast and little else." David R. Goldfield, *Cotton Fields and Skyscrapers: Southern Cities and Region, 1607-1980* (Baton Rouge: Louisiana State University Press, 1982) 69.

[12]James R. Crew to Louisa (Mrs. James R.) Crew, 18 June 1862, James R. Crew Collection, Atlanta Historical Society.

[13]William P. Robinson as told to Nellie P. Black in *Richard Peters*, 48; Fulton County Deed Book 11, Fulton County Courthouse.

Thirteen separate shops throughout Atlanta produced almost all of the different types of war material as the arsenal geared up to full capacity.[14] Scavenger drives brought to hand lead, brass, beeswax (a lubricant for bullets), and copper. Cannon, shot, and shell were turned out, as were matches (used as fuses in artillery pieces) and percussion caps. The Atlanta arsenal became the largest south of Richmond, and through it were channeled all munitions from Macon and Augusta.

Atlanta's heavy industry tried desperately to keep up with demand. The Confederate Iron and Brass Foundry and Winship's Foundry expanded their production of forgings, including bolts and plating. The Empire Manufacturing Company built railroad cars. The Confederate Rolling Mill revved to full production; it made some of the iron sheathing used on the C.S.S. *Virginia*. But the city's most important heavy industry was the Atlanta Rolling Mill, which specialized in the production of rails, and was second only to

---

[14]A pistol manufacturing company set up operations in Peters's mill building when the firm of Spiller and Burr secured a contract with the Confederate government to manufacture 15,000 navy revolvers. Edward N. Spiller ran a commission business in Baltimore before the war, and David J. Burr, a native of Richmond, was a builder of steam engines. Associated with Spiller and Burr was Colonel James H. Burton, a machinist assigned to the Bureau of Ordnance with the title of Superintendent of Armories. He was to supervise the construction and operation of the factory and machinery, for which he would receive $5,000 and one-third of the profits of the firm, an obvious conflict of interest overlooked by the government. Spiller, who at first expected to manufacture the pistols in Richmond, suddenly turned up in Atlanta during 1862 to arrange for relocating the firm and decided on the mill building, evidently leasing it from Peters. A lack of patterns for building production machines, scarcity of skilled workers, and a tendency to go for quick profits were problems that plagued the firm. Although government officials were impressed with the first samples, actual production did not begin until the spring of 1863 when only seven of forty passed inspection. By January 1864 the firm was so far behind in deliveries that the government purchased the company for $125,000 and moved it to Macon. Many of the firm's problems remained unsolved and the war ended before the government could begin full operation. In all, Spiller and Burr manufactured 762 revolvers in Atlanta, and the government produced perhaps another 689 in Macon, for a total of 1,451 at the most—a far cry from 15,000 pistols ordered initially. Miscellaneous documents, Spiller-Burr Papers, Atlanta Historical Society; *Southern Confederacy* (15 May 1863); Stephens Mitchell, "Atlanta: The Industrial Heart of the Confederacy," *Atlanta Historical Bulletin* 1:3 (May 1930): 21; Beverly M. Dubose III, "The Manufacture of Confederate Ordnance in Georgia," *Atlanta Historical Bulletin* 12:4 (December 1967): 19; Josiah Gorgas, "Ordnance Department of the Confederate Government," *The Confederate Soldier in the Civil War* (n.p.: The Fairfax Press, n.d.) 327; William A. Albaugh, et al., *Confederate Handguns, The Men Who Made Them, and the Times of Their Use* (Philadelphia: Riling and Lentz, 1963) 61-77; Franklin M. Garrett, *Atlanta and Environs: A Chronicle of Its People and Events* 2 vols. (Athens: University of Georgia Press, 1969) 1:52.

Richmond's Tredegar Iron Works as a producer of iron products for the South.

By the same token, Atlanta's role as a hospital center mushroomed. Since Atlanta was considered a safe distance from the front, had rail connections to and from the front lines, had good water available, and had a temperate climate with little disease, the army authorized the construction of forty buildings in addition to the large General Hospital (later Fair Ground Hospital Number One) already built on the fairgrounds. The Gate City Hotel, on the corner of Alabama and Pryor streets, became the Receiving and Distributing Hospital, a reception center and clearinghouse for new arrivals. Other land and buildings were pressed into medical service and smaller hospitals were set up in tents. A special hospital was erected on "Markham's Farm" for the treatment of contagious diseases such as pneumonia, venereal disease, measles, and the dreaded smallpox, which broke out regularly among the soldiers.

Confederate troops, workers attracted by war industries, and refugees flocked into the city, raising the population to some 17,000 people. Among the influx were "numbers of ill disposed persons" who caused an increase in crime and Union spying. To deal with these undesirables, the army proclaimed Atlanta a military post in May 1862. Colonel George W. Lee, Atlanta's military commander, posted guards around the city to protect military property and "examine and arrest all suspicious persons." Lee also ordered billiard and gaming houses closed, prohibited the sale of liquor to military officers and men, and placed all slaves and free blacks under a nine o'clock curfew. At the same time, the city council, under the leadership of Mayor James M. Calhoun, appointed a twenty-five man Vigilance Committee to help local police maintain law and order.[15]

At the beginning of 1863, food shortages became widespread. The South could no longer import hay from Maine, Irish potatoes from Nova Scotia, apples from Massachusetts, butter and cheese from New York, flour and pork from Ohio, or beef from Illinois. Meat supplies were diminished

---

[15]Coulter, *Confederate States*, 337; Singer, "Confederate Atlanta," 120-23, 136-38, 148-54, 159-68; Wiley and Milhollen, *Embattled Confederates*, 110; Albaugh, *Confederate Handguns*, 67. A sensational episode occurred on 7 June when Captain James J. Andrews, a Kentucky Unionist spy, and six of his raiders went to the scaffold—two of the unfortunates fell to the ground when their ropes broke and had to face the ordeal again. *Southern Confederacy* (24 May 1862); Singer, "Confederate Atlanta," 146-48.

first by the loss of supply from the North, then by Union armies that threatened Vicksburg on the Mississippi River, which consequently halted the supply from the West. To meet the emergency, Confederate leaders proselytized the food strategy. In order to encourage King Cotton to give way to King Corn, the growing of food crops was equated with patriotism—diversified farming would create economic independence from the North, while the war would bring political independence.[16]

A major hindrance to food production was the Confederate government's impressment policy. Farmers did not want to sell to the government, which offered prices that were not fair or it paid in inflated paper money. E. Merton Coulter wrote: "The ubiquitous activities of the 'pressmen,' who conducted veritable raids on the private property of Confederate citizens, stirred up a storm of bitterness as they seized food, horses, wagons, and anything else they wanted, and too often left worthless promises to pay."[17] Staple foodstuffs were almost impossible to obtain at any price, and some farmers, to even the score, hoarded food in order to drive prices even higher. But Peters was not an extortionist. Among the supplies he sold to the Confederate Quartermaster Corps were 82 bushels of corn and 1,500 pounds of hay; he also made two separate sales of firewood, one for 86 cords, and soon afterward the largest sale of all, 318 cords at $25 a cord (the market price was $50), the latter evidently used in Atlanta hospitals.[18]

In July 1863, the South, having fought toe to toe with the Union, suffered two staggering blows. Union General George G. Meade repulsed General Robert E. Lee at Gettysburg and General U. S. Grant forced the surrender of Confederate General John Pemberton at Vicksburg. In Richmond, General Josiah Gorgas confided to his diary the implications of the twin disasters: "Events have succeeded one another with disastrous rapidity. One brief month ago we were apparently at the point of success. . . . It seems incredible that human power could effect such a change in so brief a

---

[16]James C. Bonner, *A History of Georgia Agriculture, 1732-1860* (Athens: University of Georgia Press, 1964) 147; Coulter, *Confederate States*, 239-40. For a brief look at the question of pork in the Old South, see my "Republic of Porkdom Revisited: A Note," *Proceedings of the American Philosophical Society* 114:5 (October 1970): 407-408.

[17]Coulter, *Confederate States*, 251-52; Singer, "Confederate Atlanta," 94-96.

[18]Bills of Sale, 1863-1864, Record Group 109, Papers Relating to Citizens and Firms, War Department Collection of Confederate Records, Military Archives Division, The National Archives, Washington D.C.

space. Yesterday we rode on the pinnacle of success—today absolute ruin seems to be our portion. The Confederacy totters to its destruction."

If Gettysburg caught the eye, Vicksburg was probably the more mortal wound. Capture of that western stronghold secured the Mississippi River for the Union and divided the Confederacy. This certainly had the greatest ultimate effect on Atlanta. As the Confederate nation grew weaker, Atlanta became more significant, gaining immense political as well as industrial and transportational importance in the final months.[19]

Following the fall of Vicksburg, concern for Atlanta's safety intensified. The Confederate War Department directed L. P. Grant, chief engineer of the Department of Georgia, to survey and map Atlanta's outlying area and devise a plan for defensive works around the city consisting of a series of earthworks and trenches. Seventeen redoubts, built on hills and connected by rifle pits, would be the basic line of defense. Each redoubt would have five faces and was to contain five artillery pieces. Grant began with a military labor force, then added civilian labor and when, he was still short of workmen, he hired slaves. The offer of $25 a month, plus meals and medical care for each slave, found owners receptive. Finally, to insure a permanent labor force, the army required a quota of slaves from surrounding counties and housed them in barracks.

To further provide for the defense of Atlanta, General Howell Cobb, commander of the Georgia State Guard, set up headquarters in the city. Several occupational groups, including the city police force, employees of the Georgia Railroad and Western and Atlantic Railroad, and a group of boys under eighteen years of age, organized into military units (of varying degrees of seriousness) as part of the State Guard. Cobb was determined to whip the state's army of five thousand men into shape, but was only moderately successful because of lack of arms, equipment, and poor discipline.[20]

As Confederate General Braxton Bragg attempted in vain to maintain a foothold in middle and, failing that, eastern Tennessee, bloody fighting occurred near Chattanooga. The newly formed Atlanta Soldiers Executive

---

[19]Bruce Catton, *Short History of the Civil War* (New York: Dell Publishing Co., 1960) 140-41; William C. Everhart, *Vicksburg National Military Park, Mississippi* (Washington: Government Printing Office, 1954) 52-53.

[20]Singer, "Confederate Atlanta," 208-10, 212-16.

Aid Committee established a commissary in Atlanta to help supply the Army of Tennessee. In September 1863, this committee ordered a large supply depot be established at Ringgold in northwest Georgia, "or as near the battlefield as convenient," and placed it under Peters's care. Peters also supervised the transportation of casualties from the Chattanooga battlefields, and each returning train poured hundreds of sick and wounded men into Atlanta. The passenger depot became so glutted that it was almost impossible to wade through the dead and dying to board a train. Hospitals utilized almost every available building, warehouse, shed, tent, and vacant field.

The magnitude of the task of caring for the infirm soldiers is suggested by the figures: eighty thousand sick and wounded in Atlanta during the war, of whom five thousand died.[21] The influx turned Atlanta into "a dreary succession of canteens for soup and coffee, greasy ladles, ever-swarming flies, and bearded, smelly, terribly hurt men." The work of the women was magnificent. One of the most important organizations to relieve the suffering was the St. Philip's Hospital Aid Society, established in affiliation with the Georgia Relief and Hospital Association. It was highly organized; each member contributed at least fifty cents a month to buy hospital supplies and held weekly meetings to assign sewing quotas and cooking and nursing duties. The group distributed supplies in Atlanta sent from many parts of the South. Mary Jane Peters, a leading member, made donations to the society; visited the hospitals daily, usually with her daughter, Nellie, and houseslave, Mose, who carried on his arm a hamper filled with food, including fresh vegetables and fruits; and she provided kettles of hot coffee to the soldiers as they arrived in the city. But her most difficult duty was speaking words of comfort and reading the Bible to the dying in their last hours, and then writing letters to their families.[22]

---

[21]James M. Crew to Louisa Crew, 22 September 1863, Crew Collection; *Southern Confederacy* (2 April 1862; 29 September, 2 October 1863); *Atlanta Intelligencer* (26 September 1863); A. A. Hoehling, *Last Train From Atlanta* (New York: T. Yoseloff, 1958) 28-29.

[22]Scrapbook, Nellie P. Black Collection; John Henderson to William L. Calhoun, 6 August 1895, William L. Calhoun Collection, Atlanta Historical Society; *Southern Confederacy* (11 January 1863); Hoehling, *Last Train*, 40; Bryan, *Confederate Georgia*, 179, 233-34; Coulter, *Confederate States*, 133; Singer, "Confederate Atlanta," 73-74, 205-206.

CHAPTER EIGHT

GEORGIA AT WAR: BLOCKADE RUNNING, SIEGE OF ATLANTA

I cicles hung from Atlanta buildings during the winter of 1863-1864 and sheets of ice covered the streets. The frigid blast was one of the coldest in the city's history. The temperature on New Year's Day rose to only six degrees and that night plunged below zero. The citizenry huddled near their fires to keep from freezing. The arsenal's great need for charcoal caused a shortage of firewood and drove the price to $80 a cord. Desperate souls chopped and smashed furniture and used it for fuel. Domestic animals such as cows and horses, half starved already, fell victim to the cold unless they were wintered inside the homes of their owners where they were secure from frequent raids by both civilians and the military.

People desperately tried to find food. Wholesale prices were at ruinous levels—corn was $10 a bushel, Irish potatoes $20 a bushel, and flour $120 a bushel. One restaurant advertised a breakfast of ham, eggs, and coffee for $25. City Marshal O. H. Jones unsuccessfully fought crime with old men and draft rejects. Teenage boys, many of them orphans and runaways from the surrounding area, roamed the city and made thievery a certainty of life in Atlanta.[1]

Convinced more than ever of the ultimate outcome of the war, Peters concentrated on being able to save his property when the end did come. His assets in Fulton County alone—approximately $200,000—consisted of real property, nine slaves, cash and debts, merchandise, and household goods.[2] Like other investors during the war, Peters favored livestock and land, and he held some Confederate bonds. But he was not content with merely trying to save his existing property; as a hedge against its loss, he invested in a blockade-running company in order to create new wealth as a potential replacement.[3] The prewar moratorium on cotton caused the fiber to sell for much less in the South than it did in England, and many goods, especially coffee and quinine, could be bought low in England and sold for fabulous prices in the South. A ship could clear about $250,000 or more each way. Therefore, with rail transportation and a market for manufactured goods, many Atlantans became interested in blockade-running ventures. Jonathan Norcross was a founder of the Fulton County Export and Import Company, in which William Peters invested. Like the Peters brothers and Norcross,

---

[1]Ralph B. Singer, "Confederate Atlanta" (Ph.D. dissertation, University of Georgia, 1973) 220-21, 224, 229-30.

[2]Fulton County Tax Digest, 1862(?), Atlanta Historical Society.

[3]Richard Peters, "Personal Recollections," *Richard Peters: His Ancestors and Descendants*, comp. Nellie P. Black (Atlanta: Foote and Davies, 1904) 28; James L. Roark, *Masters Without Slaves: Southern Planters in the Civil War and Reconstruction* (New York: W. W. Norton and Company, 1977) 88-89. By 1864 small importers were forced out of business by the increasingly effective Union blockading squadrons, with the result that blockade running became concentrated in the hands of the larger companies that could afford to purchase vessels especially designed to run the blockade and at the same time absorb the loss of some ships. After the loss of the western Confederacy, most of the trade was limited to the port of Wilmington, North Carolina, which was easily accessible by rail from the interior and where two Cape Fear River inlets, both defended by forts, made enforcement of the blockade more difficult. The Confederate government encouraged blockade running, but at the same time shortages and inflation in the South caused heavy regulation of this single, critical lifeline to the outside world. Frank E. Vandiver, ed., *Confederate Blockade Running Through Bermuda, 1861-65: Letters and Cargo Manifests* (Austin: University of Texas Press, 1947) xv, xxxvi; Hamilton Cochran, *Blockade Runners of the Confederacy* (Indianapolis: Bobbs-Merrill, 1958) 49-50, 190; Philip Van Doren Stern, *The Confederate Navy: A Pictorial History* (Garden City: Doubleday, 1962) 225; Ralph V. Righton, "Greyhounds of the Confederacy," *Atlanta Historical Bulletin* 18:1 and 2 (Spring-Summer 1973): 31, 36; Richard D. Goff, *Confederate Supply* (Durham: Duke University Press, 1969) 55.

Sidney Root and John N. Beach were former Northerners who recognized it as a potentially profitable enterprise, and the merchandise and real estate firm of Beach and Root did a prodigious business. Indeed, Atlanta capital invested in shipping increased from $2,500 in 1862 to $73,000 within two years.[4]

In 1864, a group of capitalists led by Peters, Vernon K. Stevenson, and Richard T. Wilson, in association with the Crenshaw brothers of Richmond, began blockade-running operations. Peters, Stevenson, and Wilson formed the executive committee of the company.[5] Stevenson, a native of Kentucky, had accumulated wealth as a Tennessee merchant and, as a leading force in building the Nashville and Chattanooga Railroad; he also had experience in transportation. During the war Stevenson held the rank of major in the army and rose to assistant quartermaster-general. He was the object of some controversy for his part in the panic-stricken evacuation of Nashville, during which he had abandoned warehouses filled with Confederate supplies. Stevenson established headquarters in Atlanta, purchased clothing material for the military, and was responsible for the Army of Tennessee being "tolerably well shod."[6]

Wilson's antebellum career also directed him toward a wartime position in supply. Born in Georgia, he prospered as a merchant in Loudon, Tennessee, and later in Louisville, Kentucky. Appointed major in the Commissary Department, he purchased bacon for the Army of Tennessee. Perhaps because he was the youngest of the three executive committee members and had less influence in railroad affairs but more experience as a commission merchant, Wilson ran the blockade and represented the company in England. Peters's reputation as one of Atlanta's most respected businessmen was another plus for the company and he proved "extremely

---

[4]Minute Book of the Fulton County Export and Import Company, McNaught-Ormond Papers, Atlanta Historical Society; Sidney Root, "Memorandum of My Life," Atlanta Historical Society, typescript; *Atlanta Constitution* (19 October 1884).

[5]Peters, "Personal Recollections," 28.

[6]*Journal of the Congress of the Confederate States of America, 1861-65* 7 vols. (Washington: United States Government Printing Office, 1904-1905) 6:137; *Official Records of the Union and Confederate Armies in the War of the Rebellion* 128 vols. (Washington: United States Government Printing Office, 1880-1901) ser. 1, 7:429-31, 23:759, 765, ser. 2, 7:831; *Atlanta Constitution* (19 October 1884); *New York Times* (18 October 1884; 31 May 1908); Goff, *Confederate Supply*, 56-58.

competent at this risky business." Peters and Stevenson moved cotton forward by rail to Wilmington, North Carolina, for export; Wilson sold the cotton in England and purchased the return cargoes, mostly beef, pork, and coffee, as well as gunny cloth and iron hoops to wrap and tie cotton for export. The trio agreed at the outset that the company would use most of the profits for new ships contracted by Wilson, establishing a company policy of reinvesting to build a fleet.

James R. Crenshaw, a stockholder, was company agent in Nassau. He, too, had had experience in the Commissary Department during the early part of the war, and in 1864 was associated with his brother, William G. Crenshaw, importing for the Confederate government. The role of William G. Crenshaw in the company is obscure. A Richmond merchant by trade, he had raised an artillery battery and served with distinction in the Army of Northern Virginia after which he went to England and entered into a contract as purchasing agent for the Confederacy. He apparently represented private companies as well, and engaged in personal speculation. Wilson and William G. Crenshaw knew each other and both were interested in the shipbuilding firm of J. and W. Dudgeon Company, located on the Thames, which built for the company of Peters, Stevenson, and Wilson.[7]

The captains who commanded the ships were also key figures in the success of the company. British captains, prominent in the trade early in the war, became quite scarce when patriotism became a necessary adjunct to profits due to the increased risk of capture or destruction, although when the company began importations in the spring of 1864, one of its captains, George M. Horner, was described as "an Englishman by birth." Captain Michael P. Usina of Savannah, a Confederate naval officer, was the company's best-known captain. In 1864, the twenty-five-year-old "boy captain" rose to ship commander and was, by his own account, the youngest man to command a blockade runner. While nearly all the company's captains and crews were Southerners, the firm of Peters, Stevenson, and Wil-

---

[7]*Official Records of the Union and Confederate Navies in the War of the Rebellion* 30 vols. (Washington: United States Government Printing Office, 1894-1922) ser. 1, 3:725-26; *Official Records of the Armies*, ser. 1, 11:857-58, 21:1088-91, 12:674, 19:955, 980, 25:635-36, ser. 4, 2:481, 497-98, 3:527-28; *Atlanta Constitution* (19 October 1884); *New York Times* (31 May 1908); Michael P. Usina, "Blockade Running in Confederate Times," *Addresses Delivered Before the Confederate Veterans Association* (Savannah: United Confederate Veterans, 1895) 38: Vandiver, *Blockade Running Through Bermuda*, 130-31, 135, 137; Singer, "Confederate Atlanta," 97-98.

son, followed the usual practice of registering its ships, merchandise, and destinations as British.

The company experienced immediate success with its first two ships, the *Celeste* and the *Atlanta*. On his first voyage as captain, young Usina set an outbound course from Wilmington to Bermuda in the *Celeste*, a new side-wheeler with a capacity of approximately one thousand bales of cotton. The ship was fully loaded when she entered the Gulf Stream in rain and heavy seas. The rain cleared to reveal a powerful Union steamer, with canvas set, bearing for the small blockade runner. The blockader took in sails when Usina headed into the wind; still the *Celeste* would soon be fired on or overtaken. Usina ordered forty-five bales of cotton from forward cut open and thrown overboard. This allowed the *Celeste* to move easier through the water and the loose cotton floating in her wake hampered the progress of the pursuit vessel. The *Celeste* survived the ordeal, but was later lost to the company in a boiler explosion at Nassau.[8]

The *Atlanta*, at five hundred tons burden, was a large blockade runner (another ship, the ironclad C.S.S. *Atlanta*, fell into Federal hands near Savannah). A Dugeon-built vessel of advanced design completed in March 1864, the *Atlanta* was destined for an eventful career. The ship had twin screws with engines capable of independent action, and by reversing one screw, she could turn around on her center. More remarkable was her top speed of seventeen knots, which left every Union pursuit vessel in her wake. Considered one of the finest of a series of twin screws, the *Atlanta* reached Bermuda in April and, during the next three months, made four trips to Wilmington.

Captain Usina was in command of the *Atlanta* on two voyages, and on one, he saw that several blockade runners had returned to Bermuda after unsuccessful attempts to get into Wilmington. However, the *Atlanta* was loaded with her fourth cargo of badly needed supplies, so he weighed anchor. As Usina told it, the coastal waters were alive with blockaders and, worse yet, the moon was nearly full. He ordered the boiler safety valves closed to prevent the noise of escaping steam at a time when the ship was forced to proceed slowly in order to locate the inlet. Boiler pressures

---

[8]Peters, "Personal Recollections," 28; *Addresses Before the Confederate Veterans Association* (1895) 26, 28-29; *Papers Relating to the Foreign Relations of the United States: Geneva Arbitrations* 20 vols. (Washington: United States Government Printing Office, 1872) pt. 2, 3:144.

mounted as Usina approached the Union blockaders. Soon enough, she was spotted and the flagship of the fleet fired across her bow and ordered her to heave to. However, Usina's engineer "threw her wide open and she almost flew from under our feet." Union guns thundered without effect as the *Atlanta* stood into the Cape Fear River.

Inbound cargoes provided the owners of the company and their families with abundant supplies. But Peters shared his with many of the less fortunate in Atlanta. He explained that "my good wife visited the hospitals daily, carrying delicacies for the sick and wounded Confederate soldiers."[9]

As Peters's blockade-running venture began, the war on land entered its final phase. Federal General-in-Chief Ulysses S. Grant had recently sent a confidential dispatch from Washington to General William T. Sherman, whose armies were encamped at Chattanooga. Grant directed the red-haired Sherman "to move against Johnston's army, to break it up, and to get into the interior to the enemy's country as far as you can, inflicting all the damage you can against their war resources." Sherman's strike into Georgia was the major military development of 1864, and before the year ended he would punish Southern soldiers and civilians, men and women, adults and children, with hellish fury.

On 5 May, Sherman opened the campaign against Confederate General Joseph E. Johnston, who had replaced Bragg as commander of the Army of Tennessee, joining the army in its strongly fortified winter quarters at Dalton. Sherman, who had numerical troop strength (approximately 99,000 to Johnston's 43,000—later reinforced to some 64,000), would use the Western and Atlantic Railroad as his supply line from Tennessee and flank the Confederates to force their withdrawal, then catch them in "the confusion of retreat." Johnston, for his part, hoped to lure Sherman into a full-scale attack on entrenched Confederates, perhaps at some point far from the Union base of supply. The Confederate general, the Fabius of the Confederacy, hoped the North would eventually despair of winning the war and force the Lincoln administration to accept peace. Most Southerners did not know of, and probably would not have appreciated, Johnston's strategy. Nonetheless, only a few days into the Georgia campaign, Johnston evacu-

---

[9]Peters, "Personal Recollections," 29; *The Illustrated London News* (2 April 1864); *Official Records of the Armies*, ser. 2, 1:268; Vandiver, *Blockade Running Through Bermuda*, 130-31, 135, 137; *Addresses Before the Confederate Veterans Association* (1895) 25, 29-30; *Savannah Morning News* (5 July 1903).

ated Dalton and moved southward to Resaca. This set the scene for the spring and summer of 1864 between Dalton and Atlanta, as Sherman attempted to "knock Joe Johnston."[10]

Peters had a friend in one of the Confederate generals, Leonidas Polk, who was also Bishop of Louisiana. A religious conversion was going through the Southern army at the time, and the "fighting bishop of the Confederacy" occasionally held services for the troops. He baptized a number of senior officers, including General John B. Hood and Johnston, as the contending armies moved down the line of the Western and Atlantic. During the running fight, which was almost continuous skirmishing, Polk's corps was involved with holding action against the Federals. Polk had a military reputation for slowness, a trait which apparently served him well at the moment. He could often be seen viewing the engagements, his rotund frame clad in an old gray hunting shirt and slouch hat, a part of his dress that became something of a trademark. "He sat his horse and received the leaden compliments of the enemy with complacent yet not indifferent good-humor. He had a habit of shrugging his shoulders when a Minie-ball came too close to his ear, and sometimes he would drop a chance word as though in reply."[11]

After two days of savage battle at Resaca, Sherman sent a division across the Oostanaula River at Lay's Ferry at the rear of Resaca, causing Johnston to withdraw and burn the railroad bridge over the river. South of the Oostanaula, Northern troops saw a striking change in the landscape. The steep, barren, and rocky mountain ridges north of the river trended away to the west. Before the invader lay broad and fertile fields, luxurious at that time of year with clover and other crops maturing in the sun; fields that in a short time would present a picture of desolation and ruin.[12]

---

[10]William T. Sherman, *Memoirs* 2 vols. (Westport: Greenwood Press, 1957) 2:26, 31-32; Stanley F. Horn, *The Army of Tennessee: A Military History* (Indianapolis: Bobbs-Merrill Co., 1941) 324-28.

[11]Nita Black Rucker, Notes on Nellie Peters Black, Nellie P. Black Collection, University of Georgia Libraries, Athens; William M. Polk, *Leonidas Polk: Bishop and General* (New York: Longmans, Green and Co., 1915) 351-52.

[12]Henry Stones, "From the Oostanaula to the Chattahoochee," *The Atlanta Papers*, comp. Sydney C. Kerkiss (Dayton: Press of Morningside Bookshop, 1980) 69-70.

Gordon County, in direct line of Sherman's army, experienced a great deal of brushfire fighting.[13] The center of Sherman's troops, including General John W. Geary's Second Division of the Twentieth Corps of the Army of the Cumberland, moved near the line of the railroad. Geary (later governor of Peters's native Pennsylvania) led his division across the Coosawattee River at McClure's Ferry and during the night of 17 May 1864 reached Calhoun. The Federals were in high spirits. Speeches, cheers, and band music rang out from their campfires. Colonel Adolphus Buschbeck's brigade of Geary's division, a brigade that had a notable history having been in the thick of combat at Chancellorsville, camped on Peters's plantation.

Peters, in anticipating army movements, had shipped his prized flock of Angoras to the Florida line near Quitman, Georgia, and kept it there until after the war. Local tradition in Gordon County has it that the Federals visited with the Peters family at the plantation, and that young Nellie Peters was there when the man she was destined to marry, Lieutenant George R. Black, moved through the area with the retreating Confederates. The bluecoats used but did not destroy Peters's plantation buildings as they passed through Gordon County.[14]

Although Sherman had yet to develop his "total war" concept, great numbers of North Georgians left their homes and scurried toward Atlanta as the contesting armies continued southward. Soldiers and civilians alike made their way past almost deserted towns, promising grain fields, and the fruit trees in full bloom. Adding to the mass of humanity in Atlanta were more and more sick and wounded soldiers. The famous Confederate nurse, Kate Cumming, arrived for a visit and saw brief duty in the Receiving and Distributing Hospital. The local press reported that "the Yankees are com-

---

[13]William F. Holmes, "Whitecapping in Late Nineteenth-Century Georgia," *From the Old South to the New: Essays on the Transitional South*, ed. Walter J. Fraser, Jr. and Winfred B. Moore, Jr. (Westport: Greenwood Press, 1981) 127.

[14]Jewell R. Alverson to Royce G. Shingleton, 3 March 1975; Rucker, Notes on Nellie Peters Black, Black Collection; James C. Bonner, *A History of Georgia Agriculture, 1732-1860* (Athens: University of Georgia Press, 1964) 144; Burton J. Bell, comp., *1976 Bicentennial History of Gordon County* (Calhoun: The Gordon County Historical Society, Inc., 1976) 409; Norman D. Brown, ed., *One of Cleburne's Command: The Civil War Reminiscences and Diary of Captain Samuel T. Foster, Granbury's Texas Brigade, CSA* (Austin: University of Texas Press, 1980) 77-78; Carroll P. Scruggs, ed., *Georgia Historical Markers* (Valdosta: Bay Tree Grove Publishers, 1973) 273.

ing" and chided the "long faces," urging them to help defend the city, while L. P. Grant worked at an exhausting pace to complete Atlanta's defense perimeter.[15]

Among the city's refugees was the energetic Dr. Charles T. Quintard of Connecticut, who had been a physician and minister in Nashville and was now a chaplain in the Army of Tennessee. Quintard's combined talents as physician and chaplain were much in demand. His personal magnetism, especially his bighearted charity and quick repartee in conversation, earned him a wide circle of friends that included Peters. Quintard soon discovered that many of his fellow refugees in Atlanta were from Tennessee, among them members of his former church in Nashville. Because St. Philip's was too small for the great numbers of refugees who were Episcopalians, Quintard began preaching in a theater. He quickly secured Peters's aid in obtaining donations to establish a new parish. The church was named St. Luke's. Built by Confederate military labor on donated land at the corner of Walton and Broad streets, St. Luke's rose from an all-volunteer effort. The interior effects were gifts from friends of the new parish, including a pair of silver goblets from Mary Jane. Quintard, the rector of the little church, wrote: "Within its portals devout worshippers—many distinguished Confederate officers among them—were delighted to turn aside from the bloody strife of war and bow themselves before the Throne of Grace."[16]

Rumors of war abounded in Atlanta and the crowded conditions were fertile ground for producing panic. Peters was not the type to flee on impulse, nor on rumors and half-truths that preceded the invaders. He was not

---

[15]Mary E. Massey, *Refugee Life in the Confederacy* (Baton Rouge: Louisiana State University Press, 1964) 134; Richard Harwell, ed., *The Journal of Kate Cumming, a Confederate Nurse* (Savannah: The Beehive Press, 1975) 182; Singer, "Confederate Atlanta," 238-40, 243-44.

[16]Scrapbook, Black Collection; Mary S. Mallard to Mary Jones, 22 February 1864, in Robert M. Myers, ed., *The Children of Pride: A True Story of Georgia and the Civil War* (New Haven: Yale University Press, 1972) 1142; Harwell, *The Journal of Kate Cumming*, 180; Charles Todd Quintard, *Doctor Quintard, Chaplain C.S.A. and Second Bishop of Tennessee; Being His Story of the War (1861-1865)*, ed. Arthur Howard Noll (Sewanee: The University Press, 1905) 4, 8, 95, 153-56; Franklin M. Garrett, *Atlanta and Environs: A Chronicle of Its People and Events* 2 vols. (Athens: University of Georgia Press, 1969) 1:587-88; Bell I. Wiley and Hirst D. Milhollen, *Embattled Confederates: An Illustrated History of Southerners At War* (New York: Bonanza Books, 1964) 188.

a political nor military figure, had not been a "fire-eater" secessionist, had no sons old enough for military service, and was not especially sought by the enemy. Perhaps he could have lived fairly comfortably on his plantation during the invasion and occupation, although a breakdown in law and order in North Georgia in the wake of Sherman's columns would have been a threat. For the time being, he decided to stay in Atlanta and await military developments.

Johnston was soon forced to abandon the defensive perimeter he had constructed at Cassville because Sherman continued flanking movements instead of a direct assault. By 8 June, the Confederate forces were near Marietta, occupying high ground in the area, with the center on Pine Mountain. Within a few days, dreadful news reached Peters—General Polk was dead, having met death suddenly on 14 June at Pine Mountain. The news relayed that a heavy rain had just slackened, and Sherman, riding along his lines, noticed a group of high-ranking Confederates in plain view on the crest of the mountain. The Union general ordered several volleys from his artillery in an effort to scatter the group, which included Johnston and Polk, who were reconnoitering. The Confederate officers observed the Federal battery preparing to fire and began to seek cover. "But General Polk," wrote Sherman, "who was dignified and corpulent, walked back slowly, not wishing to appear too hurried or cautious in the presence of the men, and was struck across the breast by an unexploded shell, which killed him instantly."[17]

Peters joined with Quintard, who had served as chaplain on Polk's staff, in having the fallen general's remains transported to St. Luke's Church and placed in front of the altar. There he lay in state for several hours. Polk's body was clad in his gray uniform. On his breast rested a cross of white roses and beside the casket lay the general's sword. Thousands of soldiers and citizens slowly filed past the bier and Quintard delivered the eulogy. Following the services in St. Luke's, Polk's body was shipped to Augusta for interment.[18]

Less than two weeks later another funeral was held at St. Luke's Church when on 25 June 1864 Peters's eleven-month-old son, Stephen Elliott Peters, for whom Polk had stood as sponsor, died. The loss of two babies during the war (Joseph Thompson Peters, age one, had died 6 September 1862)

---

[17]Scrapbook, Black Collection; Sherman, *Memoirs*, 2:52-53.

[18]Quintard, *Doctor Quintard*, 98; Garrett, *Atlanta and Environs*, 1:587-88.

compounded the strain of the times for the family. The funeral of this infant son, held in St. Luke's Church, seemed especially sad. Little Stephen had been nursed with "tender solicitude" and many had said prayers for him. Nellie dropped a handkerchief at her infant brother's funeral, where it remained as the mourners left the church.[19]

Near Marietta, Johnston had abandoned Pine Mountain but remained entrenched at Kennesaw Mountain. Here Sherman launched a concentrated attack on 27 June 1864 and was hurled back with 2,500 casualties to Johnston's loss of approximately 800 men. Even when Sherman lost men in the extreme excess of a two-to-one ratio, he believed that such losses were justified considering he outnumbered Johnston two-to-one in troop strength. Although Sherman had lost—killed, wounded, captured, or missing— some 17,000 men since invading Georgia and Johnston had lost about 10,000, Sherman maintained his relative superiority. But the Union general quickly realized his mistake in forcing the issue at the bloody battle of Kennesaw. He resumed his flanking action, forcing Johnston to fall back, and by the morning of 3 July, the Confederates abandoned Kennesaw and Marietta, taking up positions near the Chattahoochee River, the last major defensive perimeter outside Atlanta.

Still outflanked, Johnston crossed the Chattahoochee River barrier on the night of 9 July and burned the Western and Atlantic Railroad bridge and his pontoon and trestle bridges. This action created a wild flurry of excitement in Atlanta. Merchants liquidated their stocks at reduced prices, packed any remaining goods, and fled. Confederate officials moved government machinery and stores to Macon, Columbus, and Augusta, and evacuated the less severely wounded soldiers from the city's hospitals.[20] Peters quickly moved his entire family and many valuables to the home of John P. King in Augusta before the Georgia Railroad could be cut by Union troops; he remained in Atlanta.[21]

Peters spent the next few days in restless anxiety. War news was hard to obtain because newspapers were shutting down. "Panic, fear, and confusion gripped Atlanta" as Sherman continued his relentless march. Every

---

[19]Genealogy Notes, Black Collection; *Atlanta Journal* (6 October 1935); Quintard, *Doctor Quintard*, 99.

[20]Sherman, *Memoirs*, 2:63-64; Singer, "Confederate Atlanta," 246-48.

[21]Peters, "Personal Recollections," 29.

southbound train of the Macon and Western Railroad was packed with refugees. Anticipating his own evacuation, Peters gave his power of attorney to a young friend and business associate, James R. Crew, who was general ticket agent for the Atlanta and West Point Railroad. Reliable and able, Crew had served as wartime aide to Mayor Calhoun and was active in Atlanta politics. (An outspoken critic of secession, Crew had been harassed by the Confederate military, including a brief arrest. Prophetically, he had written earlier in the war: "Our Sech friends are much exercised as to what they will do in the event the Yanks come here. It is quite amusing.") According to the agreement made between Crew and Peters, Crew was to care for all of Peters's Atlanta property and Gordon County plantation after Peters left for Augusta, but was prohibited from selling or otherwise disposing of any of the property without Peters's written orders.[22] Still, Peters seemed reluctant to depart the doomed city; instead, he turned his attention to corporate property as he tried to learn the condition of the Georgia Railroad.

The Confederate high command in Richmond frowned on Johnston's withdrawal strategy. Johnston was thinking as much in political as military terms; he wanted to prevent Sherman from winning a victory before the November 1864 presidential election in the North. But Jefferson Davis was under great public pressure for a victory in Georgia, which apparently did not seem possible while Johnston was in command. Among those demanding Johnston's removal was Secretary of War James A. Seddon, and on 13 July 1864 Davis's military advisor, General Braxton Bragg, arrived in Atlanta under the guise of a routine inspection tour, but actually to get a firsthand look at the situation. Bragg was convinced that Atlanta, which Davis considered vital to the Confederacy, would soon be captured unless there was a change in strategy. Accordingly, on 17 July Davis ordered Johnston to relinquish command of the Army of Tennessee to General John B. Hood. Greatly vexed at this, Johnston quit the area altogether and retired to Macon. Polk was missed more than ever at this critical juncture because he had been a buffer between the cautious Johnston and the maimed, but young and "itching-to-fight," Hood.

This change in command caused widespread controversy both then and today. A few days before President Davis acted on the matter, General Rob-

---

[22]James M. Crew to Louisa Crew, 2 May 1862, 10, 19 July, 9 December 1864, Crew Collection, Atlanta Historical Society.

ert E. Lee had astutely counseled him via telegram: "It is a bad time to re-
lease the commander of any army situated as that of Tennessee. We may
lose Atlanta and the army too. Hood is a bold fighter. I am doubtful as to
other qualities necessary." Many of Hood's contemporaries spoke of him as
having the "heart of a lion, head of wood"—an assessment of Hood upheld
by many of today's historians. Johnston had mounted a skillful resistance
against great odds and had the full confidence of his troops, and "when
news of his replacement reached the soldiers, many of them openly wept."
Sherman learned of the change of commanders from a Union spy out of Atlanta on 18 July and inquired of one of his generals, John M. Schofield, who
had been a classmate of Hood at West Point, as to Hood's general character.
Schofield characterized Hood as "bold even to rashness, and courageous in
the extreme." Sherman concluded that the change of commanders meant
"fight."[23]

The Federals, having crossed the Chattahoochee, moved toward Atlanta from the north and east. A lone Confederate scout, watching for the
enemy from a point three miles east of Decatur, observed locomotive smoke
rising above the Georgia Railroad tracks from the west. He turned his horse
to face the approaching engine and held up his hand. As the locomotive
ground to a halt, a man greeted him from the cab. It was Peters. Having
heard rumors that the Georgia Railroad had been cut, Peters had comman-
deered a locomotive for a personal inspection of the line. As Peters told it:
"We fortunately saw a mounted scout who advised us to return as quickly
as possible to Atlanta, as he was looking for the Yankees to appear every
moment." The scout was referring to Union General James B. McPherson's
forces, which had reached the railroad between Stone Mountain and Decatur four miles to the east and had begun tearing up the rails toward Atlanta. Peters immediately returned to the city, passing through Decatur only
one hour before the arrival of Union supply wagons. It was a close call for
Peters because Sherman was increasingly contemptuous of civilians and
was developing a very broad definition for the word "guerrilla."[24]

---

[23]Sherman, *Memoirs*, 2:72; Emory M. Thomas, *The Confederate Nation, 1861-65*
(New York: Harper and Row, 1979) 272n; David G. Chollet, "Advance and Retreat: Rage
or Reason?" *Atlanta Historical Bulletin* 20:1 (Spring 1976): 53; Lloyd Lewis, *Sherman:
Fighting Prophet* (New York: Harcourt, Brace and Co., 1932) 358-60; Singer, "Confederate
Atlanta," 250; Wiley and Milhollen, *Embattled Confederates*, 56.

[24]Peters, "Personal Recollections," 29; Sherman, *Memoirs*, 2:71-72.

As the Federals pressed toward Atlanta, Hood decided to strike. Actually, he was attempting to carry out a plan of Johnston, who had expected to take advantage of a gap in the Federal lines. On 20 July, Confederates poured out of their trenches near Peachtree Creek north of the city and pounced on the Federals at their noon rest. The Rebels came through the woods "yelling like demons." For several hours the action was savage as the troops became commingled and fought hand-to-hand. Union General George H. Thomas, who happened to be in the area, set up some field batteries and directed a furious fire on Confederates attempting to flank the Federal left. Slowly the Confederates retired to their trenches. They had lost about 5,000 men—killed, wounded, and missing—which they could ill afford to lose; Union losses accounted for 1,800 men. Hood was probably the victim of poor staff work, upsetting Confederate timing. Polk's old corps, now commanded by General A. P. Stewart, fought well, but General William J. Hardee has been severely criticized by history. Had Hardee been able to crush the Union left, as Hood wanted, "there would have been a different story to tell of Peachtree Creek."[25]

With the battle of Peachtree Creek, the siege of Atlanta began. The first shell, which was lobbed into the city on 20 July, prophetically demonstrated Sherman's concept of total warfare by killing a little girl at the corner of Ivy and Ellis streets as she walked with her parents. (The child's identity is unknown.) The Union commander was altering his objective from destruction of the Confederate army to capturing the hub of Southern transportation and supply. A precursor of modern warfare, Sherman deliberately moved against the civilian population. He accused Hood of hiding behind women's skirts in occupying the line of fortifications built around Atlanta by L. P. Grant, but at the time the siege began, Hood's army was still in the vicinity of Peachtree Creek.

During the night of 21 July, Hood occupied the fortifications around Atlanta. The next day the famous battle of Atlanta took place just east of the city toward Decatur. At 1:00 P.M. the order came down the line: "Advance!" Hood struck the enemy in a large-scale, fierce assault. At first the scene was impressive as the regimental colors fluttered above the advancing

---

[25]Oliver O. Howard, "The Struggle for Atlanta," *Battles and Leaders of the Civil War*, ed. Robert U. Johnson and Clarence U. Buel, 4 vols. (New York: Castle Books, n.d.) 4:313; Sherman, *Memoirs*, 2:73; Chollet, "Advance and Retreat," 59; T. Conn Bryan, *Confederate Georgia* (Athens: University of Georgia Press, 1953) 162.

Confederates. But Union batteries from strategic Bald Hill "made the earth tremble" as they began to mow "great swaths in the advancing columns." Then hot lead gave way to cold steel as officers met officers with drawn swords and enlisted men clashed with bayonets. Dense smoke filled their eyes and the groans of wounded and dying could be heard amid the roar of battle.

The sun was high and hot over Atlanta. Hood, at his field headquarters, a table and tent on Decatur Street, already knew that the sound of battle came too late, yet couriers rode up to report: "We've got 'em . . . whipping them like hell. . . . We'll capture Sherman's whole army." Nearby in City Park in front of the Atlanta Hotel, black-covered ambulances began arriving by the dozens. The wounded were placed on tables. That medical science was "woefully, incredibly imperfect" was soon demonstrated once more. "The grass in the park changed from green to red as surgeons sawed through bones. Hundreds of gory arms and legs were thrown into the baskets prepared to receive them." At this ghastly sight, the civilian onlookers slowly disappeared, leaving the surgeons and their patients in the park; a few yards away the grim general awaited battle reports.

The Confederates were desperately trying to recapture Bald Hill, a strategic point because the elevation brought Atlanta into view and also within range of Union artillery. Sherman utilized only his Army of the Tennessee, one brigade of which remained in Decatur to protect the wagon trains. His army was positioned with its right flank near the Howard House (Sherman's headquarters), extending to Bald Hill, with a division southward from there along a road. The fighting continued until well after dark and ended at different times in different places as the Confederates, many of them without rest for two days due to night marching, became completely exhausted. "By midnight the cannon and rifle fire faded like a curtain being slowly lowered on the battlefield."

The battle of Atlanta was over and the Federals retained possession of Bald Hill, having repulsed five strong Confederate thrusts up the crest and into Union trenches. Had the Army of the Tennessee been defeated, no doubt Sherman would have employed the armies of the Cumberland and the Ohio. The Federals lost General McPherson and 3,500 men; the Confederates lost General William H. T. Walker and a devastating 8,000 to 10,000 men. Sherman wrote of the seven-mile battleground: "I rode over the whole of it the next day, and it bore the marks of a bloody conflict. The enemy had retired during the night inside of Atlanta, and we remained masters of the situation outside." Whereas Hood had been thrown back with heavy losses in his efforts to rout the enemy before Atlanta, Sherman had not been allowed to reach the railroad south of the city.[26]

The Confederates settled into the defensive works at the edge of Atlanta and the siege began in earnest. Day and night for six weeks shells rained upon the city, bringing the horrors of war to the civilians. Families burrowed into eight-feet-deep pits and covered them with cross-ties; some of these "bombproofs" or "dug-outs" were multi-family shelters. Thousands sought safety in the rock-walled basement of Peters's old mill building.

Life in Atlanta became increasingly wretched. Punctuating the heavy cannon noise was the sharp crack of rifle fire as pickets constantly skirmished, day and night. An uninterrupted flow of wounded was brought in from the works around the city and blood-spattered surgeons, without medicines and anesthetics, continued to hack off arms and legs in front of the Atlanta Hotel. People walked blocks out of the way to avoid the scene. Polluted water caused a typhoid fever epidemic. The scarcity of goods and the accompanying high prices, and the drunken rabble in the streets added to the misery. City functions ceased and the only symbol of authority became the army.

Sherman soon precipitated a third battle for the beleaguered city. Still attempting to cut the railroad to the south, he sent part of his troops southward around the western edge of town. Confederate forces moved out to check this latest effort to isolate Atlanta, resulting in the battle of Ezra Church (Battle Hill). Amid some apparent confusion on the part of their leaders, the Confederates advanced on 28 July into a withering Federal fire delivered from strong defensive works. Hood again suffered heavy losses— nearly 5,000 Confederates compared to 700 for the Union. But the railroad, which was Atlanta's single lifeline to the outside, remained in Confederate hands.

On 9 August, Sherman added to his artillery two powerful siege guns that had just arrived from Chattanooga. The new guns were capable of

---

[26]Sherman, *Memoirs*, 2:79-82; Robert N. Adams, "The Battle and Capture of Atlanta," Grenville M. Dodge, "The Battle of Atlanta," Gilbert D. Munson, "The Battle of Atlanta," *The Atlanta Papers*, 421, 477, 489, 494-95; Samuel Carter, III, *The Siege of Atlanta, 1864* (New York: St. Martin's Press, 1973) 218-28, 294-95; Avalon Woodruff Bryant, "A History of Medicine in Atlanta and Fulton County, Georgia," *Journal of the Medical Association of Georgia* 69 (April 1980): 277.

knocking down buildings, leaving few places of safety. That day was recalled by Atlantans as the "red day in August." "A family of six fled to their 'bombproof' which seconds later suffered a direct hit. No one could be identified." Shells hit every section of the city, leaving hardly a block undamaged. The northern section was hardest hit, where by mid-August nearly every building was partially damaged. Least damaged was southwest Atlanta, Peters's section. Craters dotted the streets making travel difficult. Everywhere there was "an inferno of noise swollen at intervals by the roar of a falling building. The very air was loathsome with the odor of burned powder, while a pall of dust and smoke overhung the city."

Behind the Federal lines to the north and east of the city, troops held their ears as the big guns roared. Occasionally, they called out as the shells whistled overhead: "There goes the Atlanta Express!" Other Union soldiers referred to each soaring shell as "a kiss for Jeff Davis." Sherman ordered an increased rate of artillery fire on Atlanta because he knew, as he later wrote, that "its capture would be the death-knell of the Southern Confederacy." All told, an estimated five thousand shells hit Atlanta.[27]

Church buildings were potential targets for destruction because the South's churches had severed their national affiliations and actively supported the Confederate war effort, including Southern Episcopalians—at the urging of Bishop Polk and Bishop Elliott. In Union eyes, therefore, Atlanta's churches were unholy. When a pensive Quintard found Nellie Peters's handkerchief in St. Luke's, he thought of the recent funerals in the church and his scattered flock, and was moved to write a booklet, *Nellie Peters' Pocket Handkerchief and What It Saw*, in which he described the siege. Quintard's brief account tells of a shell that penetrated the building and struck a prayer desk containing a Bible, but failed to explode. In explaining the incident, Quintard wrote: "The prayer desk was broken and the Bible fell under it and upon the shell so as apparently to smother it and prevent its exploding." He removed the shell from the church. Then Quintard sadly gathered the prayer books for distribution to the Confederate troops and sent the handkerchief to Nellie in Augusta. It was the last time he visited

---

[27]Sherman, *Memoirs*, 2:99; Carter, *Siege of Atlanta*, 269; Singer, "Confederate Atlanta," 251-58; Walter G. Cooper, *Official History of Fulton County* (Atlanta: Walter W. Brown Publishing Co., 1934) 71, 135, 140, 151-52, 170-72.

St. Luke's; when he later made his way from Atlanta, he headed south on a general pass from the army.[28]

It was probably at this time, the middle of August, that Peters made his departure from Atlanta. It is not clear when or how he evacuated, but he was last reported in the city on 29 July and the railroad was the logical mode of travel for him. The depot was so crowded with refugees intent on moving southward on the Macon and Western Railroad that incoming trains had to stop outside to keep from running over people. By the end of August less than three thousand people remained in the city. Peters probably traveled an all-rail route through Macon to Millen, then northward to Augusta, a route used by quite a number of refugees from Atlanta. Once in Augusta, he joined his family at the King home.[29]

---

[28]"The Convention and General Councils of the Protestant Episcopal Church in the Confederate States of America," Georgia Department of Archives and History, Atlanta; Charles T. Quintard, *Nellie Peters' Pocket Handkerchief and What It Saw* (Sewanee: The University Press, 1907) 1-7; Quintard, *Doctor Quintard*, 100-101.

[29]*Augusta Chronicle and Sentinel* (22 July 1864); A. A. Hoehling, *Last Train From Atlanta* (New York: T. Yoseloff, 1958) 186. Peters's decision to evacuate perhaps saved his life, because near the end of the siege a forty-two pound Sawyer shell crashed into his Atlanta home and exploded, killing an officer of the Fourteenth Texas Cavalry and two children, and wounding several women. *Augusta Chronicle and Sentinel* (31 August 1864).

PICTORIAL ARCHIVES

George Washington's coach arriving at Belmont, the home of Judge Richard Peters on the Schuylkill River in Pennsylvania.
(University of Georgia Libraries)

116

The Coatesville, Pennsylvania, bridge. Peters built this bridge over Valley Creek in the early 1830s. It probably had a new top portion when shown in this 1860 photograph. (Railway Age)

The Peters home at 99 Forsyth Street. (Atlanta Historical Society)

118

Mary Jane Peters with Mary Ellen "Nellie" (left) and Richard Peters, Jr., circa 1853. (Mrs. Ralph Peters Black, Jr.)

The Atlanta City Hall-Fulton County Courthouse. Built on "Peters's Reserve," it was the center of local government, business, and civic life for three decades, and served briefly as the state capitol in 1868. The building was demolished in 1885 and replaced by the present capitol building. (Atlanta Historical Society)

120

Peters's six-year-old Devon cow, "Cherry," in an 1861 plantation sketch. With her second calf at side, she gave twenty-five quarts of milk a day. (Southern Cultivator)

The blockade-runner Atlanta. *Built of iron, she was 220 feet in length, 24 feet in width, and was painted gray to blend with the horizon at night.* (Illustrated London News)

The second "R. Peters"; built by Danforth in 1870. It was a Georgia Railroad locomotive (4-4-0 wheel arrangement) that was one of several in the South named for Peters. (Raymond B. Carneal)

The first Kimball House Hotel, 1870-1883. Located conveniently near the railroad, the passenger depot is to its right (not in photo). (Atlanta Historical Society)

An Atlanta Street Railroad car operating on Whitehall Street in 1872. Across the tracks on Peachtree is Peters's Railroad Block building, which was replaced by today's Peters Building (Number One Peachtree Street) in 1901 and later remodeled. (Atlanta Historical Society)

124

"Mahomet," Peters's celebrated Angora goat, and two ewes. "Mahomet" was imported from Asia Minor at a cost of $1,000. (Atlanta Historical Society)

The Peters second Atlanta home, 1881-1928. Located at Peachtree, Cypress, Fourth, and Fifth streets, it occupied the entire block. The First Baptist Church is situated on this block today. (Atlanta Historical Society)

Interior of Peters's Peachtree Street home. (Atlanta Historical Society)

The second St. Philip's Church, 1882-1936. (Atlanta Historical Society)

The Bishop's chair from the second St. Philip's Church, to Rector Robert C. Foute's left. It is among several items from the first two churches that are preserved in present-day St. Mary's chapel, Cathedral of St. Philip. (Atlanta Historical Society)

CHAPTER NINE

BURNING OF ATLANTA: PETERS RETURNS TO ATLANTA AS REFUGEE

Peters found conditions in Augusta much as they had been a year earlier in Atlanta. Refugees from Atlanta and North Georgia poured into the river port, where life was difficult for most of them. Those who, like Peters, had a friend's home for their families were fortunate—especially when the friend was someone like King, who was quite wealthy. As a devoted family man, Peters made sure that refugee life for his children was relatively normal; they enjoyed riding in King's impressive carriage and were also taken to church on Sundays. Their relatives, the Clarke family and a favorite aunt (Peters's sister Ellen who, like King, was a strong Unionist), were also temporary residents of Augusta.[1]

The Peters family learned the latest war news from newspapers, other refugees, and sometimes by letters via a courier system established when the railroads were severed. Among their correspondents were Bishop Elliott

---

[1]Nita Black Rucker, Notes on Nellie Peters Black, Nellie P. Black Collection, University of Georgia Libraries, Athens; Florence F. Corley, *Confederate City: Augusta, Georgia, 1861-1865* (Columbia: University of South Carolina Press, 1960) 84-86.

and Dr. Quintard. Sympathizing with the refugees, Elliott wrote from Savannah that the Peterses had enjoyed a married life of "almost unbroken
sunshine" until lately when "clouds at last have overspread your sky, and
you must bow in meekness to the storm." In a reference to the Peters infants, one of whom was named for him, he reflected that "it is very sad to
be driven from the home of our affections and from the graves of those we
love." Elliott, a staunch Rebel, still expressed hope for Southern
independence.

Quintard was in exile in a rented house two miles from Columbus,
where he was suffering from a "fit of the blues" (referring to Union troops
in Georgia). He wrote that he was tired of running and wished the war
would end; he longed to gather again around Peters's hearthstone and discuss with him the "situation," including army movements and prospects for
peace. As it was, Quintard wanted to resume his duties as chaplain, but
could not because of the necessity for providing for his family. "I don't
know that any man has the right to sit still and expect to be provided [for]
without exerting his own strength. I rather think this is Mr. Peters's philosophy. . . . Bless the dear man."[2]

Augusta provided Peters a favorable geographical base from which to
forward cotton to Wilmington, although shortly before he arrived, his
blockade-running company lost another ship. When Captain Usina docked
the sleek *Atlanta* on her fourth inbound voyage at Wilmington, the Confederate Navy Department pressed the ship into service as a cruiser. Three deck
guns were mounted aboard the vessel and Confederate Secretary of the
Navy Stephen R. Mallory assigned the new commerce raider to Commander John Taylor Wood, a hard-hitting and highly competent officer and
aide to President Jefferson Davis (Wood's uncle). The *Atlanta* was rechris-
tened the C.S.S. *Tallahassee*. The flamboyant Wood ran the Union blockade off Wilmington on 6 August and during the next twenty days alarmed
the entire Northeast by capturing thirty-three Union merchant vessels along
the north Atlantic coast before returning to Wilmington for lack of coal. The
exploits of the *Tallahassee* were widely publicized throughout the country.

The Confederate government compensated the firm of Peters, Stevenson, and Wilson for the *Atlanta*, paying $125,000 for a ship that originally
cost $85,000, but this almost certainly represented a major loss to the com-

---

[2]Stephen Elliott to Mary Jane Peters, 26 September 1864; Charles T. Quintard to Mary
Jane Peters, 21 October 1864, Black Collection.

pany. Each round trip would have provided sufficient profits to purchase a new ship, and five months remained for running the blockade which, according to the ship's established schedule of runs, made possible up to five more round-trips. As for her value to the Southern cause, the vessel's subsequent career successfully reflected Mallory's policy of destroying Union commerce ships as the *Tallahassee* ranked fourth most successful of all the Confederate raiders. The cruiser also raised Southern morale in the wake of the recent defeat at Mobile and the sinking of the C.S.S. *Alabama*. However, considering the South's desperate need for supplies, the *Atlanta* would probably have served the Confederacy better by continuing as a blockade runner. This is particularly true in view of the fact that on all four inbound voyages from Bermuda the cargoes of the ship consisted primarily of meat (four hundred tons on the last trip), bulky cargo that was avoided by the altogether profit-minded firms, a condition that had served to increase blockade running by the government. Finally, the success of the *Atlanta* as a converted sea raider caused the Union government to plan an amphibious assault that would close the cruiser's base of operations at Wilmington.[3]

---

[3]Vessel File A-168 and Vessel File T-30, Record Group 109, War Department Collection of Confederate Records, Military Archives Division, National Archives, Washington, D.C.; *Papers Relating to the Foreign Relations of the United States Geneva Arbitrations* 20 vols. (Washington: United States Government Printing Office, 1872) part 2, 3:144; Scrapbook, John Taylor Wood Papers, Southern Historical Collection, University of North Carolina, Chapel Hill; *Official Records of the Union and Confederate Navies in the War of the Rebellion* 30 vols. (Washington: United States Government Printing Office, 1894-1922) ser. 1, 3:308-309, 701-14; ser. 2, 2:804-806; J. Thomas Scharf, *History of the Confederate States Navy* (New York: Rogers and Sherwood, 1887) 806-808; John Taylor Wood, "The 'Tallahassee's' Dash into New York Waters," *The Century Magazine* 56 (July 1889): 408-17; "Bohemian" (diary of a *Tallahassee* crewmember), *New York Times*, 29 September 1864. After another brief cruise as the C.S.S. *Olustee* under Lieutenant William H. Ward, the ship was reconverted into a blockade runner named the *Chameleon*. Captain John Wilkinson, one of the war's most successful blockade runners, took her out for the government on 15 December 1864 but was unable to breach the blockade on the return trip with supplies from Bermuda. A final effort by Wilkinson to enter at Charleston from Nassau also failed. With all Southern ports closed and the Confederacy on the verge of collapse, Secretary Mallory wrote from Richmond to Commander John N. Maffitt in Nassau on 24 February 1865 instructing Maffitt to sell the *Chameleon* if possible so that the proceeds could be used to purchase a shallow-draft vessel of between five and six feet to run supplies into St. Marks or other Florida ports and then into Southern rivers, but Maffitt could not sell the vessel in a buyer's market, and the *Chameleon* sailed to Liverpool. After the war, Union officials in England sold her to Japan. *Official Records of the Navies*, ser. 1, 3:37, ser. 2, 1:268; 2:368, 707, 804-806; Clement A. Evans, ed., *Confederate Military History* 12 vols. (Atlanta: Confederate Publishing Co., 1899) 12:104; V. C. Jones, *The Civil War At Sea* (New York: Holt, Rinehart, Winston, 1960) 3:263-68.

Federal plans regarding Wilmington were unknown to Peters, whose immediate concern was news from Atlanta. On the morning of 25 August 1864, Sherman's guns were silent for the first time in forty days. The night before, Sherman had abruptly marched his army west of the city to cut the railroad to the south. Hood rushed Hardee to check Sherman at Jonesboro, but on 31 August-1 September the Confederates were repulsed and Atlanta's single supply-line was cut; Hood decided to evacuate. September 1, the day Hood withdrew his troops, was one of confusion and terror for the civilians remaining in Atlanta. Among the military supplies destroyed by the Confederates was a long train of ordnance stores along the Georgia Railroad. At nightfall the tremendous explosion of the munitions, said to have been heard over forty miles away, created near panic among Atlantans who did not know the cause.

As the Confederates left the city, the last cavalry units heading south on McDonough Road early on 2 September, Union troops entered along Marietta Street. Mayor James M. Calhoun rode out and, since Hood had merely evacuated, surrendered the city to Colonel John Coburn. The fall of Atlanta was of great political significance to the Lincoln administration because it insured the president's reelection. Mary Boykin Chesnut, the famous Southern observer, summed up the loss of the city for the South: "We are at sea. Our boat has sprung a leak."[4]

A few days after Sherman had established headquarters in Atlanta, he sent Crew and another Atlantan, James M. Ball, with a communique to Hood. Sherman demanded a ten-day truce for the evacuation of the remaining civilian population to Rough and Ready, a station five miles south of Atlanta where Hood was to receive them. Hood was incensed, but since he had no choice, he complied with Sherman's terms. Upon completion of the evacuation, 446 families—some 1,600 people, including 860 children—were uprooted. One of the evacuees was Crew, who passed through Rough and Ready on 12 September and continued to West Point. Those who went southward from Atlanta started the journey by wagon because the rails had been destroyed, while some boarded the Western and Atlantic for travel northward. Most blacks remained with the Federal troops. Approximately

---

[4]John Henderson to W. L. Calhoun, 6 August 1895, W. L. Calhoun Collection, Atlanta Historical Society; C. Vann Woodward, ed., *Mary Chesnut's Civil War* (New Haven: Yale University Press, 1981) 669.

fifty white families, evidently Union sympathizers and foreigners, were allowed to remain in the city.

Atlanta could now be held with a relatively small Federal garrison and Sherman returned to North Georgia, where he successfully defended against Hood's efforts to break the Union supply line along the Western and Atlantic Railroad. When word reached the Union commander that Hood was withdrawing through Alabama toward Tennessee, he sent General George Thomas in pursuit. As Hood moved into Tennessee, Sherman cut away from his line of supply in order to strike across Georgia for a southern port. Once communication with Washington was severed, he was, in effect, supreme commander in an area that lay defenseless before his horde, and Georgia north of Atlanta began to experience the full force of Sherman. Some civilians were arrested and held as hostages for the return of captured Federal troops. He not only ordered destruction of property, but also that citizens be killed in areas where attacks were made on his positions.

On 15 November 1864, Sherman was back in Atlanta. The streets were empty. Roses bloomed in the gardens of fine houses, but a terrible stillness and solitude prevailed. Before continuing the march against Southern morale and war-making capacity, Sherman ordered his Engineer Corps under Colonel Orlando M. Poe to burn the city. As Poe's engineers applied the torch, Father Thomas O'Reilly of the Church of Immaculate Conception, one of the citizens who had remained in the city, apparently saved his and other churches (as well as City Hall and several blocks of nearby residences) by threatening to call all Catholic soldiers from the Union ranks (some even volunteered) to protect the sacred buildings. St. Philip's, used first as a Confederate hospital and then as a commissary and kitchen during the occupation, was spared, although the rectory was burned, the lot ditched, and barracks and fortifications erected on the property. St. Luke's was burned because Quintard, a Northerner, was a Confederate chaplain who had held services in the "Rebel church" built by Confederate soldiers. The ill-fated church had existed only a few tempestuous months.

Business and industrial establishments were hard hit. The Car Shed, depots, machine shops, foundries, rolling mills, arsenals, and armory were swept away. The conflagration destroyed several hotels, including Thompson's Atlanta Hotel. The Concert Hall and the Athenaeum were doomed. For a long stretch along the Georgia Railroad no building was spared—the machine shop, depot, bank agency, and Peters's mill building which had housed the pistol factory became smoldering heaps of rubbish. Through the night the fire raged across two hundred acres, filling the air with burning cinders. In nearby camps, sixty thousand Union troops witnessed the burning as military bands played martial airs and operatic selections.[5]

Within a day or two, news from Atlanta reached Augusta. Peters realized that the Augusta Powder Works might be a target that could draw the invader to Augusta. Sherman, however, had no intention of attacking a fortified position. He divided his army for the march, personally accompanying the left wing via Decatur, Madison, and Milledgeville to Sandersville, where it joined the right wing, which marched out of Atlanta through Jonesboro and Gordon. In this way the army was able to cut a path from forty to sixty miles wide as it advanced from ten to fifteen miles a day. Explained Sherman: "These divergent lines [were] designed to threaten both Macon and Augusta at the same time, so as to prevent a concentration at our intended destination . . . Milledgeville, the capital of Georgia."

Sherman departed Atlanta on the crisp and clear morning of 16 November, riding alongside the marching troops on Decatur Road. He reined in his horse at the site where the battle of Atlanta had been fought and turned to look back on the smoldering and ruined city. The scene represented what he would be best remembered for, but he was now on another venture that would secure his place in history. The march could be tracked by the fires as ginhouses, railroad depots, bridges, and houses went up in smoke. The grim and ruthless general's special field orders for the march included the notorious: "The army will forage liberally on the country during the march." Each brigade organized a party of foragers—known to Southerners

---

[5]William T. Sherman, *Memoirs* 2 vols. (Westport: Greenwood Press, 1957) 2:119; James M. Crew to Louisa Crew, 12 September 1864, Crew Collection, Atlanta Historical Society; *Augusta Chronicle and Sentinel* (22 July 1864); *Atlanta Constitution* (2 September 1884); John C. Palfrey, "General Sherman's Plans After the Fall of Atlanta," *The Atlanta Papers*, comp. Sydney C. Kerkiss (Dayton: Press of Morningside Bookshop, 1980) 179; Daniel Oakey, "Marching Through Georgia and the Carolinas," *Sherman in Georgia: Selected Source Materials for College Research Papers*, ed. Edgar L. McCormick, et al. (Boston: D. C. Health and Co., 1961) 62; John T. Trowbridge, *The Desolate South, 1865-66: A Picture of the Battlefields and of the Devastated Confederacy*, ed. Gordon Carroll (Freeport: Books for Libraries Press, 1956) 238; John B. Walters, *Merchant of Terror: General Sherman and Total War* (Indianapolis: Bobbs-Merrill, 1973) 137-53; Burke Davis, *Sherman's March* (New York: Random House, 1980) 25; Emory M. Thomas, *Confederate Nation, 1861-65* (New York: Harper and Row, 1979) 276; T. Conn Bryan, *Confederate Georgia* (Athens: University of Georgia Press, 1953) 163, 165; Ralph B. Singer, "Confederate Atlanta" (Ph.D. dissertation, University of Georgia, 1973) 258-61.

as "bummers"—who were the "most venturesome in the army" and were apparently encouraged by their superiors to do as they pleased. Sherman admitted there was a "charm" about this looting that attracted his soldiers and they delighted in taking corn, meal, bacon, and sweet potatoes. They found sugar cane molasses in abundance and developed a liking for the "Confederate syrup." Many of the invaders "ransacked houses, ripped open featherbeds, smashed looking glasses and crockery, bayonetted family portraits, and tumbled tables and chairs, frightening women and children." They were often successful in locating personal valuables buried or hidden in swamps. At nearly every farmhouse, the troops slaughtered the livestock and burned the barns without respite.

As Sherman approached Milledgeville, Governor Joseph E. Brown and other state officials fled. Once in the capital, some Federal officers held a mock session of the Georgia legislature and repealed the ordinance of secession. On 24 November, Sherman moved toward Millen, using part of his forces to attack Confederate cavalry under General Joseph Wheeler's command. Fought on the branch railroad between Millen and Augusta near Waynesboro, the battle drove the Confederates back toward Augusta, adding to the delusion that Sherman was advancing on that city.[6]

When Lincoln proclaimed 25 November Thanksgiving Day, Peters was among those who thought Sherman might well be in Augusta for the holiday dinner. That he would not be a welcomed guest was attested to by a galaxy of Confederate military leaders who suddenly appeared in the city. Among the more famous were Generals Braxton Bragg (with 10,000 troops), William J. Hardee, and James Chesnut, Jr. Peters saw other reinforcements arriving daily. With characteristic dash, the daring Colonel John S. Mosby and his cavalry outfit arrived in town to aid the effort. The Confederates mobilized thousands of the city's idle blacks to build fortifications and Augusta took on the appearance of a military camp. The city remained on the alert for ten days, but the closest Sherman's raiders came was Waynesboro, twenty-five miles away. On 3 December, word came that the Federals were at Millen and were headed for Savannah. At this, Confederate troops quickly evacuated Augusta to concentrate near the coast.[7]

---

[6]Sherman, *Memoirs*, 2:175-82, 190-92; James C. Bonner, *A History of Georgia Agriculture, 1732-1860* (Athens: University of Georgia Press, 1972) 83-86; Bryan, *Confederate Georgia*, 166-70.

[7]Corley, *Confederate City: Augusta*, 73, 75, 86.

Early in December some Atlantans began to return home, realizing that they were going back to wrecked or burned buildings. Among the uprooted who were returning was James R. Crew. On 1 December, two weeks after the fire, he made his way back from West Point and reported some sixty families in the city. People who six months earlier had lived in humble style now occupied the unburned houses—many of them Atlanta's finest homes. These homes were filled with looted goods such as furniture, carpets, pianos, and mirrors, all awaiting removal by deserters and robbers who came as far as fifty miles to carry such plunder away. Crew managed to get word to Augusta that Peters's house, although damaged by shelling, was among those left standing. However, every panel of his fence was gone, evidently used for firewood during the occupation, and a Peters acquaintance, Tom Ware, had sold Peters's furniture to a Union officer and then departed for the North.[8] Many Atlantans whose houses were not destroyed became suspected collaborators, but Peters's good fortune need not have been an embarrassment since he had openly supported the Confederacy. His house was spared because a woman had taken up residence in it (occupied houses had a much better chance of escaping the torch) and it was in a section of the city least burned because of the efforts of Father O'Reilly.

Reports also reached the Peters family concerning widespread Union depredation in Atlanta, and Mary Jane became worried that the graves of their two infant sons had been disturbed. She had good reason for concern because the Federals had robbed graves in the city's Oakland Cemetery. They stripped silver fittings from coffins and dumped bodies from metal caskets, which were used to transport their own dead to the North. Ornaments of graves such as marble lambs and miniature statues representing departed children were broken and scattered. A commission established by Governor Brown to investigate the damage in Atlanta confirmed such reports and the vandalism was widely reported in Southern newspapers, including those of Augusta.

In mid-December Mary Jane joined a group who wanted to return to Atlanta. The party included her brother-in-law, William P. Orme, treasurer of the Atlanta and West Point Railroad, and Louisa Crew, who wanted to

---

[8]James M. Crew to Louisa Crew, 1 December 1864, Crew Collection; Report of General W. P. Howard (Georgia Militia) to Governor Brown, 7 December 1864, in the *Augusta Chronicle and Sentinel* (21 December 1864).

join her husband. Aware that rail travel beyond Athens was impossible and food difficult to obtain, Mary Jane and her companions boarded a train for Athens equipped with provisions, a rockaway (a popular vehicle because its light weight and high, narrow wheels enabled it to move through mud), and a driver. In Athens they passed the night with a friend, Ferdinand Phinizy, from whom they borrowed a pair of mules. The party proceeded to Atlanta the next day, walking the sixteen miles of farmlands recently pillaged by Sherman's army.

The small group of weary travelers approached the ruins of Atlanta in the wintry cold and sleet; what lay before them was repulsive to both eye and nostril. The suburbs resembled a "vast, naked, ruined, deserted" camp. Two-thirds of the timber, including that on Peters's four hundred acres north of the city, was destroyed. The center of Atlanta was a sad and dreary spectacle: "Piles of brick from which purple smoke lazily curled up told of the ravished city and over it all the silence of death brooded." A stench, at first overwhelming, rose from the putrid carcasses of two or three thousand animals. Birds avoided the city until the following summer.

Mary Jane found a family friend who would loan her some furniture for her two-day stay. During her visit she moved through the bleak streets, viewing the ruins of the commercial and residential areas as well as the twisted rails of the railroad. At Oakland Cemetery, she approached the graves of her children to find that their burial places had not been desecrated and even found some flowers as she had left them. Satisfied that they rested in peace, Mary Jane left the desolation of Atlanta and returned to Augusta.[9]

Among the news reports circulating in Augusta were accounts of depredations in North Georgia. In the wake of Sherman's columns, virtual anarchy existed in that portion of the state. Thousands of deserters from both armies found natural protection in the hilly area. They prowled the high country, some on horseback, exacting a lawless livelihood. To make matters worse, veritable guerrilla warfare erupted between locals. "Secesh" and Union men, referring to themselves as "independent scouts," devastated, marauded, and ambushed. Peters read with alarm that "bushwhacking tories are doing considerable mischief. They are composed of the low classes,

---

[9]*Augusta Chronicle and Sentinel* (21 December 1864); *Atlanta Constitution* (2 September 1884); Carrie M. Berry, Diary, Atlanta Historical Society; Scrapbook, Black Collection; Walters, *Merchant of Terror*, 151-52.

whose object is plunder, rather than any particular regard for the success of either party." Conditions grew so chaotic that the Confederate War Department appointed General William T. Wofford to break up the unauthorized military units, restore law and order, and distribute corn to the people. Peters was glad to learn that although his plantation sustained heavy damage, the main house survived this internecine mountain warfare.[10]

While Sherman had not taken Thanksgiving dinner in Augusta, he did celebrate Christmas in Savannah. On 21 December, the Union general rode into the city in triumph. It gave him obvious pleasure to present the captured city to Lincoln as a Christmas present. In early 1865, Sherman moved into South Carolina, "the hell-hole of secession." Rumors again reached Augusta that he would attack the city. Since it was thought the Federals would attack through Hamburg on the other side of the river, citizens tarred the bridge and piled upon it stacks of combustibles to be ignited when a bell tolled the enemy's approach. Again Augusta's defenders waited, and again the citizens climbed out of the trenches without firing a shot when Sherman bypassed the city. He marched between Augusta and Charleston, which allowed him to move easily into the South Carolina capital of Columbia. He had swept in a huge semi-circle around Augusta.[11]

Moving through the Carolinas, Sherman's troops cut the rails on which Peters depended for cotton exports and, on 15 January, Federal troops assaulted and captured Fort Fisher at the mouth of the Cape Fear River, closing the port of Wilmington. With this, the activities of the Peters, Stevenson, and Wilson blockade-running firm abruptly ceased. The end came at a most inopportune time for the company. In spite of the loss of their first two ships, the *Celeste* and the *Atlanta*, Peters and his associates had added ship after ship until their fleet included ten steamers, making them an important firm. Their estimate of the length of time that the port of Wilmington would remain open, however, proved a costly error in judgment. After operating less than a year, the executive committee was about to divert profits from ship purchases to stockholder dividends when Fort Fisher fell. Several of the company's ships were captured at Wilmington. Another, the

---

[10]*Augusta Chronicle and Sentinel* (29 July, 14 December 1864; 4 January 1865); Frances T. Howard, "In and Out of the Lines," *Sherman in Georgia*, 57; Bryan, *Confederate Georgia*, 151-52, 154-55.

[11]Corley, *Confederate City: Augusta*, 77, 89-93.

Rattlesnake, a large steamer with a capacity of two thousand bales of cotton, was unable to enter at Wilmington and steamed to Charleston where, deep in the water with coffee, she was trapped in Bull's Creek and burned, either by her captain or Union shells. The remaining ships were sold in South America. Coffee, bacon, quinine, and other goods valued at nearly $1,000,000 were lost or stolen at Nassau. Although the firm had made approximately $3,000,000, barely enough was salvaged to close the accounts of the company, and each stockholder received in greenbacks the amount he had originally invested in gold. Peters commented simply that thus closed a business "which was hazardous, but very interesting and exciting. Had the port of Wilmington remained open a few months longer we would probably have made a very large fortune."[12]

Although Peters had failed to gain new wealth to replace the potential loss of his property, he had again served the Confederacy well. In using profits to increase its fleet and concentrating on needed supplies instead of luxuries, the company helped keep the Army of Northern Virginia in the field. After Union forces sealed Wilmington, Lee's army melted away, in large measure from want of food and concern on the part of the soldiers about shortages at home. Although the Confederate government should have taken over blockade running early in the war, it is generally agreed that this was one of the things Southerners did best, which for much of the war "made the difference between disastrous shortages and nagging deficiencies."[13] To this effort the firm of Peters, Stevenson, and Wilson made a significant contribution.

----

[12]Richard Peters, "Personal Recollections," *Richard Peters: His Ancestors and Descendants*, comp. Nellie P. Black (Atlanta: Foote and Davies, 1904) 28-29; Robert U. Johnson and Clarence U. Buel, eds., *Battles and Leaders of the Civil War* 4 vols. (New York: Castle Books, n.d.) 4:625n; Frank E. Vandiver, ed., *Confederate Blockade Running Through Bermuda, 1861-65: Letters and Cargo Manifests* (Austin: University of Texas Press, 1947) 130-31, 135, 137, 145; *Addresses Before the Confederate Veterans Association* (Savannah: United Confederate Veterans, 1895) 29. The Wilmington *Daily Journal* (30 July 1864) lists blockade runners operating at Charleston and Wilmington from 1 January 1863 to mid-April 1864, giving trips in and out and the disposition of each ship. This source, when compared with Confederate agent John T. Bourne's Letterbook (in Vandiver, *Blockade Running Through Bermuda*) serves to determine that the company, Peters, Stevenson, and Wilson, operated from May 1864 to January 1865.

[13]Robert E. Lee to J. A. Seddon, 16 January 1865, in *Augusta Chronicle and Sentinel* (25 January 1865); Richard D. Goff, *Confederate Supply* (Durham: Duke University Press, 1969) 52.

With the end of the blockade-running venture and after it was clear that Sherman was finished with Georgia, Peters concentrated on railroad repair and prepared for his return to Atlanta. The rails of his two companies were broken a combined total of some one hundred miles. The Atlanta and West Point Railroad had been destroyed to Fairburn, twenty-four miles southwest of Atlanta. The Georgia Railroad, partly by the company itself on Hood's orders and partly by Sherman, had been destroyed almost to the Oconee River in the vicinity of Madison, eighty miles east of Atlanta. The bridge over the river was also demolished as were several depots, scores of locomotives, and hundreds of cars. James R. Crew was in charge of rebuilding the Atlanta and West Point Railroad, and L. P. Grant supervised the rebuilding of the Georgia Railroad. Because the extensive destruction and lack of materials slowed progress, the primary objective was to replace track on the principal routes of both roads at the expense of branch lines; permanent rebuilding would follow.

During the cold, dismal winter of 1865, food was so scarce and costly that most people resorted to barter. Peters, planning his return to Atlanta as carefully as he did everything else, wrote Crew that he would return the following spring and sent funds with instructions to purchase provisions and to arrange for curing meat and storing corn. Peters decided to bring his family back in April for several reasons—winter would be over, he anticipated that the railroads would be rebuilt by then, and perhaps he thought that the war would be over, which it was. Service was restored on the Georgia Railroad at the end of the war, and life as refugees ended for the Peters family as they returned by rail to Atlanta and their damaged home at 99 Forsyth Street.[14]

The Civil War fascinates Americans to this day because it has such unusual human interest and drama and a tremendous range of military characters—heroes as well as failures. The war represents a great tragedy, a breakdown of the political process, a national failure, but most importantly it was the pivotal event in American history, one that "compelled change in

----

[14]Richard Peters to James R. Crew, 17 December 1864, 1 February 1865, Crew Collection; Sherman, *Memoirs*, 2:228; Richard E. Prince, *Steam Locomotives and History: Georgia Railroad and West Point Route* (Green River WY: Privately printed, 1962) 11, 15; Corley, *Confederate City: Augusta*, 89. In the upstairs bedroom of his daughter Nellie, Peters found an unexploded shell that had come in through the roof. Nita Rucker, Notes on Nellie Peters Black, Black Collection.

important areas of national life."[15] The cost of the war was staggering. The nation suffered over 1,000,000 casualties, including 600,000 dead, and expended $20 billion to free approximately 4,000,000 slaves and preserve the Union. It would have taken about $2 billion to have provided compensated emancipation at full value. "The intangible costs—dislocations, disunities, wasted energies, lowered ethics, blasted lives, bitter memories, and burning hates—cannot be calculated." Human suffering was so great that "if the cost of the Civil War in terms of casualties alone is calculated as part of the price of national unity, then perhaps the cost of national unity in the American experience is not one that many national leaders would be willing to pay."[16]

Peters was fortunate; with no sons old enough to serve in the armed forces and, being wealthy and vigilant, he had actually suffered little as a result of the war. Although motivated at times by the profit incentive, he had still contributed a great deal to the Southern war effort. He had provided engines to power the Confederate's biggest powder factory, transported troops and supplies by rail for the western theater, and imported through the blockade—all of which improved fighting ability and raised morale in the South. Basically, Peters had aided his adopted section industrially and commercially—New South activities desperately needed by Southerners during the Civil War.

[15]T. Harry Williams, *The History of American Wars: From 1745 to 1918* (New York: Alfred A. Knopf, 1981) 198-99.

[16]Thomas B. Alexander, "The Civil War as Institutional Fulfillment," *The Journal of Southern History* 47:1 (February 1981): 30-31.

CHAPTER TEN

RESURGING ATLANTA: LOCAL GOVERNMENT LEADER, CONCILIATOR

In May 1865, the center of Atlanta was a burned desolation. The ruins loomed through the spring fog and drizzle, and rain-drenched vagrants huddled around outdoor fires amid the litter. Bent and rusty railroad iron lay by the roadbeds near piles of brick. For months there were no funds for clearing rubble from the streets; civil authority was yet to be established. Visitor John R. Dennett considered the people as unpleasing to the eye as the city: "A great many rough-looking fellows hang about the numerous shops and the shanties among the ruins where liquor is sold, and a knot of them cluster at each street corner." Added to this was a Federal garrison that had taken control from Confederate forces and had reoccupied the city at the end of 1864.

Almost no one seemed to question whether the city should be rebuilt because Atlanta was still a "perfect crow's-foot of railroads." While the Federals had torn up the rails, the roadbeds themselves had not been heavily damaged. Even if the hinterland to be supplied with goods was poorer and less productive, the mere storage and trans-shipment of freight would cause Atlanta to boom. One of the first actions of the city council when it resumed operations was to levy a two-dollar "street tax" on all males; work then began to fill in the washed-out gaps, clean up the debris, and plant shade trees. Commerce was given priority over residences as in Atlanta's early years, and again it had the raw character of a frontier town as merchants built stores with their own hands. At first they lived in tents left by the armies or "calico houses" built with scraps of cloth, tin, bricks, and lumber. The new business blocks consisted mostly of one-story structures, with cheap, temporary roofs, designed to be raised in more prosperous times. By the end of the year, some 250 stores had a total volume of trade one-third larger than that of antebellum Atlanta.[1]

Peters set about restoring his home from the ravages of wartime shelling and looting. He recovered his losses on the flour mill by selling the mill lot to the Georgia Railroad.[2] In another transaction, he sold his calf and goat lot (between Hunter, Thompson, and Mitchell streets) to the Macon and Western Railroad as a site for its new depot, the original one being located in the center of Atlanta and consequently burned. This transaction helped make the center of the city more attractive to commerce. Peters's remaining property in Atlanta was worth over $100,000 (down from about $200,000 when the war began, mainly as a result of depreciated property values); his holdings consisted of his residence, some fifteen or twenty scattered city lots, and Land Lots 49 and 80 at the northern edge of the city.[3]

The Federal threat to Southern property rights posed a dilemma for Peters. Under the Confiscation Acts, lands of every supporter of the Confederacy were subject to forfeiture. Although President Andrew Johnson, under his Amnesty Proclamation of 29 May 1865, halted all proceedings and issued a sweeping amnesty and pardon that restored land titles, for Peters there were complications. The commander of the Atlanta garrison, who

---

[1]John Richard Dennett, *The South As It Is, 1865-1866* (New York: The Viking Press, 1965) 268; John T. Trowbridge, *The Desolate South, 1865-66: A Picture of the Battlefields and of the Devastated Confederacy*, ed. Gordon Carroll (Freeport: Books for Libraries Press, 1956) 242; Arthur R. Taylor, "From the Ashes: Atlanta During Reconstruction, 1865-1876" (Ph.D. dissertation, Emory University, 1973) 51, 129-30, 256-58; James M. Russell, "Atlanta, Gate City of the South, 1847 to 1885" (Ph.D. dissertation, Princeton University, 1971) 164-65.

[2]Richard Peters, "Personal Recollections," *Richard Peters: His Ancestors and Descendants*, comp. Nellie P. Black (Atlanta: Foote and Davies, 1904) 27.

[3]Fulton County Tax Digest, 1866; Fulton County Deed Book TT; *The Weekly Atlanta Intelligencer* (27 June, 10 October 1866).

was responsible for administering the amnesty oath, slapped Atlantans under a 10:00 P.M. curfew and withheld mail and dispatch service from all citizens until they signed the oath—first published in an Atlanta newspaper extra on 2 June, but it was months before the document was offered to the citizens. Adding to Peters's anxiety was the president's refusal to automatically include those whose taxable property exceeded $20,000; instead these wealthy ex-Confederates had to apply for individual pardons by petition.[4]

Into this difficult situation stepped Union Major Eugene B. Beaumont, a gallant young adjutant-general on the staff of cavalry leader James H. Wilson. A West Point graduate, Beaumont was from Wilkesbarre and was a friend of Peters's relatives in Pennsylvania. Beaumont had written to Peters from Wilson's headquarters in Macon to offer his assistance during the occupation. Shortly afterward, when Beaumont was en route to Pennsylvania on leave, he visited Peters in Atlanta and obtained for him rail transportation to the North on the Western and Atlantic, which was then under Federal military control and tight security. Once in the North, Peters was reunited with his kinfolk, and perhaps took the opportunity to apply for his individual pardon from President Johnson. Peters was unaware of it at the time, but the Federal effort to dispossess Southerners was relatively minor because the Radicals in Congress recoiled from confiscation as too obvious an attack on property rights. He was able to retain his real property, including his Gordon County plantation.[5]

On 9 September 1865, after Peters returned to Georgia, Provisional Governor James Johnson appointed him one of five directors of the Western and Atlantic Railroad to receive the road on behalf of the state from U.S. military authorities, being so ordered by President Johnson. While the military had control, their policy was "to spend no money on railroad repairs in rebellious States, except where absolutely necessary to supply posts and

---

[4]James L. Roark, *Masters Without Slaves: Southern Planters in the Civil War and Reconstruction* (New York: W. W. Norton and Co., 1977) 182; Taylor, "From the Ashes," 36, 110, 315-16.

[5]Kenneth M. Stampp, "Radical Reconstruction," *Reconstruction in the South*, ed. Edwin C. Rozwenc (Lexington: D. C. Heath and Company, 1972) 53-54; Charles Todd Quintard, *Doctor Quintard, Chaplain C.S.A. and Second Bishop of Tennessee; Being His Story of the War (1861-1865)*, ed. Arthur Howard Noll (Sewanee: The University Press, 1905) 144-46.

garrisons," and they had been operating the Western and Atlantic in a dilapidated condition. This appointment was temporary, but in the next few months the directors rebuilt the road, including fourteen bridges, and purchased nine engines and approximately one hundred cars.[6]

As a director of the Georgia Railroad and the Atlanta and West Point Railroad, Peters faced many company problems, but of primary importance was restoration. Trains moved slowly and circuitously at first due to the lack of material for repairs, but the roads were restored to good working order within two years of the war. Peters and his fellow directors also built a splendid Georgia Railroad depot, constructed of brick on a foundation of Georgia granite. Located at Alabama and Lloyd streets in Atlanta, the building's third floor was embellished with a large board of directors' room with a view of the city and Stone Mountain. (Although a fire destroyed its upper floors and cupola in 1935, the Georgia Railroad depot is apparently downtown Atlanta's oldest standing building.)[7]

Peters had barely regained his usual optimistic spirits when one of his friends and associates was murdered. Late in 1865 the criminal element in the city viciously assaulted Atlanta and West Point Railroad agent James R. Crew. After returning to Atlanta from West Point, Crew had resumed his interest in public affairs and was running for mayor at the time of the attack. He returned home one evening in November with a gaping head wound caused by a blow with a blunt instrument and, as the Peters and L. P. Grant families kept a vigil over him, Crew died.[8] He was an early victim of the

---

[6]Allen D. Candler, ed., *The Confederate Records of the State of Georgia* 6 vols. (Atlanta: C. P. Byrd, 1910) 4:32, 38-40; *Official Records of the Union and Confederate Armies in the War of the Rebellion* 128 vols. (Washington: United States Printing Office, 1880-1901) ser. 1, 49:816.

[7]*Atlanta Constitution* (24 July, 3 October 1869; 26 July 1870; 30 April, 3 May 1871; 15 May, 26 July 1873); *The Weekly Atlanta Intelligencer* (23 May 1866; 18 May 1870); *The Daily Atlanta Intelligencer* (15 September 1867; 20 May 1868; 5 February, 28 April, 15 May, 14 July, 11 August 1869; 18 May 1870).

[8]The Crew murder remained a mystery for over a year, but then a black man, "Bill," facing the gallows in Milledgeville for an unrelated murder, confessed that he had taken part in the Crew murder. The confession created something of a sensation when it was published in pamphlet form and sold in Atlanta. According to the publicized account, three blacks had conspired to obtain Crew's keys to the depot ticket office in order to rob it, and one of the men, Dennis Harris of Atlanta, had struck Crew with an iron bar picked up at the depot.

widespread violence in the post-Civil War South.

The crime and violence in Atlanta highlighted the urgent need for reviving the moral tone of the city. "The churches had stood while nearly all else had crumbled, and now they served as a bedrock of inspiration for Atlanta's renaissance." Although Peters and the scattered congregation of St. Philip's returned to find that Federal troops had desecrated the church, they were ready to resume services under Reverend Charles W. Thomas when Bishop Elliott reconsecrated the building in January 1866. The restoration of burned St. Luke's was not mandatory at that early date, so Quintard, after a visit with Peters in Atlanta, returned to Tennessee where he became bishop and played a major role in rebuilding the University of the South.[9]

Christian principles had their place, but Peters came to realize that unusual public leadership would be needed to control the undesirable element in Atlanta during the postwar era. Furthermore, vindictive Northern politicians might find a way to confiscate Southern property and Peters believed their attitude would be influenced by the kind of political leaders that were elected in the South. Since a former Union man would be better received than an ex-Confederate leader, Peters sounded Alexander H. Stephens on the possibility of the state legislature selecting John P. King for United States senator. In his reply to Peters, Stephens wrote that he personally favored King for the senate, but could not say whether the legislature would select him since "men's opinions these days are so fickle, strange and unaccountable that it is impossible to form any rational conjecture concerning them," but he declared his own intention not to participate in the election.[10] However, Stephens's election as senator in 1866 was one of the reasons why Congress rejected President Johnson's lenient policies and insisted on its

---

They failed to find the keys, however, and when their robbery scheme went awry, the three had gone on a looting spree for several days in Atlanta. *The Daily Atlanta Intelligencer* (13, 15 January 1867). Jane Louisa Crew, Diary, Crew's "Funeral Services," Crew Collection, Atlanta Historical Society; *Southern Confederacy* (5 December 1862); T. D. Killian, "James R Crew," *Atlanta Historical Bulletin* 1:6 (January 1932): 14.

[9]*The Daily Atlanta Intelligencer* (7 June 1866); Bishop Stephen Elliott, Diary, Georgia Department of Archives and History, Atlanta; Charles R. Wilson, "The Religion of the Lost Cause: Ritual and Organization of the Southern Civil Religion, 1865-1920," *The Journal of Southern History* 46:2 (May 1980): 235-37; Taylor, "From the Ashes," 166, 205; Quintard, *Doctor Quintard*, 143, 148-67.

[10]Alexander H. Stephens to Peters, 27 December 1865 in Black, *Richard Peters*, 32-33.

own brand of Reconstruction. By that time, Peters was a member of the Atlanta city council, initially agreeing to serve "to keep down gamblers and low-dive fellows."

Peters had become involved in local politics in 1867 after City Treasurer J. T. Porter resigned under fire. Atlantans, including Peters, signed a petition calling for a public meeting to be held on the morning of 30 January "to take into consideration the condition of our municipal affairs." At the appointed hour, the city's rich and poor mingled in the largest crowd ever to assemble in City Hall on a local question; shortages in the city treasurer's book during the past two years were then made public. Of particular importance were the pressing claims upon the city's credit, especially outside the South, which had to be quickly resolved. George W. Adair referred to the matter as a heavy blow "coming right after Sherman," but believed that with a competent man at the helm of city government, Atlanta could rise above this new problem. Adair was suggesting that the mayor resign; it was alleged he should have monitored the financial books more closely. But Mayor James E. Williams, builder of the city's first theater, the antebellum Athenaeum, said he had done no wrong and refused to step down. In view of the mayor's position, a citizens' committee was established to investigate the city's finances during the preceding two years.

Four members of the city council resigned as a result of the citizens' action; the resignation of First Ward Councilman D. P. Ferguson created a vacancy in Peters's home ward. To fill the office, residents met on 19 February 1867 in Davis Hall on Broad Street. One of the largest theaters in the South before its destruction by fire in 1865, Davis Hall could seat 1,600 people. The ward's residents filed into the theater and took their seats on long pine benches amid the numerous kerosene lamps on the wall. There, in grassroots fashion, they unanimously elected Peters to fill the vacancy. Then, at a council meeting on 22 February, Peters took the oath of office from Mayor Williams. Peters's committee assignments were impressive. He filled the key position of chairman of the Finance Committee, and also served as a member of the vital Public Buildings and Grounds Committee, and on Ordinances, Lamps and Gas.

Peters soon learned that former Treasurer Porter had begun fraudulent operations in 1865; that year he failed to report $7,462.68 due the city and in 1866 stole $47,006.48 in a total of forty-eight defalcations during the two years. Porter used the money to assume an extravagant life-style and build tenement houses to rent. Attacks on the mayor subsided as his negligence came to be viewed as "somewhat unintentional"; he still refused to resign. He refuted the superintendency theory altogether, saying the treasurer reported to the council with inspection by the Finance Committee, and therefore the mayor was not responsible for everything that was done. Basically, Williams remained in office because he was not charged with dishonesty and there was no firm legal recourse to a charge of incompetency. Yet four councilmen and the treasurer had resigned and steps were taken to put city finances under a trusted individual—Richard Peters.[11]

As chairman of the Finance Committee, Peters kept a tight rein on city expenditures. The council demonstrated its faith in him by directing his committee to approve all funds spent by the city and it began to examine all quarterly and annual reports of the clerk of council, treasurer, marshal, deputy marshal, tax collector, and clerk of the city market. Next, the council authorized the Finance Committee to fund the debt of the city by issuing $30,000 in city bonds, followed by $400,000 at the end of the year. (Before the new bond authorizations, the bonded debt of the city was $250,000, of which Peters held $60,000 at eight percent interest.)[12]

Peters's tight-money policy made relief for the poor a controversial subject. Because of Atlanta's reputation for providing charity, the city attracted indigents from a wide area and it became known as "the Poor House of the State." Merchants began voicing displeasure at what they considered high relief figures, which amounted to $29,580 in 1866, a figure that almost matched the $32,934 collected by the city's private relief organizations

---

[11]Atlanta City Council Minute Books, 25 January, 22 February 1867; *The Daily Atlanta Intelligencer* (13, 30, 31 January, 2, 6, 9, 10, 14, 17 February, 2 March 1867; 8 June 1869); Taylor, "From the Ashes," 159; Helen K. Lyon, "Peters: Atlanta Pioneer—Georgia Builder," *Atlanta Historical Bulletin* 38:10 (December 1957): 34. Peters was one of the first councilmen elected by the machinery of ward politics, probably due to the fact that it was a special election. The ward system was formalized in October 1870 when the Republican legislature replaced the city's at-large arrangement with a ward election system. That year two blacks, George Graham and William Finch, were elected to the council as a result of voting by wards. By December 1871, however, this was reversed by the Democratic legislature and the Democratic municipal ticket regained complete control of city government. The Radicals never controlled Atlanta. Howard N. Rabinowitz, "From Reconstruction to Redemption in the Urban South," *Journal of Urban History* 2:2 (February 1976): 170, 172, 177-78; Russell, "Atlanta," 257-58, 275.

[12]Atlanta City Council Minute Books, 6 January, 22 March, 7 June, 26 July 1867, 3 April, 3 July 1868; Taylor, "From the Ashes," 157, 295; Kenneth Coleman, ed., *A History of Georgia* (Athens: University of Georgia Press, 1977) 217.

during the same period. The merchants wanted city funds spent on projects related to commercial interests. The working class, becoming gainfully employed in a resurging Atlanta in 1867, was also unsympathetic toward helping the poor. While it was difficult for city officials to completely ignore the poor whites because many were related to Confederate veterans, constraint was the order of the day. Peters occasionally acted in council on the subject. In order to make Atlanta less attractive to the poor, he had a law passed that prohibited peddlers from being licensed, except the disabled who had resided in the city for two years. He also officially expressed gratitude to the superintendent of the city-operated almshouse, the major contribution of local government to poor relief, for his "very efficient and economical management of the institution."[13]

Private relief was more popular but usually seasonal, operating only during the winter months. Fairs, lectures, and suppers provided funds for the poor. Mary Jane and Nellie, resuming the active social life of the Peters family, helped organize the especially popular calico balls to which women wore calico dresses and men wore extremely long scarves. On the day following the ball, all the calico material was donated to the poor in addition to merchants' contributions of coal, wood, cloth, and other useful material (no money). From these calico balls grew the capable Ladies Relief Society. The success of private relief perhaps explains why the Freedmen's Bureau left Atlanta after being in the city for about two years.[14]

Shortly after Peters began dealing with the Porter scandal, Radical Republicans in Congress, as Peters had foreseen, changed Reconstruction from occupation by a leftover military garrison to aggressive military dictatorship. Overriding the presidential veto, Congress superimposed this military rule over civil authority in the South in a series of acts beginning 2 March 1867. Reconstruction by the sword saw the South divided into five military districts, each commanded by a Union general backed by troops; the acts swept away the Johnson governments and the disfranchised Southern white leaders. The bitterest pill for whites was the stipulation that

---

[13]Atlanta City Council Minute Books, 25 October 1867; Taylor, "From the Ashes," 117; Russell, "Atlanta," 260-61.

[14]*The Daily Atlanta Intelligencer* (28 February 1867); *Atlanta Constitution* (8 February 1871); *Atlanta Daily New Era* (16, 17 February 1871); Taylor, "From the Ashes," 120; Eula T. Kuchler, "Charitable and Philanthropic Activities in Atlanta During Reconstruction," *Atlanta Historical Bulletin* 10:40 (December 1965): 48-50.

Southern states could not be readmitted to the Union until new state constitutions guaranteed the vote to blacks. Although the acts imposed Federal restrictions on municipal government, their primary impact was at the state level and Peters decided much more could be gained for Atlanta by cooperation than antagonism. He was among the Fulton County residents who petitioned for a public meeting to be held on the morning of 4 March in City Hall to consider the duty of Georgia in the "political troubles which now agitate the country." Meeting only two days after the passage of the first Reconstruction measures, the citizens were necessarily confused as to the new status of the South.

A large, excited crowd packed City Hall. Peters, a councilman for less than two weeks, accepted the call to the chair and explained the object of the meeting. Was it the duty of the people of Georgia to form a government according to the Sherman Act (Reconstruction) or should Georgians wait for the establishment of a military government over them? Peters believed that immediate compliance would result in less severe military rule and he wanted Atlanta to lead Georgia through this new phase. Looking over the crowd, he saw seventy-five or more freedmen. The presence of a large number of blacks at a civic meeting must have been a novelty to white Atlantans. The blacks asked if they could vote in the proceedings and Peters ruled that only those who could previously vote could do so in the meeting. Since he was for cooperation with the Reconstruction policy of Congress, Peters perhaps would have welcomed the black vote, but his decision was wise under the circumstances. It was not yet clear who could vote and to personally enfranchise the blacks might have driven some cooperationists into the ranks of antagonists. Furthermore, it would have dangerously fueled an already tense atmosphere.

Peters appointed pro-Union Henry P. Farrow, a United States senator during Reconstruction, as chairman of a committee on resolutions to prepare a statement expressive of the import of the meeting. The assignees retired from the hall and, when they returned, the citizens listened in stern disapproval as Farrow read recommendations for submission to the Union. He observed that "indiscretion has already delayed the work of restoration until the interests of the entire people of Georgia are bleeding at every pore, and that all passion and prejudice should be forthwith cast aside, and reason once more permitted to ascend the throne." Farrow said there were enough Georgians of sufficient integrity and ability, who were not barred from voting or holding office by the new law, who could perform the functions of government. He concluded that the citizens of Fulton County should try to heal the wounds of war and the people of every state were welcome in Atlanta. A copy of the proceedings would be sent to the Reconstruction Committee of Congress in Washington.

Wartime mayor James M. Calhoun moved adoption of the report, but Luther J. Glenn, a former mayor and battle-scarred veteran of Chancellorsville, offered counterresolutions resisting congressional authority. After some amendments were offered to the Glenn resolutions, followed by a motion to table the Glenn resolutions as amended, great confusion and excitement prevailed, rendering orderly proceedings impossible. On motion, Peters adjourned the meeting and, along with the friends of the Farrow resolutions, retired from the hall. The rump of the meeting remained and passed the Glenn resolutions. Glenn wanted the South to test the Sherman Act in the United States Supreme Court. Copies of this resolution were ordered sent to President Johnson.

That evening Peters, clearly the leader of the cooperationists, returned with his followers to City Hall. Glenn and a few of the antagonists were also present at this night meeting. After taking the chair, Peters added to the Farrow resolution a request that Georgia Governor Charles Jenkins immediately convene the state legislature for the purpose of calling a convention in full compliance with the terms of the Sherman Act. Glenn asked Peters if the opponents of Farrow's report would be allowed to vote. Peters said they would not, whereupon Glenn and his followers left the hall. The Farrow report as amended by Peters was then unanimously adopted. Such fragmented public meetings as this pointed up the acrimonious division among Southerners caused by the Reconstruction tangle.[15]

President Johnson, who had the duty of executing the program of Congress, appointed General John Pope to command the Third Military District—Georgia, Alabama, and Florida. As the head of an army of occupation, it was his duty to enforce the Reconstruction Acts. He could make laws simply by issuing them in the form of military decrees; he would decide what officials stayed in office and whether elections would be held, giving him considerable power. Peters quickly secured Pope's good will

---

[15]*The Daily Atlanta Intelligencer* (2, 5 March 1867); *Southern Confederacy* (8 May 1863); Howard N. Rabinowitz, *Race Relations in the Urban South, 1865-1890* (New York: Oxford University Press, 1978) 263; Walter G. Cooper, *Official History of Fulton County* (Atlanta: Walter W. Brown Publishing Co., 1934) 216-17.

"by a stroke of policy and good tact." At his suggestion, a reception committee traveled up the Western and Atlantic Railroad 31 March 1867 to greet the general and welcome him to Atlanta, a reception quite different from that expected by the general. Pope was so receptive to this demonstration of cordiality that he discarded his uniform for civilian dress and favorably impressed those who called at the hotel to pay their respects. That evening Pope departed for Montgomery, Alabama, where he issued General Order Number One ordering civil officers retained unless otherwise directed. In a few days, he returned to Atlanta and opened permanent headquarters in the city. The cooperationists, realizing the importance of that decision, honored him with a banquet at the National Hotel. Toasts such as *"Our Pope—may he prove to be as infallible as he is powerful"* mellowed his attitude. In his speech, Pope admitted that he had anticipated hostility but the hearty welcome assured him of mutual cooperation and as a result he expected that his distasteful mission would be brief.[16]

By now Peters was the most influential figure in local government. Not only did Atlanta have a weak-mayor form of government, but because Mayor Williams had been implicated in the Porter scandal, his role was essentially reduced to that of bystander. Too, Peters, as chairman of the powerful Finance Committee, was returning the city to solvency. He had also found common ground with the Republican military regime, allowing Atlantans to maintain control of local government. In believing that the law should be obeyed as a practical matter, he again found himself in a minority just as he had been in his anti-secession stand prior to the war; however, this time he rejected the majority view, with the result that Atlanta would make important new gains. But to many, Peters's acceptance of Congressional Reconstruction bordered on treasonable behavior and it would be years before his detractors would see the common sense of his actions.

---

[16]Black, *Richard Peters*, 31; *The Daily Atlanta Intelligencer* (12 April 1867); Franklin M. Garrett, *Atlanta and Environs: A Chronicle of Its People and Events* 2 vols. (Athens: University of Georgia Press, 1969) 1:733-37.

CHAPTER ELEVEN

ATLANTA NAMED CAPITAL: PETERS MAKES IT HAPPEN

The most delicate and least understood situation faced by Peters as an Atlanta city councilman was the proposal by James L. Dunning, president of the newly formed Lincoln National Monument Association, to erect a monument to Abraham Lincoln in Atlanta. Dunning, a former councilman, was a foundryman from Connecticut. As superintendent of the Atlanta Machine Company during the war, he had refused Confederate contracts and, accused of holding secret meetings in his home to abet the Union, had been imprisoned for several weeks in the Kiles Building. When the Federals occupied the city, he had climbed a pole and tacked up a Union flag amid the cheers of a small crowd. Since he was an important figure during the early postbellum years in Atlanta, General Pope sought his advice before appointing officials in Georgia. Dunning was judge of the Fulton County Freedmen's Bureau at the time he proposed the monument honoring the martyred president. The proposal, coming at a time when many Southern Democrats were losing the vote to Republicans, was, at the least, insensitive.

On 20 September 1867, the council took up the petition requesting the city to finance the Lincoln monument and Dunning was present to press the issue. Peters, realizing the situation called for careful handling, suggested that the petition be referred to a special committee. Mayor Williams obligingly named Peters, Alexander W. Mitchell, and Edward E. Rawson to a Select Memorial Committee. Like Peters, both Mitchell, a banker, and Rawson, a cotton dealer, were "old Atlanta," having arrived during the antebellum period. Mitchell had successfully led a vigilante force in the street battle against the Rowdy party that had ended the town's frontier era. Rawson, as a councilman during the war, had protested the forced evacuation of Atlanta civilians by Sherman.

At the next weekly meeting of the council, the Select Memorial Committee reported its findings. Coupling the monument question with the need for a new city park, Peters and the other members recommended that the city purchase ten acres of land for transfer to the Lincoln Monument Association to be used as a city park. Acreage in the eastern suburbs of the city, near Oakland Cemetery and the site of the battle of Atlanta, had been examined and found to be a suitable place for the monument because it commanded a splendid view of the city and surrounding country. However, Peters stipulated that the association must first demonstrate its good faith by erecting a 145-foot tower of Georgia marble and improving the grounds on a scale of expenditures from $750,000 to $1,000,000; he noted that the importance of the project justified the high expenditure for the park and monument. After heated debate, the council approved the committee's recommendation by a six-to-four vote.

This action created a tempest in Atlanta and throughout Georgia that could hardly have been more intense had the Georgia legislature resolved to include Sherman's likeness in the Stone Mountain carving. A letter to the editor of the conservative *Intelligencer* said that Peters created no surprise in the mind of any who reflected upon his background, "for it is well known that a Yankee must be caught very young in order to forget his cunning." Editorially, the *Intelligencer* blasted the affirmative vote. The paper linked Peters and some of his fellow councilmen with Republicanism: "No excuse can be made for their vote; no wealth they may possess; no social nor public position they may fill; can justify the act in the minds of this indignant community." Without regard for where they came from or where they may go, according to the editorial, when future historians record the Reconstruction period there could be no better example of the "degeneracy of this day and time in the South" than the vote of these six councilmen to erect a Lincoln monument "perhaps over the bones of Confederate dead." Atlanta's Republican newspapers, the *Daily Opinion* and the *New Era*, supported Peters, saying the *Intelligencer* assaulted his respectability. The Republican papers defended the vote chiefly on economic grounds, saying that since the project would indicate Atlanta's willingness to cooperate with the North and thereby attract Northerners, who were heretofore wary of an antagonistic reception, the council had expressed sensible business principles. The *Intelligencer* responded that a dead man's memory was not a "merchantable commodity."

Outside the city, the incredible news spread quickly and the reaction was highly unfavorable. It was believed that Atlanta was the only city in the South to consider such an outrage. The supreme blast came from a village paper in southwest Georgia, the *Lacross Democrat*: "A Lincoln monument at Atlanta! Great God, what an insult! There is a monument of hate in every heart of every honest American for his vices and misdeeds."

Sudden in origin, the late-summer storm over Atlanta just as quickly dissipated. Dunning himself defused the controversy. He wrote a letter to the council, read at its next meeting, in which he expressed his gratitude for the council's action, but declined the offer.[1] Why did the council vote to provide ten acres toward the Lincoln monument project? Perhaps a few who voted yes were trying to effect a commercial reunion with the North by offering ten acres in honor of the Northern statesman, but it is doubtful that many councilmen who approved the project really expected the monument to be built. If it had been erected, the conservative Democrats, especially the Ku Klux Klan type, probably would have destroyed the memorial. But that is not why Dunning declined the offer; he did so because of the financial condition set by the council. And Peters led the affirmative vote with a

---

[1]Atlanta City Council Minute Books, 21 January 1859, 20, 27 September 1867; *The Daily Atlanta Intelligencer* (4 October 1866; 3 September, 2, 4 October, 1 November 1867—quoting *Lacross Democrat*); Ralph B. Singer, "Confederate Atlanta" (Ph.D. dissertation, University of Georgia, 1973) 232; Arthur R. Taylor, "From the Ashes: Atlanta During Reconstruction, 1865-1876" (Ph.D. dissertation, Emory University, 1973) 20. David Goldfield, in an incorrect assessment of the monument question, wrote that "the city council first supported the idea but changed its mind after a group of Confederate veterans understandably objected to such use of public funds." David R. Goldfield, *Cotton Fields and Skyscrapers: Southern Cities and Region, 1607-1980* (Baton Rouge: Louisiana State University Press, 1982) 120.

tongue-in-cheek attitude. For him, it was deliberate financial overkill. He knew that Dunning could not raise the outlandish sum required to accept the ten acres proffered by the city. By placating both sides, Peters, Mitchell, and Rawson had handled the controversy extremely well. They had avoided potential violence from conservative Democrats by rejecting the project, and in such a way that had alienated neither Republicans nor the military commander.

During his work on city council, Peters was moving toward cinching one of his most important contributions to the development of Atlanta. However, his efforts at the time were most unappreciated and misunderstood because of his close work with General Pope. For example, when Pope ordered that the contract for city printing go to a newspaper favorable to Congressional Reconstruction, Peters recommended awarding the contract to the lowest bidder provided the bidding paper was "not obnoxious" to Reconstruction. The contract, predictably enough, was awarded to the *New Era*. Pope's attempt to muzzle Democratic newspapers by withholding government patronage, and his "cock-sure" demeanor, infuriated the conservative Democrats, who began to agitate for his removal. Leading the movement was former Confederate General John B. Gordon, a leader of the Fulton County Democratic Club, and the anti-Reconstruction *Intelligencer*. Peters's plans were stymied when President Johnson, sympathetic to the complaints against Pope, recalled him in December 1867 and appointed as his successor General George G. Meade. One of Pope's last official acts was convening the Georgia Constitutional Convention in the friendly atmosphere of Atlanta City Hall. To insure a continued welcome for the convention, he directed the mayor and council to continue in office for 1868 and the usual year-end election was cancelled. On 2 January 1868, Pope departed via the Western and Atlantic Railroad amid the fanfare of friends, a military band, and a staff in dress uniform.

Meade arrived three days later and was accorded a welcome similar to that given Pope. His gentlemanly conduct and Democratic tendencies made him initially more popular than his predecessor. His popularity was nipped, however, when he removed state officials for failure to fulfill the Reconstruction Acts and his enforcement of the hated acts caused his name to be anathema to conservative Georgians. The first test for Atlanta came in February 1868 when the council passed Peters's resolution requesting Meade to permit local appointment of city tax assessors. As chairman of the Finance Committee, Peters had drawn up the city tax ordinance, which exacted one dollar on every assessed valuation of $100, but it was crucial that the assessed valuation be reasonable. Meade allowed the council to appoint two assessors provided those selected could take the "iron-clad" oath of past loyalty to the United States as declared by Congress. In this way Atlanta property remained safe from confiscation through excessive valuation and taxation, and Meade had proven cooperative in dealing with the city council.[2]

Meade, an Episcopalian, also proved cooperative as a member of St. Philip's. Bishop Elliott had died shortly after the war ended and Peters supported the election of John W. Beckwith, a native of North Carolina who had ministered to the wartime sick and wounded in Atlanta. He resigned as rector of Trinity Church in New Orleans to become the second Episcopal Bishop of Georgia. Noted for his oratorical gifts, Beckwith became one of the most eminent men ever produced by the Episcopal Church in the South. Visiting Peters in Atlanta, Beckwith commented that St. Philip's had been "defiled and desecrated until the very spirit of insult seemed to have exhausted itself." This prompted Meade to write to Northern friends requesting funds to rebuild the church, a gesture he thought would prove to Atlantans that the North regretted the consequences of the war. The general raised $5,000 in contributions and when added to receipts from the annual auction rental of pews, St. Philips' congregation not only restored but also enlarged the church building, so as to accommodate the 150 new members brought in by the military.[3]

Peters had also overcome the temporary regression of his plans caused by Pope's recall—Peters hoped to move the state capital from Milledgeville

---

[2]Code of the City of Atlanta, 1899, Atlanta Historical Society; Atlanta City Council Minute Books, 16, 23 August 1867, 21, 28 February 1868; Scrapbook, Nellie P. Black Collection, University of Georgia Libraries, Athens; Atlanta Daily New Era (3, 12 January 1868); The Daily Atlanta Intelligencer (7 January 1868); Franklin M. Garrett, Atlanta and Environs: A Chronicle of Its People and Events 2 vols. (Athens: University of Georgia Press, 1969) 1:772-74.

[3]Atlanta City Directory (1867); Atlanta Daily New Era (14, 21 April, 14 May 1868); The Daily Atlanta Intelligencer (23 February, 23 April, 12 May 1867; 4 April 1869); National Cyclopedia of American Biography, s.v. "Beckwith, John W."; Walter G. Cooper, Official History of Fulton County (Atlanta: Walter W. Brown Publishing Co., 1934) 886; Alex H. Hitz, A History of the Cathedral of St. Philip (Atlanta: Conger Printing Co., 1974) 22-23, 25-26.

and conditions favoring Atlanta were finally irresistible.[4] Meade was friendly toward Atlanta, the Georgia Constitution was being rewritten, and the convention (referred to by some as the "Georgia Unconstitutional Convention" because its membership included freedmen) was meeting in Atlanta City Hall. In addition, Fulton County Representative James L. Dunning wielded great influence in the convention and Meade had the power to manipulate the statewide vote to insure ratification of the new constitution. In February 1868, Dunning introduced an amendment to the constitution proposing removal of the capital to Atlanta, but before acting on Dunning's proposal, the convention suggested that both Atlanta and Macon offer inducements.

Acting quickly, city council met 26 February in a special session. Peters voiced the convention's proposal to relocate the capital and resolved that Atlanta should furnish for ten years suitable buildings for the general assembly, a governor's residence and statehouse office space, a state library room, and a supreme court room. Peters also included an offer of twenty-five acres for the capitol site at the city's old fairgrounds or ten acres of unoccupied land chosen by the general assembly. Unanimously adopted by the city council, Peters's resolution found quick acceptance in the state convention. Dunning, who as president *pro tem* was in the chair on 27 February, took up the city's offer and, after an effort by some members to reconsider, it passed by a 99-to-30 vote. By including a provision in the constitution (Article X) for a new capital site, the delegates pointed out that Atlanta would be held to a "just and full compliance" of its promises made to the state.

---

[4]As early as 1847, when Atlanta was a small village, its citizens had asked the legislature to move the capital to their city. In 1851, the Georgia Senate offered some encouragement when it passed a resolution to gather information on the cost of moving the capital from Milledgeville to either Macon or Atlanta. During 1853, the Atlanta city council sent a lobbying delegation to Milledgeville, but that year Atlanta had to settle for the lesser distinction of becoming the county seat of Fulton County. The following year, as Atlanta City Hall neared completion, the council created an expense-paid commission that soon totaled fifty members, including Peters, "to urge before the people of Georgia the propriety of the removal of the capital from Milledgeville." In January 1855, the new mayor, Allison Nelson, struck just the right note when he said the issue could not be left to the people, the press, nor Atlanta's natural advantages, but must be a question of continuing importance to members of the city council. *Georgia Laws*, 1851; Atlanta City Council Minute Books, 28 November 1853, 18 January, 21 April, 19 May 1854, 19 January 1855; *Atlanta Daily Examiner* (23 September 1857).

The convention then adjourned on 11 March after nominating as the Republican gubernatorial nominee Rufus B. Bullock.

There were some good reasons for keeping the capital at Milledgeville, the seat of state government since 1807. Most notable at the time was the in-progress $25,000 renovation of the buildings, plus Milledgeville had more hotel accommodations than Atlanta. Furthermore, the removal of records, papers, books, and furniture would entail considerable expense and perhaps result in some damage and confusion. Milledgeville was also in the geographic center of the state—within thirteen miles by actual survey. For these reasons, the people of Milledgeville seemed confident they would retain the capital. To Middle Georgians, the removal provision was a foolish act by a "Mullatto Convention" in Atlanta and, in a reference to the coming vote for ratification of the new state constitution, one newspaper predicted that "the people are not such a set of asses as to listen to a foolish idea."

Atlanta, however, had some attractions in addition to the inducements offered by Peters's resolution. The Gate City boasted four railroads with two more anticipated, while Milledgeville had only two with one anticipated and, unlike Milledgeville, Atlanta's were the main arteries of Southern rail travel. Furthermore, the terminus of the Western and Atlantic Railroad, one of the most important state institutions, was located in Atlanta. The city's healthful climate would allow summer sessions of the legislature; and when a new capitol building became necessary, Atlanta had access to nearby building materials such as Stone Mountain granite and North Georgia marble. Finally, Atlanta's business was thriving and the city's population was increasing rapidly. The *Atlanta New Era*, elated with recent developments, informed its readers that the capital was coming out of the woods from "swampy, mosquito-infested" Milledgeville. Calling the members of the state convention and city council in Atlanta a "capital set of fellows," the paper predicted that "the ratification of the Constitution is by no means a question of debate. He who doubts is already damned." The *Atlanta Intellingencer* evidently favored the move, but strongly opposed Bullock for governor and the remainder of the new constitution made by "infamous and ignorant men."

Of central importance in the ratification vote was General Meade's determination to enforce the Congressional Reconstruction Acts in his military district. He had promised the state convention on 11 January that he would allow qualified voters to vote on the state constitution without fear of influence, fraud, or restraint. This meant that while many whites were proscribed, blacks would be protected in their right to vote. And to insure that rural Georgians, including many blacks, could vote without walking as far as forty miles, Meade ordered three voting locations situated in each county with only one in the county seat; the other two had to be located at different points in the county in a way that would result in a fairly even geographic distribution of the polls.

When all was ready, Meade submitted the new state constitution for ratification. On 20-23 April 1868, Georgians approved the document containing the capital-removal provision by a vote of 88,123 to 69,750, and Bullock was a somewhat less impressive victor over the Democratic candidate, John B. Gordon. Fulton County voters barely approved the constitution by a vote of 2,169 to 2,019, and repudiated Bullock for Gordon. (Some of the disfranchised whites expressed themselves in unofficial balloting in the rooms of the Fulton County Democratic Club. This microcosmic white vote stood eighty to five against the constitution; and eighty-five to none, Gordon over Bullock.) The four-day voting period allowed ample time for any necessary travel and Meade undoubtedly would have held the polls open longer if necessary. The Ku Klux Klan countered the Republican effort to persuade blacks to vote. Yet the disfranchisement of former Confederates probably nullified more anti-constitution votes than favorable votes suppressed by the Klan. Therefore, blacks played a significant role in Peters's successful effort to make Atlanta the capital of Georgia.

The capital-removal question continued to boil. In Macon, the press claimed that if removal had been voted on separately it would have failed, which is probably true. Certainly the vote would not have been so favorable to Atlanta. The people of Milledgeville, realizing too late the danger, attempted in vain to prevent removal, including their proposal of a state constitutional amendment and of a memorial to the United States Senate.[5] The legislature intended to hold Atlanta to its promise of space, but if Atlantans failed to please the solons, the remodeled buildings at Milledgeville might prove too inviting. Should the legislature convene in the old capitol, just the physical presence of the legislature would be a serious setback for Atlanta.

------

[5]Atlanta City Council Minute Books, 9 August 1867, 26 February 1868; *Atlanta Daily New Era* (11, 28 February, 3 March—quoting *Macon Journal and Messenger*, 5, 7, 8 May, 2 June 1868); *The Daily Atlanta Intelligencer* (15 December 1867; 7 January, 22, 29 April, 20 May 1868); *Atlanta Constitution* (10 March 1869; 13 July 1870); *Athens Banner-Herald* (7 June 1931).

To prevent this, Peters suggested in council that Mayor Williams appoint a committee to plan quarters for the state government, and Williams, having been reduced to the role of sycophant by the Porter affair, appointed Peters chairman of the Committee on Capital Removal.

At first Peters intended to enlarge City Hall by expanding the building 50 feet on the east end and 115 feet on the south side, but he soon realized the additions would never be completed in time—the legislature would convene ninety days from the adjournment of the convention. Instead, he suggested interior changes in the building's upper rooms. A major problem for Peters was the absence of the legislature, which made it impossible for him to determine the members' needs and desires. He suggested that when the legislature assembled, the councilmen should consult with the members to learn their wants and satisfy them—alterations of City Hall, new buildings, different lots—until a permanent capitol could be built. Peters believed that once ascertained, such needs should be met "let them be what they may." In the meantime, carpenters altered the interior of City Hall by arranging partitions to increase the size of the rooms and erected a gallery in the House Chamber that would accommodate 250 people. Other workmen added exterior blinds to the upper story of the building and repainted the interior and parts of the exterior. By 23 July 1868 the work was completed. On that day Meade ended the military regime and over ten thousand conservative Democrats celebrated the lifting of the occupation with a huge rally, later called the "Bush Arbor meeting," in City Park.[6]

When the legislature convened in cramped quarters in City Hall, space limitations caused immediate dissatisfaction. The solons, seated on reed-bottomed chairs at pine desks, quickly established the Joint Committee on Public Buildings to locate adequate facilities for state government; members of the committee met with the city council on 5 August to discuss the prob-

---

[6]Scrapbook, Black Collection; Atlanta City Council Minute Books, 6 March, 15, 22 May, 12, 26 June 1868; *Atlanta Daily New Era* (17 March, 12 May, 27 June 1868); *Atlanta Constitution* (21 August 1870); Taylor, "From the Ashes," 293. At the "Bush Arbor meeting," where an immense bush arbor shaded the speakers' platform, Robert Toombs, Howell Cobb, and Benjamin Hill excoriated the Radicals. Among the crowd that sweltered in the sun for five hours was young Henry Grady, already an accomplished orator at the University of Georgia, who took time out from classes to make the trip to Atlanta. Grady was very much impressed with Hill, of whom he wrote: "Such a speech, of such compass, pitched upon such a key, was never made in this state before or since." Raymond B. Nixon, *Henry W. Grady: Spokesman of the New South* (New York: Alfred A. Knopf, 1943) 51.

lem. Peters, able now to ask about space requirements, was told that a room
for a state library was needed immediately as the legislature had passed a
resolution ordering the state library moved from Milledgeville. A few committee rooms would be needed; the secretary of state needed two rooms in
the statehouse; and two rooms each were needed for the state treasurer and
comptroller general, but not necessarily in the statehouse. Then, on motion
by Peters, the council gave its Committee on Buildings and Grounds authority to procure the needed space, working in conjunction with the legislature's committee.

Peters offered two proposals—his earlier plan of additions to City Hall
or renting the opera house then under construction at Forsyth and Marietta
streets by the brothers Edwin N. and Hannibal I. Kimball. The latter was
one of the most controversial figures of his day, but a "specimen of the class
of Northern men" that postwar Atlanta was beginning to welcome. Born in
1832 the son of a Maine carriage-maker, Kimball had managed a carriage
factory in New Haven, Connecticut, then moved to Chicago after the war to
plan a Southern branch of George Pullman's Sleeping Car Company. The
branch opened in Atlanta in 1867 and, from then to the end of the Radical
regime, Kimball "reigned supreme as Atlanta's financier." The opera
house had definite appeal as a capitol. The building was located in the center of the city, plus it could be completed to the desired specifications. Adequate space for state officials could be located on its four floors. The
House Chamber would be 70-by-75 feet with a ceiling 38 feet high, and
have a 500-seat gallery. The smaller Senate Chamber would contain a 200-
seat gallery. Water closets would be conveniently located on each floor, and
other modern fixtures and features would enhance the structure.

The legislature's Joint Committee on Public Buildings, after studying
plans presented by Peters for increasing the size of City Hall and the Kimball brothers' proposal for completion of the opera house, reported the two
options to the full legislature. That body selected the opera house, provided
the choice proved agreeable to the city council. In August the council requested Peters to negotiate with the Kimball brothers for the lease of the opera house, and after meeting with the owners, he returned with a document.
Two rooms on the first floor and all of the second, third, and fourth floors
of the opera house would be used by the legislature. The lease would cost
the city $6,000 a year with a five-year renewal option, and there would be
no city tax on the entire building. Peters pointed out that these terms seemed
favorable when weighed against the $40,000 in city bonds which would be
necessary to finance the proposed additions to City Hall; he also took into

consideration the fact that the legislature wanted the opera house. The council then adopted Peters's report and sent it to the legislature. To publicize the terms of the lease to Atlantans and the solons, the council ordered four hundred copies printed in handbill form.

There was an urgent need to complete the opera house as soon as possible. In September, to allay continued grumbling because of lack of space, an Atlanta council-citizens group sponsored a lavish pacification gala for the solons. Still the issue remained a source of discord, which was only exacerbated when the conservative Democrats ejected the black legislators that same month.[7] In December Peters's Finance Committee issued non-interest bonds to H. I. Kimball in payment of the lease. On the evening of 12 January 1869 the public, agog with the glitter of the new capitol building as construction neared completion and eager for a first look at the interior, were allowed inside prior to the opening of the legislative session. The completion of the Kimball Opera House did much to sustain Atlanta as Georgia's fifth capital.[8]

---

[7] On 22 December 1869, because of the expulsion of blacks from the legislature and on the advice of Governor Bullock, the Federals reinstituted military rule in Georgia under General Alfred H. Terry. Georgians had to ratify the Fifteenth Amendment to the U.S. Constitution before the state could again be readmitted to the Union. In January 1870, the new military commander restored the expelled blacks to the legislature, and at the same time ousted twenty-nine conservative Democrats ("Terry's Purge"). In February, the Fifteenth Amendment was ratified and in July Congress again readmitted Georgia, but Republicans retained control for the next eighteen months. Although the Bullock administration and the legislature as reconstituted by Terry became the most corrupt in Georgia history, it paled in comparison to the Tweed Ring in New York, which made the scandal in Georgia "look like a crooked card game between two near-broke cotton merchants." Kenneth Coleman, ed., *History of Georgia* (Athens: University of Georgia Press, 1977) 214-16.

[8] Atlanta City Council Minute Books, 5, 14, 17 August, 18 September 1868; *Atlanta Daily New Era* (27 February 1868); *The Daily Atlanta Intelligencer* (5 August, 8 September 1868; 12 January, 5, 18, 20 February, 17 November 1869); *Atlanta Constitution* (19 December 1877); James C. Bonner, *Milledgeville: Georgia's Antebellum Capital* (Athens: University of Georgia Press, 1978) 219; Taylor, "From the Ashes," 71. The lease of the opera house by the city was followed by the purchase of the building by the state. The latter was accompanied by financial excess that helped produce the Kimball-Bullock scandal. H. I. Kimball, gaining title to the building from his brother, installed magnificent interior appointments and sold it to the state in 1870 for $380,000, a highly profitable sum. In order for Atlanta to meet its contract obligations to provide space, the price included $130,000 in bonds paid by the city to Kimball, although he apparently never turned the bonds over to the state. To make up for the missing funds, the city offered the state City Hall square (formerly "Peters's Reserve"), which eventually became the site of the permanent Georgia State Capitol. *Atlanta Constitution* (11 March 1869; 1, 6 August 1870); *The Daily Atlanta Intelligencer* (26 February 1869; 10 August 1870); Taylor, "From the Ashes," 162-64.

When city government changed hands in January 1869, Peters returned to private life, choosing not to stand for re-election.[9] His two years on the council had been ones of solid accomplishment. His conciliatory stand under military occupation helped Atlantans elude the worst features of Reconstruction,[10] but because of his role in capital removal, he has been denounced by a Milledgeville historian as a member of "the Atlanta Ring." James C. Bonner described him as a real estate developer and councilman who, along with other businessmen and politicians, worked "quietly with

---

[9]Peters had worked on ad hoc council committees for other city improvements. In an attempt to insure an adequate city water supply to extinguish fires, he carefully monitored city contracts for digging and walling cisterns. When a contractor used oversized rocks in a street resurfacing project, Peters specified that in the future all rocks used to macadamize streets must be small enough to pass through a three-and-a-half inch ring. He was a member of a joint citizens-council committee to name and rename streets, and one important action of the panel was to redesignate part of Whitehall Street—from the railroad crossing to Marietta Street—Peachtree Street.

During his years on the council, Peters also found time to serve as foreman of the grand jury of the United States District Court of the Northern District of Georgia, join and support the Young Men's Library Association (later Atlanta Public Library), and was a member of the Board of Commissioners of the Georgia State Orphan's Home. Further, he attempted, without success, to attract Mercer University and establish a women's college with personal inducements of money and land. Atlanta City Council Minute Books, 1 March, 3, 24 May, 23 August, 1, 13, 22 November 1867, 10 April, 29 May 1868, 1 January 1869; *Atlanta Constitution* (9, 17 July, 5, 7, 28 August, 3, 13 September 1870); *The Daily Atlanta Intelligencer* (11 July, 11 September 1867); Nita Black Rucker, Notes on Nellie Peters Black, Black Collection; Young Men's Library Association Collection, Atlanta Historical Society; Paul W. Miller, ed., *Atlanta: Capital of the South* (New York: O. Durrell, 1949) 83, 199-200; Franklin M. Garrett, *Atlanta and Environs: A Chronicle of Its People and Events* 2 vols. (Athens: University of Georgia Press, 1969) 1:750.

[10]Peters did display some of the characteristics of a scalawag. The term probably came from Scalloway, a county consisting of the Shetland Islands off the northeastern coast of Scotland, known for its runty cattle and horses. Finding its way into Reconstruction politics, the term became a synonym for rascal. A scalawag was characterized as disloyal, cowardly, motivated by greed or lust for power, and despised as a traitor to his race and section. Perhaps a general definition would be a white Southerner who supported Congressional Reconstruction and by that definition Peters was a scalawag. To be a scalawag was to pay a price. Peters merely suffered heavy criticism, but many throughout the South were shot, hanged, drowned, burned, or flogged. Peters also demonstrated the injustice of the term scalawag, that some among this group were men of exceptional quality. Allen W. Trelease, "Who Were the Scalawags?" *Journal of Southern History* 29:4 (November 1963): 443-47; John S. Ezell, *The South Since 1865* (Norman: University of Oklahoma Press, 1978) 84, 95; Grady McWhiney, *Southerners and Other Americans* (New York: Basic Books, Inc., 1973) 128; William Warren Rogers, *The One-Gallused Rebellion: Agrarianism in Alabama, 1865-1896* (Baton Rouge: Louisiana State University Press, 1970) 35-36.

the radicals to obtain primarily for themselves and incidentally for their community anything which was possible for the military regime to grant." On the other hand, E. Merton Coulter wrote that Peters, "being a loyal Atlantan, saw no harm in helping to snatch the state capital away from sleepy little Milledgeville." These opposing viewpoints serve to illustrate a common theme—Peters's greatest achievement as a councilman was the primary role he played in capital removal inasmuch as becoming the seat of state government was a dramatic symbol of Atlanta's future as a regional metropolis and center of the New South movement.[11]

[11]Athens *Banner-Herald* (7 June 1931); Bonner, *Milledgeville*, 218; Taylor, "From the Ashes," 162.

CHAPTER TWELVE

STREET RAILROADS: PETERS BUILDS TRANSIT SYSTEM

C ity services boomed in the South during the decade following the Civil War as cities and private companies financed water and gas works, bridges, public buildings, and paved streets. But most important was the appearance of horse-drawn streetcars—Atlanta's first mass transit system. It was built by Richard Peters. Indeed, Peters was best known by most Atlantans in the postwar years as a traction magnate. Peters realized that street railroads in other cities had proven practical and profitable, and had seen them in operation in the North.[1] He considered a system for his

---

[1] The older horse-drawn omnibus (without rails) began service in 1827 in New York, and although the city experimented with horsecars in 1832, it was the 1850s before they became the national vogue. Except in New York, Boston, and Philadelphia, progress was spotty, totaling five hundred miles nationwide at the close of the decade. In the South, only New Orleans and Mobile had horsecars in the antebellum period, but in 1865 lines began operating in Richmond, Charleston, and Memphis, for a Southern total of five of the forty-eight cities with street railroads in America. Systems began in 1866 in Nashville, 1868 in Houston, 1869 in Savannah, 1870 in Norfolk, 1871 in Atlanta, and 1873 in Dallas. Howard

own city as being feasible: it would increase the real estate values near the lines; it would reinforce Atlanta's rapid growth; and the demand was building—even then inhabitants of West End outside the city limits needed commuter service to Atlanta. Peters decided that with proper charter specifications and adequate financing, a street railroad could be successful in Atlanta.[2]

Shortly after the war, the state legislature had authorized a charter incorporating the Atlanta Street Railroad Company under the stewardship of the city council. Unfortunately, the council had burdened the charter with a host of strict provisions that had delayed action on the project for years. It was, therefore, no coincidence that during the last session of the council on which Peters served, the group passed an ordinance that eased the charter regulations in order to encourage development by the inert street railway company. The new guidelines allowed the company to construct lines on any street; fare ceilings would be twenty cents for through passengers and ten cents for short trips; rolling stock would be exempt from taxation for fifty years; and macadamizing requirements were reduced from the entire street to the area between and three feet on each side of the tracks. To insure compliance with these new provisions, the company was placed under the general supervision of the council's Committee on Streets.

A few months later, on 30 April 1869, with the city's press calling for action, the stockholders of the Atlanta Street Railway Company met in James's Bank and elected Peters president. He was also a director, along with George W. Adair, who doubled as company secretary, John H. James, B. E. Crane, Lewis Scofield, and B. H. Broomhead. Peters's major challenge was raising sufficient capital of an estimated $50,000 to build the first line to West End—a street railroad was an experimental project to Atlantans. He had the Whitehall Street portion of the route surveyed, but it was

---

N. Rabinowitz, "Continuity and Change: Southern Urban Development, 1860-1900," *The City in Southern History: The Growth of Urban Civilization in the South*, ed. Blaine A. Brownell and David R. Goldfield (Port Washington: Kennikat Press, 1977) 98; Gunther Barth, *City People: The Rise of Modern City Culture in Nineteenth-Century America* (New York: Oxford University Press, 1980) 53-54; Blake McKelvey, *The Urbanization of America, 1860-1915* (New Brunswick: Rutgers University Press, 1963) 14.

[2]*Atlanta Constitution* (13 August 1869). The first known reason given for a street railroad in Atlanta was to provide the citizens some relief from the shoe-top deep mud that often mired the streets. *The Weekly Atlanta Intelligencer* (7 June 1860).

two years later in 1871 before the company declared the line sufficiently subscribed—most likely due to heavy investment by Peters.

Under Peters's leadership, the revitalized Atlanta Street Railway Company began construction of its first line to West End. Treasurer William P. Orme called in twenty-five percent of each share and let bids for four-by-eight-inch stringers and four-by-six-inch cross-ties, all from the heart of long-leaf pine. Carloads of iron for the line began to arrive in Atlanta. Peters, who personally supervised construction, used a crescent rail because macadam rocks could not rest on top of it and upset the cars. This early type of construction raised the rails above the level of the street, which inconvenienced other vehicles when crossing, but it was the most inexpensive method. Peters placed the rail line in the middle of the street to facilitate parking on either side.

A big day for Atlanta and the street railroad company was 7 September 1871 when the West End line began partial operation. The horse-drawn cars, operated by L. P. Thomas, ran smoothly along the one-and-a-quarter miles of completed track. (Peters used some horses but he preferred mules because they were more durable, purchasing quality animals from the bluegrass region of Kentucky.) The following day Atlantans crowded on board to take advantage of free rides in a combined celebration and promotion by Peters. When fully operational, the line extended from the Whitehall Street railroad crossing to McPherson Barracks in West End, a distance of two-and-a-half miles.[3] Following steam-driven railroads, the telegraph, and gas lights, "rapid transit" was a reality, and in three of the four ventures, Peters had been a prime mover.

The inevitable criticism of the street railroad began even before Peters completed the first line to West End. Early complaints centered on both the inconvenience caused by the raised tracks and on the motive for the lines. For example, the company could increase property values through its choice of route, which was subject to approval by the city council's Committee on Streets. During the real estate boom of the early 1870s, Adair, becoming wealthy as a real estate auctioneer, exploited the streetcar routes' accessi-

---

[3]Atlanta City Council Minute Books, 21 September 1866, 1 January 1869; Scrapbook, Nellie P. Black Collection, University of Georgia Libraries, Athens; *The Daily Atlanta Intelligencer* (23 February 1867; 6 January, 12 February, 1 May 1869); *Atlanta Constitution* (20 March 1869; 26, 30 April, 27 June, 13 July, 9 September 1871); Wade Hampton Wright, "Georgia Power Company," *Atlanta Historical Bulletin* 2:14 (July 1938): 197-202.

bility to his property as an advertising gambit, offering free rides to the sites of his sales. Furthermore, it was hardly coincidental that the first line ran by Peters's home and terminated near Adair's residence at West End. Some real estate owners leveled criticism at Peters, saying the company's tax-exempt status might otherwise serve to reduce real estate taxes, and charged Peters with leading a "ring of monopolists" to which the city had given unlimited power. Actually, the city retained control over the company, as the charter made clear: "Mayor and council reserve to themselves the right, in conjunction with the President and Directors of said company, to make all rules and regulations for the government of said company." No idle words; the city used this authority many times.

Nor were the merchants on Peters Street pleased at first. They met in M. T. Castleberry's store and selected men to complain to the council about the condition of Peters Street resulting from the building of the street railroad. Peters Street merchants historically favored the wagon trade and appeared unenthusiastic about the line, but this particular complaint, while reflecting a general attitude, dealt with the need for cleaning up construction debris. The council passed an ordinance prohibiting Peters's company from making deep cuts or heavy fills that could infringe on property rights along the lines and ordered the company to repair streets after construction. While flush times encouraged Peters to begin street railway construction, the fact remained that with meager financial backing from Atlantans, he was building the transit system almost single-handedly. He selected routes he thought would be profitable, but at the same time provide the city adequate coverage. And he built lines in areas advocated by the *Constitution*, which was rapidly becoming the most influential newspaper in Atlanta.[4]

At the beginning of 1872, Peters opened the subscription books for new lines on Marietta, Decatur, and Peachtree streets. The first line had yet to prove its success, however, and there was little risk capital proffered, so with less than $3,000 in subscriptions, Peters invested the necessary capital to build and equip the new lines. The Marietta Street line began partial operation on 14 January, only one month after ground had been broken, and when completed in March, it extended one-and-a-half miles northward to

[4]*Atlanta City Directory* (1871); George W. Adair Plat Books, 1866, Atlanta Historical Society; Atlanta City Council Minute Books, 30 August 1872, 24 January 1873; *The Daily Atlanta Intelligencer* (23 February 1867; 27 June, 13 July 1869); *Atlanta Constitution* (28 April, 30 August 1871; 12 July, 13 August 1872; 7 October 1879).

the Rolling Mill. On 3 May, the Decatur Street line opened for the one-mile trip eastward to Oakland Cemetery, and on 8 August the Peachtree Street line began service northward to Pine Street.[5]

The company purchased most of its streetcars from the North, although a few came from lines in other Southern cities. Each car carried sixteen to twenty passengers and was comfortable, moving over smooth rails at five miles an hour. This was a vast improvement over walking or, for the few who owned private carriages, riding over bumpy streets. Company regulations prohibited smoking on the cars and straw was sometimes placed on the floor to catch mud and dirt from the feet of passengers and help keep their feet warm in winter. Although the company's charter allowed a fare of ten to twenty cents, most fares were initially ten cents, but were soon, with "commendable liberality," reduced to five cents. Each car was equipped with a small glass-covered box into which the passengers deposited their nickels. The glass top enabled the driver to check receipts and an "embarrassment bell" allowed him to notify a passenger who entered the car and neglected to pay. Drivers also had to contend with accidents resulting from runaways, collisions, and people jumping on and off the cars. Peters hired respectable married men as drivers, so that women would feel safe riding the cars at any hour in any part of the city.[6]

After Peters demonstrated that the street railroad could be profitable in Atlanta, he noted with growing concern the efforts of a group of investors to establish a rival company. Led by M. G. Dobbins and A. K. Seago, the group secured a charter from the state legislature to establish the Atlanta and West End Company; Dobbins became president. Anticipating adding another line to West End, the Dobbins group said that they also intended to build a line to Ponce de Leon Springs, a popular resort northeast of the city, and applied to the city council for grades on streets not previously contracted by Peters. But Peters, who had already surveyed for a line to the springs, protested to the city council that his charter gave him exclusive

---

[5]*Atlanta Constitution* (28 September, 8, 12 October, 9 December 1871; 26 March, 1 April, 3 May 1872).

[6]*Atlanta Constitution* (28 September 1871; 15 September, 11 October, 4 November 1872; 8 October 1874; 19 July 1876; 15 August 1882); *Atlanta Sunday American* (27 June 1937); Jessie Folsom Stockbridge, "Turntable at Five Points," *Atlanta Journal Magazine* (17 December 1933); William B. Williford, *Peachtree Street, Atlanta* (Athens: University of Georgia Press, 1962) 35.

rights to build in Atlanta and vowed to oppose the new company by employing "all legal means" to protect his rights. The dispute spilled over into the press, where the Dobbins group accused Peters of "putting his heel upon the neck of all public enterprises" that interfered with his private interests. Moreover, Peters's critics aired old animosities, beginning with his role in the antebellum struggle between the Georgia Western and Air Line railroads, and ending with his determination "to have no competition" in streetcar lines. Wanting to keep aloof of the controversy until the matter was legally settled, the council on 3 January 1873 disallowed Dobbins's application. At this, an adamant Dobbins announced he would nonetheless build a line to Ponce de Leon Springs, although he too found it difficult to raise the necessary subscriptions.

At this point, Peters attempted a merger, but Dobbins refused. Peters therefore carried through with a legal volley by applying to Fulton County Superior Court for a perpetual injunction against Dobbins's proposed line. Relying on a section of the original charter that gave "exclusive rights" to the Atlanta Street Railway Company, Peters maintained the rights must be upheld in order for the company to raise funds from subscriptions. Fulton Superior Court ruled in Peters's favor and the defendants gave notice of appeal to the Georgia Supreme Court. Dobbins's appeal began while Peters was visiting Tallulah Falls in North Georgia and, upon his return to Atlanta, he learned that the Supreme Court had decided against him by overturning the decision of the county's superior court. According to the Supreme Court, Peters's company had exclusive rights only on streets already selected, because if the company had rights on *all* streets, the legislature would not have granted the charter to a second company. Elated by the Supreme Court's decision, friends of the Atlanta and West End Company celebrated with a victory barbeque at Ponce de Leon Springs. This celebration was premature, however, because another variable dominated the situation—the national financial crisis of 1873. Atlanta was hard hit and actual construction of the rival line had to be indefinitely postponed. Nonetheless, the case of the *Atlanta Street Railroad Company vs. the Atlanta and West End Company* was influential, as it established the legality of competing companies.[7]

---

[7]Atlanta City Council Minute Books, 6 September, 20 December 1872, 3 January 1873; *Atlanta Constitution* (10 September, 29 October, 11, 17 December 1872; 22, 29, 31 July, 3, 20, 27, 30 August, 5 September 1873).

While involved in litigation, Peters added two more lines, each about one mile in length: the winding Taylor Hill line to the west opened on 30 March 1873, and the McDonough Street line to the south had a 26 May opening date. On 15 February 1874, the final line took its place in the system in the form of a short run down Whitehall Street on the opposite side of the Macon and Western tracks from the West End line. That same year the company extended its Peachtree Street line two-and-a-half miles northeastward out Ponce de Leon Avenue to Ponce de Leon Springs, and Peters built a bridge, 270 feet long and 40 feet high, where the line crossed a ravine at Clear Creek.

With seven lines in operation by the beginning of 1874, Peters needed central facilities for distribution and maintenance. At Five Points in the center of the city, the company purchased two lots on opposite sides of Line Street (Edgewood Avenue) near the corner of Ivy Street. On one lot Peters built a brick-front stock barn that housed clerical offices, a harness-maker shop, a blacksmith shop, as well as stables. A "mule-book" showed a history of the earnings, expenses, and distribution of the livestock. The draft animals worked in relays after each round trip, with seven mules for each car working in teams of two each, an arrangement that gave each mule one day's rest a week.

On the opposite lot at 49 Line Street, Peters constructed a fireproof brick car-barn that contained a bookkeeping department, a repair shop, and an overnight holding area for the cars. Outside the car-barn, he installed a turntable with a length of track barely longer than a streetcar. At day's end, each driver unhitched his mules and the car was pivoted into position for storage. In this building Peters's son Ralph recorded each days's earnings of every car. In 1874, after two years of expansion, the company had grown from five cars and forty mules and horses to seventeen cars and one hundred and fourteen animals. The work force consisted of sixteen drivers; sixteen hostlers; and one each bookkeeper, blacksmith, car cleaner, harness maker, stable boss, watchman, striker, and helper. Company stock totaled $145,000, and there were eleven miles of track. Peters pointed with pride to the fact that Atlantans could travel to any part of the city for a small sum. "We have endeavored to make the system adequate to the requirements of the city," he explained, "by furnishing cheap and comfortable traveling facilities to the people, in every direction, and they appreciate it as a great public convenience."[8]

The depression of the 1870s deepened after the seven major lines were completed, yet Peters's careful management allowed the company not only to survive but to average at least ten percent per annum dividends to stockholders. Had it not been for extraordinary expenses such as damages for injuries on the road and lawyers' fees, dividends would have been higher. As was natural for that era, company policy favored dividends over wages. When receipts fell $20,000 in one year, Peters slashed expenses from $46,000 to $26,000; he admitted that the reduced workers' wages were "not more sufficient [than] to supply them with the necessaries of life," but the workers kept their jobs. For a business, even a monopoly, operating in the depths of a severe depression, the Atlanta Street Railroad Company was highly solvent. The system was one of the most extensive in the South and turned a profit while responding to the demands of the public.

While the street railroad survived the depression, one of its leading officers, George W. Adair, found it necessary to quit the company because of personal financial distress brought on by unremunerative real estate. Adair lamented that "you couldn't borrow ten dollars in New York with ten counties in Georgia as security." He stunned Atlantans by placing a notice in the 28 March 1877 *Constitution* declaring his insolvency. Adair's financial failure resulted from ten to twelve percent interest rates on an indebtedness of $140,000, and a decrease in the value of Atlanta real estate of approximately thirty percent. To cover his debt, Adair owned $200,000 in property

---

[8]*Atlanta Constitution* (30 April 1873; 14 July 1874; 2 March 1875; 18 August, 18 October 1878; 8 June 1879); Augusta Wylie King, "Atlanta's First Car Barn," *Atlanta Historical Bulletin* 4:19 (October 1939): 252-55; Louise Black MacDougald, "A Trip Down Peachtree Street in 1886," *Atlanta Historical Bulletin* 5:21 (April 1940): 137. Peters, who had a Bourbon's approach to race relations, was in no hurry to raise the barriers of racial separation, but after white passengers complained about blacks crowding into the cars, he apparently placed separate Jim Crow cars into service. George B. Tindall, *The Persistent Tradition in New South Politics* (Baton Rouge: Louisiana State University Press, 1975) 13; James M. Russell, "Atlanta, Gate City of the South, 1847 to 1885" (Ph.D. dissertation, Princeton University, 1971) 269. However, Howard Rabinowitz wrote that in 1888 the rival Metropolitan Street Railroad Company was "responsible for the first clear indication of segregation in Atlanta" by placing two cars behind its new steam-powered (dummy) engine— a yellow car for whites, a red one for blacks. *Race Relations in the Urban South, 1865-1890* (New York: Oxford University Press, 1978) 193. In 1891, Georgia's Jim Crow streetcar legislation removed any previous flexibility. Rabinowitz, "Continuity and Change," 119.

assessed for tax purposes and other investments. Consoled by Peters, who declared in a tone of hearty encouragement that "in five years time Adair will be worth $50,000," the real estate auctioneer remained gloomy as he faced the inevitable.

Adair's bankruptcy meant a severe test for the street railway stock, which had to hold its own at public auction during a depression and after it was rumored that shrinkage in the stock had injured him. Individual shares had not been sold previously except when the holder needed cash, and then the stock was sold back to the company for $100 a share and resold, sometimes at $105, to a private buyer. Adair auctioned his property himself and the sale was second only to the visit of President Rutherford B. Hayes as the notable event in Atlanta that year. The first bid for the street railroad stock was $55 a share, but before any was sold the bidding reached $100, and the bulk of it was sold at that price—ninety shares went for $8,985 in a company with $164,000 in capital stock. Since Peters and Adair had held most of the stock, Peters apparently owned almost all the company. One buyer acted solely upon his "confidence in Dick Peters," but most who purchased the stock had investigated the company and found that the street railway's dividends were among the highest of any rail in Georgia. The aggregate of Adair's property brought a disappointing $109,925. His financial reverses were temporary, but he was out of the company.[9]

As panic slowly turned to prosperity, Peters reorganized his street railroad. J. W. Culpepper succeeded Adair as secretary-treasurer, and Peters's son Edward became superintendent. Peters remained as president; the directors were Peters, Edward C. Peters, Samuel Inman, W. M. Middlebrooks, and J. R. Wylie. The press touted Peters's leadership, calling him "one of the best financiers in the South; clear-headed, sagacious, prudent, honest to the last drop of blood, and thoroughly practical, he is the very man of all others fitted to handle such a large interest. His name is a perfect guaranty wherever it is known." Young Edward, in charge of the details of management, received mention as an emerging Atlanta capitalist. He was described as "a young man of wonderful talent for business, and inherits his

---

[9]*Atlanta Constitution* (27 July 1873; 19 September 1876; 17 January, 28, 29 March, 17, 19 December 1877; 11 January 1878); Jean Martin, "Mule to MARTA (part 1)," *Atlanta Historical Bulletin* 29:2 (1975): 1-10.

father's powers." The company enjoyed good press and Peters's success lent substance to the assertion that "Atlanta has not been built by brag."[10]

Good management was needed because a plethora of new challenges arose for Peters's company, one of which was severe weather. Heavy snows sometimes halted service for days at a time and caused public consternation. In letters to the public and city council, Peters explained his problems:

> Owing to unprecedented frosts and rains last winter, the wagons and drays from all portions of the city were compelled to seek the macadamized tracks of the street railroad, the sidestreets of the city being impassable for a period of sixty days. This heavy travel, which was fully three times as much as in former years, caused the side filling of the street railroad to yield in many places and expose the stringers of the track.[11]

The poor condition of the tracks caused frequent accidents to crossing vehicles and Peters pointed out that deterioration resulting from weather and wagon travel would have been minimal if the city had carried through with its intention to macadamize the remainder of each street along the routes. Peters defended his use of the crescent rail, saying that after studying street railways in other cities, he was convinced it worked best on macadamized streets and its use had been ratified by the council. He had T-rail only on the Ponce de Leon line, where there was no interference by wagons and therefore it was practical. On 11 miles of tracks, Peters's cars ran 974 miles daily, the distance from Atlanta to New York, for an annual run of 355,500 miles. There had been no serious accident to passengers (accidents caused occasional injury and death to pedestrians and animals) and no interruption of service except during winter months when wagons left the tracks covered with ice and frozen mud that incapacitated Peters's snow plows.

Harsh weather continued to be the bane of the company at other times of the year, when rain and wind storms left knee-deep mud that drifted over the tracks, rendering the streets impassable. Passengers stranded on their way home in the dark turned into "swearing humanity," while others waiting downtown for cars that never came were "breathing vengeance" against

---

[10]*Atlanta City Directory* (1878); *Atlanta Constitution* (1 November 1872; 14 July 1874; 18 January, 27 March, 3 April 1877; 11 January 1878); Arthur R. Taylor, "From the Ashes: Atlanta During Reconstruction, 1865-1876" (Ph.D. dissertation, Emory University, 1973) 108.

[11]*Atlanta Constitution* (4 October 1881).

the company. One stranded patron suggested what was usually done if practical: "If two mules can't pull a car, Mr. Peters ought to give us four mules. We stand by the cars in fine weather—in bad weather they ought to stand by us." Peters explained that the stoppages were unavoidable: "The public should understand that we do the best we can. Our cars make six hundred trips every day. Each trip has its history—its accidents. Whoever is in a car when anything happens abuses the management. It is simply inevitable that something will happen once in a while to stop things." The situation demonstrated how dependent Atlantans had become on the public transit system and, as Peters had already suggested, the solution to the problem was to improve the streets.

Tired of ubiquitous mud and spurred by Peters's urgings, the city council launched a block-laying and macadamizing crusade. The first paving project began on Alabama Street on 3 June 1882 when Edward C. Peters, representing the Atlanta Street Railway Company, and city officials laid the first ceremonial blocks. That same month, the council made plans for macadamizing Peachtree Street to a depth of fourteen inches. The famous street was graded and macadamized a distance of four miles from the center of the city. Soon other streets received rock, stone, or blocks. The streetcar tracks usually had to be raised three to eleven inches, as was the case on Peachtree Street. The council considered the height adjustment important so that the tracks would be in a "good, smooth, passable condition" for other vehicles. When these heavy company expenses were accompanied by passenger complaints that work on improvements interrupted service, Peters could not resist a gentle reminder: "We [of the company] are all Atlanta men, fully identified with her history, and we do not yield to any of our fellow citizens the proud distinction of being more public spirited than we of the Atlanta Street Railroad Company."[12] Of the many problems confronting the company, it was ironic that the most burdensome—the council's insistence on company lines conforming with street improvements—resulted partly from Peters's admonition to the council to improve the streets.

---

[12]Atlanta City Council Minute Books, 5 September 1881, 3 April 1882; *Atlanta Constitution* (31 December 1880; 6 January 1881; 2 March, 4, 13 June, 12, 14 July 1882; 28 January 1883; 7 July 1886). Peters's comment points to his awareness of his role as builder of Atlanta; in language much less eloquent than he used in public, he admonished his sons: "Don't let these smart alecks and upstarts run the hog over you. You were here long before they were." Helen K. Lyon, "Richard Peters: Atlanta Pioneer—Georgia Builder," *Atlanta Historical Bulletin* 38:10 (December 1957): 37.

At this point, some ten years after Peters began operating the street railroad, his monopoly came to an end. The Atlanta and West End Company, delayed by the depression, had sold adequate stock and had built a line to the suburb of West End. Additionally, city council granted new charters. The Metropolitan Company constructed a line to Grant Park. The Gate City Company built a line through the country to Ponce de Leon Springs.[13] This competition for Peters heralded the end of an era. Atlanta had been fortunate in having him at the helm of the city's transit system during the 1871-1882 period because "contrasting future street railroad operations in the city, there is no evidence in the annals of Atlanta that Peters . . . abused [his] unique position by placing corporate profits above the public trust."[14]

With extensions and modifications, Peters retained most of his original lines (only the Taylor Hill line was completely discontinued, evidently because it was unprofitable) and he absorbed one rival. The Gate City Company, with seven cars and twenty-six mules, was paying a ten percent dividend on its single line to Ponce de Leon Springs when a fire destroyed its headquarters and some of its rolling stock. The $40,000 company was preparing to rebuild its stables and car shed on Fort Street amid rumors that Peters was about to "gobble up" the line. Financial problems continued for the Gate City Company when the city council directed the firm to lay block between and three feet on each side of its tracks. This crushing directive forced liquidation and Edward C. Peters and J. W. Culpepper bought the company and leased it to their own Atlanta Street Railroad Company with Peters as president of both companies.[15]

Among the recreational areas served by streetcars was a baseball field known as Athletic Park. Baseball had become popular in Atlanta after the Civil War, and by the 1870s young boys played all positions except the battery, which was usually filled by more experienced men. Edward C. Peters, with his father's consent, wisely helped a local team select grounds for their club on Peters's property on North Avenue near the Peachtree Street line, where the club constructed a new field, complete with grandstand, bleach-

---

[13]Atlanta City Council Minute Books, 21 July 1879, 6 June 1881; *Atlanta Constitution* (1 June, 20 July 1881; 27 July, 8 August 1882).

[14]Martin, "Mule to MARTA," 10.

[15]*Atlanta City Directory* (1882); *Atlanta Constitution* (4 March 1882; 24 March, 1, 9 June, 31 October 1883; 8 July, 2 September 1885; 5 January, 10 February, 11 July 1886).

ers, and a high wire fence. Atlantans developed a solid case of baseball fever the summer of 1884 when the first semiprofessional team, the Atlantas, played in Athletic Park. City newspapers gave considerable attention to the game and Peters placed numerous brief advertisements among the sports news urging fans to ride the street railroad to the games. Business boomed on the Peachtree Street line during baseball season. A matter of local civic pride, baseball drew neighborhoods and cities into wider relationships and also contributed to the rapid urbanization of America.[16]

The Atlanta Street Railroad Company remained the city's best balanced transit system in serving industrial, residential, and recreational areas. It also remained the largest. At the end of the 1880s, Peters's company was worth an estimated $350,000 and consisted of the Line Street headquarters, 18 miles of track, 50 cars, 250 horses and mules, and employed 100 men. But the company had financial difficulties. Horsecars, for years obsolete in Northern and Western cities, were quickly becoming outdated in Atlanta. Conversion to powerful steam engines, called "dummies" because they were enclosed in housings that resembled regular passenger cars, became necessary after the Metropolitan Company began using them on its line to Grant Park; steam quickly gave way to electric power. In a short time, all street railroad companies in Atlanta, unable to keep pace with the rapidly changing conditions, would no longer operate as separate entities.[17]

---

[16]*Atlanta Constitution* (19 May 1883; 24 August 1884; 20 October 1885); McKelvey, *The Urbanization of America*, 185, 193.

[17]Richard Peters to Ralph Peters, 23 June 1888, Black Collection; Atlanta City Council Minute Books, 18 October, 2 December 1886; Wright, "Georgia Power Company," 204; First National Bank, *Atlanta Resurgens* (n.p.: privately printed, n.d.) 32-33. In 1890 Joel Hurt, who first used electric cars, gained control of competing lines and formed the Consolidated Street Railroad Company. A forceful rival soon appeared in the person of Henry Morrill Atkinson. A Harvard-educated member of a distinguished Massachusetts family, Atkinson married Peters's youngest daughter, Anna May. In 1895, Atkinson gained control of Peters's former company, then bought out Hurt in 1902 and formed the Georgia Railway and Electric Company. Street railroads in Atlanta had moved full circle—from monopoly by Peters to monopoly by his son-in-law. Because the establishment of electric power in Atlanta was closely related to street railroads, Peters's Atlanta Street Railroad Company became the nucleus of the Georgia Power Company. Wright, "Georgia Power Company," 195-97, 203; Walter G. Cooper, *Official History of Fulton County* (Atlanta: Walter W. Brown Publishing Co., 1934) 857-58, 861; Franklin M. Garrett, *Atlanta and Environs: A Chronicle of Its People and Events* 2 vols. (Athens: University of Georgia Press, 1969) 2:426-27.

In the postwar years, a public transit system became a public necessity, especially in aiding Atlantans in getting to work. From the center of Atlanta the lines spread through the principal streets like the spokes of a wheel and held the city together. Property in central Atlanta became more valuable because it was accessible from the outside. Then, too, the street railroad eased the housing congestion near the center of town, causing Atlanta to become healthier and allowing business concentration at the core.

There was a critical connection between the street railroad and Atlanta's growth. The walking city became a suburban city. Peters pushed the lines so far out of town that some initially operated at a loss. This encouraged the extension of Atlanta's boundaries and necessitated street extensions, additional lamps, and wider police and fire protection. When he built a line to an unimproved part of the city, residential construction followed as wealthier Atlantans rushed to take advantage of the higher property values and increased social status which came from living on a streetcar route. As a result, there was a sorting of the population. Social class and the pastoral ideal were probably the two major forces generating suburban growth. The evenness of wealth in a suburb gave neighbors a sense of shared experiences and reinforced each family's efforts to pass on its values to its children. But the suburb also functioned as a psychological safety valve—aspiring poor families, should they earn enough money, could possess the symbols of success.

In the late nineteenth century, the street railroad was Atlanta's most significant franchised enterprise. Telephones remained the playthings of a few wealthy businessmen; electric lights illuminated the central city and the homes of the very rich; even gas and water lines left the lives of many residents unaffected. For all but the indigent, however, the streetcar was an indispensable part of urban life.[18]

---

[18]Blaine A. Brownell and David R. Goldfield, "Southern Urban History," *The City in Southern History*, 21; Barth, *City People*, 41, 55; Sam B. Warner, Jr., *Streetcar Suburbs: The Process of Growth in Boston, 1870-1900* (Cambridge: Harvard University Press, 1962) 2, 154, 157, 160, 162; McKelvey, *The Urbanization of America*, 87; Rabinowitz, "Continuity and Change," 98, 113-14; Richard C. Wade, "Urbanization," *The Comparative Approach to American History*, ed. C. Vann Woodward (New York: Basic Books, 1968) 192-93.

CHAPTER THIRTEEN

KIMBALL HOUSE: HOTEL PROMOTER, RAILROAD LESSEE

A tlanta was no longer a collection of hastily built stores beside a battlefield when the city ushered in the 1870s. Peters was pleased with the prosperity of the city's businesses, some of which were owned by his relatives. T. M. Clarke's hardware firm on Peachtree Street featured huge plate glass windows and central freight elevators. Thompson's Restaurant under the James Bank Block offered excellent food.[1] The new Union Passenger Depot, which again served all of the city's rail lines, accommodated endless arrivals and departures. On the site of the former Georgia Railroad Bank, where Peachtree Street crossed the railroad to become Whitehall Street, stood a new building containing several stores called the Railroad

---

[1]When Henry Grady transferred from Rome, Georgia, to Atlanta by buying into the *Herald*, the details of the deal were fixed one night in October 1872 over a bowl of oysters in Thompson's. As early as a year and a half later, in a 14 March 1874 editorial, Grady used the term "New South." Raymond B. Nixon, *Henry W. Grady: Spokesman of the New South* (New York: Alfred A. Knopf, 1943) 91, 109.

Block.[2] (The commercial center of Atlanta remained in this area around the Whitehall/Peachtree/railroad intersection during Peters's lifetime; this area is just south of today's financial district at Five Points.)

Atlanta had three hotels and a number of boardinghouses, but they were insufficient to meet demand, and the city's movers knew that a first-class hotel would add much to the wholesale trade of the city. Therefore in 1870, the highly persuasive H. I. Kimball decided to build an appropriately grand hotel. John C. Peck, who as a young farm boy in Connecticut during the 1850s had read of Peters's Angoras and was now an Atlanta building contractor, recommended the site of the burned Atlanta Hotel. Joseph Thompson still owned the lot, located on Pryor Street between Decatur and Wall and conveniently near the Passenger Depot, except for two small parcels that he had sold individually to John P. King and Peters. Thompson agreed to sell through his realtor, George W. Adair, but Kimball wanted the plots owned by King and Peters included in the deal. Adair sought out Peters who agreed with the idea and immediately gave a ninety-nine year lease. Peters then briefed King in a letter carried by a Georgia Railroad conductor to Augusta, and the following day King telegraphed his agreement to a similar lease of his property.

Kimball, who had little equity in the site, proceeded to build the largest hotel in the South. With Peck as construction contractor and Kimball as coordinator, the enterprise progressed well. Less of a dealer in "frenzied finance" than Kimball but an aggressive mover nonetheless, Peck lent stability to the undertaking. On 28 March, the day after King's telegram to Peters, Peck had one hundred men digging the foundation and promised completion of the building in October. Peters, doubtful the project could be completed so quickly, continued to visit the site daily to offer encouragement.

On 17 October, Kimball gave a dinner to celebrate the opening of the building to the public, although the hotel was only two-thirds completed. Constructed mostly of brick painted yellow with brown trim, the structure's six stories rose above the city's skyline. The interior consisted of an open lobby with the ceiling on the fourth floor. In the middle of this bustling interior court, plants and flowers surrounded a fountain twelve feet in diam-

---

[2]Arthur R. Taylor, "From the Ashes: Atlanta During Reconstruction, 1865-1876" (Ph.D. dissertation, Emory University, 1973) 61, 79-80.

eter. Gas-light chandeliers and band music dazzled guests during the evening. The hotel boasted elevators ("moving rooms"), a laundry, a central heating plant, a billiard hall, and five hundred guest rooms. Originally expected to cost $250,000, the hotel initially cost $650,000, with an additional $250,000 for furnishings, plumbing, corrections, and improvements over the next few years. The building was by far the most expensive structure in the city, accounting for nearly one-fifteenth of the assessed value of Atlanta's real estate.

The Kimball House was the pride of Atlanta. It was the mecca of all interested in public affairs. Robert Toombs, an unreconstructed Rebel, made it his second home as he sat in the lobby with a long, unlighted cigar in his mouth and harangued the men who always gathered around him. Performers of the day such as Tom Thumb and Edwin Booth provided celebrity aura during their visits. Political dynasties were established and overthrown in its rooms, commerce was regulated in its convention parlors, and leaders of education, medicine, and insurance met in its halls. The hotel symbolized the city's growth. The *Constitution* said the hostelry "means that the swaddling clothes are cast off, and the place is booked among capitalists and businessmen for a steady journey in the direction of metropolitan importance." Small wonder that Peters grasped Peck's hand in hearty congratulations upon completion of the Kimball House.[3]

Shortly after the opening of the Kimball House, circumstances transpired that caused Peters to join the management of the Western and Atlantic Railroad, and resign from the directorships of the Georgia Railroad and the Atlanta and West Point Railroad. The state-owned Western and Atlantic had been badly managed under Governor Bullock's administration and Bullock only compounded the scandal when, in a purely political appointment, he named Foster Blodgett superintendent of the road. Blodgett dismissed hundreds of Democratic employees in favor of Republicans who stole or squandered receipts and allowed glaring physical dilapidation of the entire

---

[3]John C. Peck to Nellie P. Black, 28 June 1901, in *Richard Peters: His Ancestors and Descendants*, comp. Nellie P. Black (Atlanta: Foote and Davies, 1904) 54-58; *Atlanta Constitution* (27 January, 25 March, 18 October 1870; 15 October 1871; 24 July 1874; 26 January 1879); *The Daily Atlanta Intelligencer* (18 May, 1 June 1870); Eugene M. Mitchell, "H. I. Kimball: His Career and Defense," *Atlanta Historical Bulletin* 3:15 (October 1938): 255-56; Franklin M. Garrett, *Atlanta and Environs: A Chronicle of Its People and Events* 2 vols. (Athens: University of Georgia Press, 1969) 1:835-38.

railroad. Although a relatively small line by national standards, misman-agement of the Western and Atlantic under Blodgett was probably the most monumental in American history and the worst stain of Georgia's postwar era.

Acting on the desire of most Georgians to remove the road from poli-tics, the legislature enacted a bill on 24 October 1870 to lease the company to private interests for twenty years. It was stipulated that rent paid the state could not be less than $25,000 a month, and the lessees were to give an $8,000,000 bond. Other provisions set the minimum number of lessees at seven and a majority had to have been Georgia residents for the preceding five years, which would give Georgians control of the company. No railroad companies could apply, but they could be used as security. The state prop-erty to be leased consisted of a single-track railroad 138 miles in length, with all turnouts, rolling stock, shops, depots, tools, and appurtenances of every character then in operation between Atlanta and Chattanooga.

On Christmas Eve, railmen and bankers assembled at the Kimball House to learn the results of the bidding from Bullock. The "rich man's treasure" would go to one of three bids: Dobbins, Seago and Blodgett Com-pany; William K. de Graffenreid Company; or the Brown, Cameron and Hill Company. Brown and Peters of Atlanta; John P. King of Augusta; Ben-jamin H. Hill of Athens; Alexander H. Stephens of Crawfordville; Simon Cameron of Harrisburg, Pennsylvania; and Thomas A. Scott of Philadel-phia were among those who represented the latter company's twenty-three shareholders. Peters, like most of the others, subscribed $100,000, which gave him one share in the venture. Since M. G. Dobbins and associates of-fered monthly rental of $31,000, Bullock's decision to award the lease to the Joseph E. Brown group for the minimum of $25,000 a month was a source of controversy.

A student of the South, U. B. Phillips, wrote that Bullock awarded the lease to "railroad presidents and politicians, Democrats and Carpet-Bag-gers." It is true that leading capitalists and politicians of varying shades of respectability composed the successful syndicate, yet Bullock must have noted that only a few of the Southeners had been ardent Confederates and most had cooperated with Congressional Reconstruction; another factor which undoubtedly swayed the governor was that the Brown group was widely representative of Georgia. The Dobbins group was almost entirely citizens of Atlanta and Bullock expressed doubt that the de Graffenreid Company had sufficient financial resources. The Brown combine offered as security eight railroads, the value of which exceeded $17,000,000 free from all corporate liabilities. The individuals filed affidavits, each saying he was worth $500,000 above his liabilities, and the overall individual worth was $16,000,000, with Georgians accounting for half the total amount. Bullock signed the lease to one of the strongest railroad companies ever formed in the South—in expertise and in financial resources.

A Georgian was the logical choice for president of the company. Brown had had experience with the road as governor during the war; later as Chief Justice of the Georgia Supreme Court, he had written the lease bill, and then resigned to organize his colleagues for the successful bid. Thus when the lessees assembled in Atlanta in January 1871, they elected Brown president, although he was not a professional railroad manager. Peters and five other Georgians sat as the executive committee. The by-laws stipulated that the lessees as directors would meet quarterly in Atlanta, but in practice the president plus the six-member executive committee, all elected for one-year terms, managed the company. The annual meeting itself seldom attracted many of the Northern lessees.

A major problem for the executive committee was criticism of the lease. Peters and King came under sharp attack from the stockholders of the Georgia Railroad and the Atlanta and West Point Railroad because they had used the two roads as part of the security for the lease. The two rail officials assured their stockholders that company dividends were not in danger, calling such fear of any loss as a result of the directors' action "imaginary, whimsical and fanciful." They pointed out that nearly every railroad company in the state had been offered as security for the lease because it was necessary to preserve the link with western trade by rebuilding the Western and Atlantic in the wake of Blodgett. It was apparently this issue that caused Peters to sever his connection with the two railroads which he had served so long and faithfully.[4]

---

[4]Western and Atlantic Railroad Minute Books, 27 December 1870, 10, 11 January 1871, Atlanta Historical Society; *Atlanta Constitution* (25 December 1870; 11, 12 January, 26 July 1871); U. B. Phillips, "An American State-Owned Railroad: The Western and Atlantic," *Yale Review* 15:3 (November 1906): 282; James H. Johnston, comp., *Western and Atlantic Railroad of the State of Georgia* (Atlanta: Stein Printing Co., 1931) 62; Derrell C. Roberts, *Joseph E. Brown and the Politics of Reconstruction* (Tuscaloosa: University of Alabama Press, 1973) 91-93.

Alexander H. Stephens, severely criticized for his participation in the lease, withdrew in a precipitate action that reflected unfavorably upon the other lessees. Then a joint committee of the state legislature thoroughly investigated a charge that $70,000 had been expended on the 1870 legislature to secure the lease. The results convinced the Georgia lawmakers that the charge of bribery was unfounded, although the report reflected unfavorably upon Bullock and Kimball.[5] All in all, Georgians seemed relieved that the state no longer operated the road—the prompt payment of the monthly rental, efficient management, and the rebuilding of the road by the lessees placated the public.

An inventory by the company completed 10 January 1871, listed the rolling stock as 44 engines; 193 box cars; 86 flat cars; 82 coal cars; 21 passenger cars; 8 baggage cars; 2 post-office cars; 2 express cars; and 1 derrick car. The lessees immediately ordered the laying of 26 miles of new iron, followed by the purchase of 7 new engines, 215 new box cars, and 12 new coal cars. The company was one of the first Southern roads to adopt the Westinghouse air brake, which served to reduce employee costs and the cost of livestock killed because the engineer could stop the train much faster and without a brakeman. Soon the condition of the rolling stock was some of the best in the South.[6]

With the Panic of 1873, the need for austerity confronted the company on every hand and Peters played a leading role in finding ways to curtail expenses. The tight-knit executive committee began to police accounts at least monthly, with Peters's touch evident in the strict economies, reminiscent of his service on the city council. He successfully urged economy in

---

[5]Western and Atlantic Railroad Minute Books, 11 July 1872, 15 April 1874, 4 February 1875; *Atlanta Constitution* (6, 9, 14 January 1871; 31 March 1874; 26 February 1876); Johnston, *Western and Atlantic*, 64-68, 336. Bullock, faced with imminent impeachment by the new Democratic legislature, resigned and fled the state in October 1871. Kimball's overexpansion of his many enterprises caused his Southern empire to collapse. Almost bankrupt, he returned to Chicago. In 1874 Kimball made his way back to Atlanta and invited indictment against himself for his earlier financial dealings, but no one accepted the challenge because the city had benefited from his genius for promotion. Instead, he was given a "vindication banquet" at the hotel named in his honor. Two years later Bullock was arrested in New York and returned to Georgia for trial, but was eventually acquitted in Atlanta. William Gillette, *Retreat From Reconstruction, 1869-1879* (Baton Rouge: Louisiana State University Press, 1979) 88-90; Nixon, *Henry W. Grady*, 109; Kenneth Coleman, ed., *History of Georgia* (Athens: University of Georgia Press, 1977) 214-16.

[6]Western and Atlantic Railroad Minute Books, 10 January 1871, 17 January 1872.

salaries, a reduction in the number of free passes, and a revision of the accounting procedures. This retrenchment program was initially coupled with experiments such as laying new steel rail, which was smoother and more durable, and using coal instead of wood as fuel. But as the depression deepened, the company drastically reduced repairs and other expenditures as profits evaporated during a four-year period.

Peters was president pro tem of the Western and Atlantic in 1876 when Brown was on a trip out west under a leave of absence, and that year the company increased the laying of steel rails (purchased from Andrew Carnegie's company, the J. Edgar Thomson Steel Works in Pittsburgh). Because damages paid to stock owners remained significant, the company fenced the road with barbed wire the next year to keep cattle and other animals from the track. Juries reflected a bias against large corporations by generally ruling against railroads in all types of damage cases. This and the depression disallowed net profits until 1878, when the company cleared $178,977, the first black ink in four years. With local tonnage increasing each year, the road became one of the state's strongest and most valuable transportation links.[7]

---

[7]Ibid., 1 February 1877, 7 February 1878, 6 February 1879, 5 February 1880. In the postwar period there was renewed interest in the proposed Air Line and Georgia Western railroad projects. A. S. Buford, a Virginia rail magnate, became president of the Air Line and, with federal and state aid, consolidated the line into the Atlanta and Richmond Airline Railroad Company. Completion of the road reduced the distance from Richmond to Atlanta by one hundred miles but it was controlled outside Atlanta and the city's merchants continued to complain of freight discrimination. On the other hand, the Georgia legislature abandoned the Georgia Western as a potential threat to the western trade of the Western and Atlantic. Since Peters was a director of the Western and Atlantic, he resigned as president of the Georgia Western, and the Atlanta city council and the Georgia Railroad withdrew their support from the project. In 1880 John B. Gordon, backed by a Richmond and Danville syndicate, bought the franchise and pushed construction through Birmingham, Alabama, and ultimately to the Mississippi River under the new company name of the Georgia Pacific Railway, another line unfriendly to Atlanta. Gordon resigned his United States Senate seat to Brown, evidently expecting Brown to lose interest in the competing Western and Atlantic, but with Peters in Atlanta, the state road continued under strong leadership. Council Minute Books, 4 September, 4, 11 December 1868, 31 January 1873; *The Daily Atlanta Intelligencer* (6 January 1869); *Atlanta Constitution* (5 January, 12 March 1869; 14, 24 May, 11, 20, 23 June, 1, 6, 7, 25 July, 5 August, 10 September, 29 December 1871; 6 January, 25 July 1872); *The West Point Route: A Story of the Atlanta and West Point Railroad and the Western Railroad of Alabama*, pamphlet (1954), Georgia Department of Archives and History, Atlanta; Walter G. Cooper, *Official History of Fulton County* (Atlanta: Walter W. Brown Publishing Co., 1934) 596.

The Western and Atlantic lease, by the hand of Republican Bullock, was unpopular both with a later Democratic legislature and with capitalists who were disappointed by their failure to secure the lease. Although hampered by almost fifty acts and resolutions of the legislature, the lessees demonstrated outstanding management ability. They made a profit after paying rent to the state, resisting litigation against the lease, paying claimants who had accident suits against the road, making improvements, rendering superior service to the public, and supporting worthwhile projects in Atlanta.[8] Peters, who presided over the annual election of officers, had a powerful voice in formulating company policy because two members of the executive committee plus the president, or three without the president, made a quorum, and since Brown served as a United States Senator during the 1880s, he depended heavily on Peters to manage the road. At Peters's urging, the lessees purchased additional steel rail until it stretched the entire length of the road; increased rolling stock to ten cars to the mile (the Western and Atlantic probably had as many cars as any Southern road); increased side tracking; and replaced wood bridges with iron structures.

Eventually, Peters was among the few original lessees and, as most of them or their heirs sold shares, rival roads attempted to gain control of the

---

[8]There were, of course, "the various turns of chance." The road sustained considerable loss in the spring of 1884 when a storm-washed roadbed collapsed over a distance of one-and-a-half miles near Big Shanty, including trestles over Proctor and Noonday creeks. The damage was compounded when a freight train piled into the washout. Peters rushed to the scene with Kimball and, as a large crowd gathered to view the spectacle, ordered the cargo of bacon, hay, and corn removed from the freight cars, after which the wreckage was burned to clear the site. Passengers were then hauled through the disaster area by carriage as service continued on the line. That same year a rival line, the East Tennessee, Virginia and Georgia Railroad, running from Bristol to Brunswick by way of Atlanta, ended the Western and Atlantic's monopoly, forcing the lessees to hire more agents to solicit business. Western and Atlantic Railroad Minute Books, 7 February 1884, 5 February 1885; *Atlanta Constitution* (20 April 1884).

Another major expense was the Southern gauge change in 1886 that cost the company an estimated $125,000, double the company's income for the year. The gauge of rails from Virginia to the Mississippi River was 5 feet, but throughout the rest of the country the gauge between the rails was generally a "standard" distance of 4 feet 8.5 inches. Since total rail mileage north of the Ohio River far exceeded that of the South, and since imitation of the North was consistent with New South philosophy, it was logical for the South to alter its gauge. *Atlanta Constitution* (8 April 1885); Johnston, *Western and Atlantic*, 68-69; Richard E. Prince, *Steam Locomotives and History: Georgia Railroad and West Point Railroad* (Green River WY: Privately printed, 1962) 81.

Western and Atlantic, causing the Georgia lessees to form a bare majority of 11-5/8 shares at one point. Peters successfully rallied their support, not only to keep rival rails from securing control, but also because he agreed the road should be controlled by Georgians as stipulated in the lease. When the lease expired, the company was considered to be a $6,000,000 concern and the legislature continued to lease Georgia's most productive property. Peters was a key figure in renovating the Western and Atlantic, a road crucial to Atlanta's commercial importance. The *Constitution* lauded him as one of the very best railroad men who was always considered an authority: "Whatever he has touched has prospered. He has rarely ever made a mistake—never a blunder."[9]

Sunday, 12 August 1883, was a fateful day in Atlanta. Shouts of alarm and dismay mingled with the clatter of hurried travel broke through the streets before daylight. The citizens left their beds to stare in horror at the city's symbol, the Kimball House, turning to a blackened ruin as flames consumed the structure in Atlanta's most spectacular fire since Sherman. The "front wall fell out from top to bottom with a terrible thud." There was no loss of life. The three hundred guests, aroused by an alert staff, saved some of their possessions, but none of the hotel's furnishings could be saved. One theory concerning the origin of the disaster was that a lemon dealer in one of the street-level shops had left a cigarette in some tissues which smoldered into flame. As for the efforts to extinguish the fire, the city's water supply was inadequate and the low-pressure fire hoses were unable to reach the upper stories of the building.

H. I. Kimball was in Chicago, where he was an occasional resident, but in response to a letter signed by Peters and other Atlantans, wired that he was returning immediately to the Gate City. Kimball thought $400,000 would be needed to construct a second, and this time fire-resistant, Kimball House. He wanted $100,000 of that from Atlanta citizens in the form of $50,000 in subscriptions and $50,000 in donations. A group of investors promptly organized the Kimball House Company, but it was difficult to raise that amount. Peters made a $1,000 donation while most investors subscribed to common or preferred stock. Six weeks after the fire, the total was

---

[9]*Atlanta City Directory* (1889); Western and Atlantic Railroad Minute Books, 3 February 1881, 2 February 1882, 20 September 1883, 3 February, 7 September 1887, 2 February 1888; *Atlanta Constitution* (6 November 1879; 10 March, 24 May 1882; 10 July 1887; 28 July 1888); Johnston, *Western and Atlantic*, 67-68, 334-38.

some $10,000 short of the goal and the funds leveled at that sum. Street talk began to predict failure of the enterprise. Kimball himself gloomily reported that the time for subscriptions had almost elapsed and stood ready to abandon the undertaking.

With Atlanta subscriptions at $89,000, Peters decided the situation called for his personal attention. He set up a reception for Kimball, who would work his fund-raising magic on a crowd of businessmen and public figures interested in the future of Atlanta. Peters issued the invitations, offering the hospitality of his home on Peachtree Street and, to help insure their attendance, dispatched special streetcars for their convenience.[10] As guests filled his halls and parlors, Peters called the group to order and said the object of the meeting was to promote the rebuilding of the Kimball House under Kimball's direction. Then Peters asked the architect to speak. Kimball dramatically stated that he owned no property in Atlanta, but would work from sentiment because he loved the city. He promised that when the $100,000 figure was reached he would organize further, select a contractor, and once again make Atlanta his home. Otherwise he would leave Atlanta, feeling he was not wanted. Rufus Bullock, James English, and Hugh Inman commented on the spirit of Atlanta and the need for cooperation in the rebuilding project. George W. Adair reminded everyone that without a good hotel, there would be few conventions. As if by prearrangement, Joseph E. Brown interrupted to increase his subscription, followed quickly by Peters: "I can afford to follow [former] Governor Brown, so I say that I will add a $1,000 donation." Applause led the way to more subscriptions and increasing enthusiasm.

Peters adjourned the meeting to serve champagne and total the pledges. When he called the group to order again, only $600 more was needed to

---

[10]In 1881, Peters had built a new residence outside the city limits facing Peachtree Street from the west side and bounded by Fourth, Fifth, and Cypress streets. Located at 488 Peachtree Street (now site of the First Baptist Church) on four acres of his own Land Lot 49, the imposing red-brick Victorian home had a large porch across the front and south side and was situated in the middle of the block amid oak trees. The grounds included a large frame barn and dependencies and was enclosed by a wrought-iron fence. *Atlanta Constitution* (15 June, 22 July 1880; 11 May 1882); Paul W. Miller, ed., *Atlanta: Capital of the South* (New York: O. Durrell, 1949) 202; Franklin M. Garrett, "A Short History of Land Lot 49 of the Fourteenth District of Originally Henry, Now Fulton County in Georgia," *Atlanta Historical Journal* 25 (Spring 1981): 19; William B. Williford, *Peachtree Street, Atlanta* (Athens: University of Georgia Press, 1962) 41.

reach $100,000 and Kimball called for six subscriptions of $100 each. On the call for the last $100 in stock, Edward C. Peters and W. A. Hemphill spoke simultaneously and both were entered to close the books. The meeting adjourned amid cheers of success. Adair unsuccessfully attempted to call the meeting together again to raise the entire $400,000. Kimball vowed he would rebuild by 12 August 1884, a year from the fire.[11]

On the morning of 4 October 1883, the stockholders gathered in the Chamber of Commerce Building.[12] Their purpose was to organize the company and get the project underway. Peters, one of twelve directors, also served on the by-laws committee that decided that the directors would meet daily in the editorial offices of the *Constitution*. The $400,000 building fund was greatly assisted when the Southern Railway and Steamship Association agreed to accept Kimball House bonds in payment for shipping building materials for the new hotel. Next, the directors secured leases from the owners of the lots on which the first Kimball House had stood, now totaling seven men. W. D. Grant owned three lots; Joseph Thompson three; and Peters, Joseph Thompson, Jr., Robert Toombs, John P. King, and J. T. Glenn owned one each. After these men had invested a total of $33,000 in subscriptions and donations to the second Kimball House, they were criticized for encouraging the development of their own property. However, some owners considered their subscriptions more of an obligation than an opportunity.

---

[11]Samuel P. Richards, Diary, Atlanta Historical Society; John C. Peck to Nellie P. Black, 28 June 1901, in *Richard Peters*, 55-56; *Atlanta Constitution* (30 August, 9, 11, 12, 23 September 1883); James M. Russell, "Atlanta, Gate City of the South, 1847 to 1885" (Ph.D. dissertation, Princeton University, 1971) 283; Harvie Jordan, "Burning of the H. I. Kimball House," *Atlanta Historical Bulletin* 5:22 (July 1940): 218-24.

[12]During 1883, the Board of Trade became the Chamber of Commerce, at which time Peters joined a smaller, more exclusive Commercial Club. City Hall was demolished to make way for a new state capitol building, and a Chamber of Commerce Building constructed at Pryor and Hunter streets housed city government as well as the two business clubs. When construction of the capitol began, Peters joined in a petition to the legislature requesting that Georgia granite or marble be used in the new building instead of Indiana limestone. The question of construction material received a great deal of attention, including a legislative committee study, with the result that the foundation was constructed of granite, and the walls built of brighter limestone. Completed 15 June 1889, the State Capitol is still in use on "Peters's Reserve." *Atlanta Constitution* (30 May, 21 June, 14 November 1883; 19 October 1884; 22 May, 4 July, 3 September, 25 August 1885).

For the most part, Peters and the other directors supervised separate contracts for various phases of interior construction, while Kimball attended to details. The directors had been inclined to omit fireproofing above the second story because of the cost involved, but finally they awarded a $30,000 contract to E. T. Barnum Wire and Iron Works of Detroit to install metal fixtures and wire lathing on both sides of all partitions. The idea was that in case of another fire the hotel would be slow-burning rather than completely fireproof. In a major decision involving the exterior, the directors decided that, at $10,000 in extra costs, pressed brick would be used for the entire front and sides of the hotel to add to the building's appearance.

On 12 November, clean-up of the burned ruins began. As in 1870, Kimball was coordinator and J. C. Peck was the contractor, but this time Kimball was also architect, later joined by a newly arrived architect, L. B. Wheeler. As two hundred men and forty animals began to clear the rubble, they found that the fire had banked in part of the ruins and remained so hot that workers could not complete the task until 6 December, almost four months after the fire. Finally on 12 December, a crowd gathered to insert a few nickels and dimes in an informal cornerstone ceremony. A small American flag attached to a nearby tool box flitted pitifully. Everyone was too busy for ceremonies. Work had hardly begun when severe weather delayed construction until the end of February 1884 when, in an effort to maintain the time schedule, the work force was increased to 240 men. Offers began to arrive from companies in New York, Cincinnati, and Louisville to furnish interior material and accept payment in stocks and bonds. It was estimated that the cost to the business community was $1,000 a day in lost sales until the famous hotel reopened, and it was of even greater importance that public confidence in the project be maintained. As a result, the directors worked day and night amid early optimism: "The directors all look happy and the goose hangs high."

The following spring, however, another crisis developed when subscribers, reluctant to pay because they wanted to see more progress, caused a shortage of funds. At this point Charles Beerman, director and auditor, whose firm of Scoville and Beerman had leased the hotel and posted the highest subscription of $25,000, proposed a solution. Beerman represented an unnamed syndicate of Atlanta and outside men who would provide financing for completion of the hotel, provided Atlantans created a $25,000 bond subscription. This bond was expected to reestablish Atlantans' faith and encourage outside investment. The directors accepted Beerman's proposal and started the task of fund-raising. On the night of 20 May, the directors met to total the bond subscriptions and found that they were $3,450 below the mark. Peters gave $500 more and the next day the balance was subscribed. With this latest financial crisis successfully resolved, the directors made Beerman a coordinator and increased the work force. But on 12 August 1884, the anniversary of the burning, the directors had to be content with a celebration on the roof of the unfinished hotel.[13]

On 12 January 1885, the Kimball House, Atlanta's rebuilt landmark, began partial operation. A month later Peters entertained a large group of Philadelphians on their way to New Orleans. To highlight the day, he treated the visitors from his native city to a meal at the Kimball House, where the dining room was used for the first time. Finally, on 30 April construction noises ceased and the directors celebrated with an opening gala, planned by their finance committee, including Peters, who sent invitations to every city in Georgia for an eight-hundred-seat banquet, concert, and ball.

Peters had helped provide Atlanta with three different hotels on the same plot of ground, two of which burned, dating from the antebellum Atlanta Hotel. The second Kimball House was regarded as a "regulator" of property values in downtown Atlanta, and Peters's property holdings, including ownership of part of the land on which the hotel was built, explains to some degree his motive for participating in the project. In a tightly drawn lease, he charged $100 a month for the use of his lot, accepting payment in company bonds for the first thirty months. Yet on two occasions, when many businessmen who would also benefit from the construction of the new hotel recoiled from financial commitment, Peters increased his subscription. He contributed a total of $2,500 to the undertaking, eighty percent of which was in the form of donations; his was second only to Brown's $3,500. Peters regarded the destruction of the first Kimball House a municipal tragedy and in the rebuilding effort he once again combined his quest for profit with his sense of civic pride. In October 1885, he retired from the board of directors of the second Kimball House, saying other busi-

---

[13]*Atlanta Constitution* (23 September, 5, 30 October, 11, 22, 23 November, 7, 12 December 1883; 3 January, 21 February, 20, 21, 27 May 1884; 20 October 1885); Thomas H. Morgan, "The Georgia Chapter of the American Institute of Architects," *Atlanta Historical Bulletin* 7:28 (September 1943): 144-45.

ness forced him to ask relief from further service.[14] Peters had rescued from oblivion the movement to rebuild the hotel, devoting himself to the project for two years and reaffirming Atlanta's resiliency in the process.

[14]Fulton County Deed Book RR; *Atlanta Constitution* (11 October 1884; 13 February, 20 March, 30 April 1885); Garrett, *Atlanta and Environs*, 2:60.

CHAPTER FOURTEEN

PETERS'S STOCK FARM: SCIENTIFIC STOCKMAN IN POSTBELLUM ERA

Peters waited several years after the war before concentrating on the restoration of his shattered agricultural enterprise. Seeds, supplies, and equipment were scarce, and unusual dedication and exertion were required for a new start. But Peters's plantation house was intact and so was his reputation as a livestock breeder. Probably most encouraging of all was that Peters's flock of Angoras had survived the war near Quitman and that Aaron Roff agreed to resume his duties as manager.[1] By 1870, his plantation consisted of 500 improved acres and 1,000 woodland acres, and was valued at $20,000 with implements worth another $1,000; the value of all livestock on hand was $6,000—including 7 horses and jacks, 55 cows, 4 oxen, 230 sheep, and 50 swine. He was growing several grains, plus peas, beans and Irish potatoes, and had on hand 900 pounds of wool and 500

---

[1]Farm Book, Peters Estate Collection, Atlanta Historical Society; *Southern Cultivator* 26:5 (May 1868): n.p. (advertisement), 26:6 (June 1868): n.p. (advertisement), 26:10 (October 1868): 290, 26:11 (November 1868): 330, 351; James C. Bonner, *A History of Georgia Agriculture, 1732-1860* (Athens: University of Georgia Press, 1964) 144.

pounds of butter. The estimated value of all his rural productions for the year was $7,000, including improvements and additions to stock.[2]

The revival of the Georgia State Agricultural Society's fair (held in Macon in 1869 with Peters's prominent involvement) gave fresh courage for agricultural recovery.[3] Peters, again on the executive committee, aided the society in setting up offices in the State Capitol (opera house) that included a library of 1,500 volumes, a collection of Georgia minerals, and a large table containing copies of all United States agricultural publications. To attract the state fair to Atlanta for the first time since the war, a new site was needed since the fairgrounds on East Fair Street was overrun with development. Therefore, the city purchased a 42.5 acre tract—twice the size of the old grounds—in the northwestern suburbs two miles from the center of Atlanta, and leased the new grounds to the society for improvement. The local press predicted that with "practical men such as Peters" planning the fair, "it can not fail to be a brilliant success."

Oglethorpe Park was the name given the new location. The omnipresent H. I. Kimball was placed in charge of improvements. He enclosed the grounds with a whitewashed fence and an enormous ornamental gate, and lined the drive around the interior with four hundred stalls for stock exhibits. The park included an elongated half-mile racetrack covered with white gravel, complete with a double-deck, 5,000-seat covered stadium. There were four main exhibition buildings of two stories each. In addition, there were two restaurants, and some twenty other buildings, including a skating rink, refreshment stands, cottages, and storehouses. Pleasure boats dotted three small lakes. When it was all totaled, the improvements carried a $125,000 price tag.

Good weather on opening day, 19 October 1870, brought out some 5,000 excited people who heard musical selections performed by the band from McPherson Barracks. There was a total of $50,000 in premiums and Peters took many of them, including several for Brahmin cows and Merino sheep. He swept the categories for Cashmere goats and Essex swine. His son, Edward C., exhibited some fowl, including Red Pouter, Silver Wing,

---

[2]*Ninth Census of the United States, 1870: Agriculture* (Washington, D.C.: Government Printing Office).

[3]Georgia State Agriculture Society, *Proceedings* (1869) n.p.; *Atlanta Constitution* (19 February, 12, 18 November 1869).

Fan Tail, and Jacobin pigeons, and won a premium for Muscovy ducks. Atlanta's first fair since the war was a success, despite the complaints by the more serious farmers of what they saw to be commercialism and the attendant circus atmosphere.[4]

Peters took an active part in a somewhat different fair held in October 1871 at Oglethorpe Park. The Georgia State Agricultural Society had decided to alternate fairs between Macon and Atlanta, and since 1871 was Macon's year, Atlanta sponsored a fair in combination with the Georgia Mechanical and Manufacturing Association. The agricultural society again held its fair at Oglethorpe Park during October 1872 and it was probably the most successful since the war. This resulted in part from the conciliatory spirit of W. L. Jones of the *Southern Cultivator*, who called for harmony between city and agriculture. Another reason for the success of the fair was Peters's outstanding stock shows. He outdid himself, winning two dozen awards. The *Constitution* lauded the effort which drew 15,000 to 20,000 people, adding: "Mr. Peters did his duty nobly in adding to the attractions of the fair."[5]

But the agricultural society fell on hard times during the depression of 1873-1877 and interest in fairs waned. Then, too, the state government favored the railroads with what little financial support it could offer during these times, so that the society had to depend to a great extent on the local citizens where the fairs were held. As a result, the fairs became carnivals with agriculture a sideline, which created its own tension. Too, the racetrack in Atlanta, which was associated with Kimball, continued to draw criticism. Finally, the society became rife with politics with some leaders using it as a stepping-stone to state office. The society continued to hold

---

[4]*Atlanta Constitution* (19 February, 5 March, 10 May, 11, 14, 20, 25 October 1870); Eugene M. Mitchell, "H. I. Kimball: His Career and Defense," *Atlanta Historical Bulletin* 3:15 (October 1938): 255-56; Arthur R. Taylor, "From the Ashes, Atlanta During Reconstruction, 1865-1876" (Ph.D. dissertation, Emory University, 1973) 266; E. Merton Coulter, *The South During Reconstruction 1865-77* (Baton Rouge: Louisiana State University Press, 1947) 229-30.

[5]*Southern Cultivator* 24:4 (April 1871): 154, 24:9 (September 1871): 359-60, 24:10 (October 1871): 403, 30:9 (September 1872): 356, 30:10 (October 1872): 396; *Atlanta Constitution* (17, 19 October 1871; 18 October 1872); Coulter, *South During Reconstruction*, 215-16.

fairs in Atlanta and Macon, but activities centered on field crop "best re-sults" of small farms, along with some stock, fruits, and homemaking.[6]

In his personal agricultural enterprise in Gordon County, Peters had fif-teen hands on the payroll, plus his three older sons took an active interest in the plantation. He planted eleven acres of lucerne—a perennial that could only be grown in relatively small plots because it required rich soil. But once set, lucerne remained productive fifteen or twenty years as its strong tap root sometimes penetrated six feet into the ground. Peters sowed it in drills, broadcast a top dressing, and ran a small plow between the drills. When planting red clover, often as much as 250 acres, Peters first used a drill to distribute 200 pounds per acre of pure bone dust, then sowed clover and wheat together. When the wheat was ripe, it was harvested and cattle were turned onto the clover/wheat stubble pasturage until December, when they were removed; the clover grew until it was ready for cutting that June. Peters was convinced that after three years of this treatment, alternated with a corn crop every fourth year, the land was fifty percent richer because red clover was excellent as a regenerator of land and as the basis of grain crops. He advertised some of these grains for sale, such as Red Rust Proof and White Grazing oats, and Georgia Rust Proof and Kingston White wheat, "all warranted true to name and unmixed."[7]

At times Peters had as many as 250 purebred Spanish Merinos on his plantation. He firmly believed that, crossed on the native ewe, these sheep afforded Southerners "the solution to the sheep question" by providing the best wool and mutton, with the progeny showing an improved constitution and fattening properties. But in spite of his belief that sheep husbandry of-fered the South a means of restoring broken fortunes, the industry was dying in the Cotton Belt, where wool was looked upon as a competitor to cotton.[8]

---

[6]*Southern Cultivator* 32:6 (June 1874): 250-51, 32:7 (July 1874): 258-59; Willard Range, *A Century of Georgia Agriculture, 1850-1950* (Athens: University of Georgia Press, 1954) 118-35.

[7]Henry W. Grady, "Forty Years All Told Spent in Live Stock Experiments in Georgia," *Richard Peters: His Ancestors and Descendants*, comp. Nellie P. Black (Atlanta: Foote and Davies, 1904) 35-38; *Southern Cultivator* 34:6 (June 1876): n.p. (advertisement), 35:11 (November 1877): 463, 36:10 (October 1878): n.p. (advertisement), 42:7 (July 1884): 219.

[8]Peters to John L. Hayes, January 1878, Nellie P. Black Collection, University of Geor-gia Libraries, Athens; Farm Book, Peters Estate Collection; Grady, "Forty Years in Live Stock Experiments," 41-43; *Southern Cultivator* 33:1 (January 1875): n.p. (advertisement), 33:12 (December 1875): 488-89, 35:11 (November 1877): 463-65; Coulter, *South During Reconstruction*, 227.

Peters's efforts to improve swine in the South was also a laborious task. The key traits for remunerative porkers were health, thrift, early maturity, and ease of fattening, and he felt that the Berkshire and Essex breeds exhibited these best and, therefore, continued to import them. In spite of the serene indifference in the South toward hog breeding, Peters did make some progress as revealed in a Georgia poll on swine raising. According to the poll, forty-one percent of those responding considered the Berkshire most profitable; twenty percent the Essex, and nine percent the common stock. Eighty-five percent agreed with Peters that black hogs were less susceptible to disease.[9]

One day in 1883 Peters walked up the stairs at the *Constitution* to the office of Henry Grady and the editor described his seventy-three-year-old friend as "rosy-cheeked, clear-eyed, steady-handed, breathing easily, and smiling like a boy of sixteen." The two men had become good friends and each undoubtedly realized by this time the distinct role the other was playing in the New South movement.[10] Peters had come to inform Grady of his recent sale of one hundred blooded Angora kids for a top price of $40 each, which was probably the largest lot of purebred kids ever sold in the United States. A Texas breeder bought them at Peters's plantation and assumed the risk and cost of loading and transporting the animals to Texas. Peters was quite popular with breeders in the Southwest. One Texan wrote that Peters's Angoras were "the finest goats we have ever handled and the finest in this country." Indeed, Peters considered his current bucks superior to those of Asia Minor.

Mohair, the Angora's fleece, was distinctive in the world of fabrics. It had the "aspect, feel, and lustre of silk, without its suppleness." Because the best mohair plushes were almost indestructible and highly resilient, they made the most enduring coverings for railroad seats and other furniture. Mohair was also used for pile in imitation sealskins; it was found in women's fur pieces, shawls, overcoat linings, French lace, Utrecht velvet, and

---

[9]*Southern Cultivator* 32:3 (March 1874): n.p. (advertisement), 42:5 (May 1884): 147.

[10]A few years earlier, during his first known interview of Peters, the subject had been beekeeping as practiced by Peters. Grady had suggested the interview and Peters actually blushed. But Peters had information to impart as an apiarist and granted the journalist an audience. In such a manner were brought together the practitioner and the publicist of the New South, each unequaled in his specialty. Scrapbook, Henry W. Grady Collection, Emory University, Atlanta.

because of its long luster, it was the essential material in the best carriage and lap robes.

Peters sold his Angora fleece first in England, then in New York, and finally to the Tingue Manufacturing Company of Seymour, Connecticut. He sent the entire annual clip in bales and fetched thirty to sixty cents a pound. Fleece shipped by Peters, graded during clipping into sorts of prime (side), shorts (belly, leg), and kemp (tail), was highly regarded at Tingue Manufacturing Company. A company official wrote: "no lot of mohair, in length of staple, fineness, lustre, and uniformity, comparable to it had ever come to the establishment." The Angora was also valuable for its flesh, milk, and butter, and according to Peters, the second cross of the thorough-bred buck on the common ewe produced skin valued for rugs, mats, and gloves.[11]

Peters had been one of America's foremost breeders of Brahmin cattle, but after finding the breed unsuitable to his purposes, he turned his attention more and more to the Jersey. This breed was related to the Guernsey, which developed into a larger, redder, coarser milker. On the British Island of Jersey, little attention had been paid to the color of their cattle, with the result that they were fawn, yellow, white, and black. Peters and other breeders worked to establish fawn as the solid color. The American Jersey Cattle Club, founded shortly after the war with headquarters in New York, helped carry on the work more systematically by recording pedigrees in its Herd Registry. This gave a greater reputation to the Jersey over the Guernsey and promoted improvement in the former until it was without equal as a butter cow. In one week, a Jersey might well give fifteen pounds of butter, often orange-yellow in color (Peters found that a determination of this color could usually be made beforehand by looking at the wax in the cow's ears). This amount of butter was the best ratio relative to the amount of feed consumed, plus the cream rose more quickly and separated more completely than that of other breeds. Peters believed the upkeep of a good Jersey was less than

---

[11]H. C. and J. C. Jacobs (Albany, Texas) to Peters, 6 March 1883, Peters Estate Collection; Grady, "Forty Years in Live Stock Experiments," 34, 43-44; *The Angora Goat: A Pastoral Bonanza*, comp. Virginia Angora Company (Boston: Alfred Mudge and Son, 1880) 15-16, 18-19, 34; *Atlanta Constitution* (10 May 1882); *Southern Cultivator* 38:3 (March 1880): 100; James C. Bonner, "Angora Goat: A Footnote in Southern Agricultural History," *Agriculture History* 21 (January 1947): 45; John L. Hayes, *Angora Goat: Its Origin, Culture and Products* (Cambridge: The University Press, 1882) 118-20, 123.

that of a poor one. He particularly stressed the importance of a quality bull—preferably fawn, with small horns and head, slender neck, and graceful movements. "It is hard to calculate," said Peters, "how much good a fine, vigorous Jersey bull can do in a country neighborhood."[12]

During the 1880s, Atlanta was encircled again, but this time by gentle Jerseys instead of a hostile army. Peters's interest in the breed supported a Southern Jersey boom that centered in Georgia—the "Realm of the Thoroughbreds." He and other leading breeders met in Macon on 21 March 1883 and organized the Georgia Jersey Breeders' Association. The group determined that "no Jersey cattle will be registered . . . unless they have been previously registered in the American Jersey Cattle Herd Registry." Under that rule, which protected both purchasers and sellers, it was possible to register almost four hundred Jerseys in Georgia. The state association printed a catalogue and began to hold sales in Atlanta (which had a local Jersey club), giving the assurance "that none but thoroughly acclimated cattle will be offered, and no animal that is defective will be sold under our management." Some Jerseys sold by Peters included "Pitty P." (17858), "Miss Alfonso" (21358), "Miss Linnett" (26769), "Signal's Favorite" (29504), "Waxwing" (18994), "Chestnut Pansy" (22738), and "Zangarina" (21361). He imported a number of strains—Signal, Dauncy Rioters, Coomassic, Stoke Pogis, and St. Helier. According to the *Southern Cultivator*, Peters was the most outstanding Southern cattle breeder: "The last decade developed a marked disposition to tone up our stock of every kind. And today we are making more rapid strides than any other Southern State in leavening our cattle with thoroughbred strains of blood. Col. Richard Peters, of Atlanta, was the pioneer in this."[13]

Peters was now convinced that any intelligent man could turn a profit in stock farming. Income from his plantation exceeded $8,600 in 1883. It was probably an unusually good year because of the sale of one hundred Angora kids for $4,000; the next highest income was from Jerseys—butter $1,800 and yearling bulls $800; wheat—$1,500; and Essex pigs—$500.

---

[12]*Southern Cultivator* 22:4 (April 1874): 146, 23:1 (January 1875): 19, 23:7 (July 1875): 267, 38:2 (February 1880): 77; *New Orleans Weekly Southland* (19 March 1870); Bonner, *A History of Georgia Agriculture*, 134-35.

[13]*Southern Cultivator* 41:3 (March 1883): 14, 41:4 (April 1883): 22, 42:4 (April 1884): 180, 42:5 (May 1884): 176, 44:3 (March 1886): 114, 44:10 (October 1886): 114, 45:4 (April 1887): 147, 46:4 (April 1888): xiv, 46:7 (July 1888): 294.

There were some small sales beyond these figures and family supplies such as chickens, eggs, butter, pork, and other foodstuffs from the plantation were consumed at his home in Atlanta. Yet it was hard for Peters to know if his plantation had paid over the years because he had spent almost $50,000 just for animals that could not acclimate to the Southern climate and conditions. He had also incurred additional expenses as he sought the best crops, implements, and fertilizers. His belief in diversification and improvement in the South dictated his constant policy to select the best, give customers the benefit of the doubt, and guarantee the quality of his stock.[14] In summing up what his plantation meant to him, Peters discounted the profit incentive, noting an added benefit:

> I have a fine herd of Jerseys on my place, the butter and calves from which pay the entire expenses of my farm. If I had put the same capital, skill, and energy that I have employed on my farm in any other business, I would have made more money perhaps. But I have had a great deal of pleasure. I have raised my children in health, with a knowledge of riding, driving, farming, hunting, fishing, etc., and the investment in a "fancy farm" has been, perhaps, the best of my life.[15]

Many others enjoyed Peters's "fancy farm" as it awed its continual visitors; he had built a larger house a few years after the war, known to this day in Calhoun as "the big house," where he entertained guests. Among those who enjoyed his hospitality were Atlanta's young ladies, friends of Peters's daughters, who joyfully rode in Peters's carriage drawn by his horse "Whirlwind" through the streets of Calhoun.[16] Peters sometimes invited members of the state legislature, who traveled up in the directors' car of the Western and Atlantic. This was undoubtedly good for Peters's livestock (and railroad) investments. On one such occasion, the solons were "charmed and delighted with the elegant and hearty hospitality of Mr. and Mrs. Peters" and returned to Atlanta full of admiration for the plantation and stock. The Angoras were especially impressive—"the finest animals of the kind in America." Guests realized that their host had an unblemished reputation throughout the country "for the purity of his stock and the integ-

---

[14]Grady, "Forty Years in Live Stock Experiments," 42-44.

[15]*Southern Cultivator* 40:11 (November 1882): 2-3.

[16]Jewell R. Alverson to Royce G. Shingleton, 3 March 1975; Farm Book, Peters Estate Collection; Jewell B. Reeve, *Climb the Hills of Gordon* (Privately printed, 1962) 27, 34.

rity of his dealings. He guarantees everything he sells and is able to make his guarantees good."[17]

Perhaps the most significant visitor of all was Henry Grady. In October 1884, Peters learned that his young friend was ill with fever, to which the famous editor seemed susceptible, so he went to visit. Grady awoke to see the prominent stockman standing beside his bed. Peters told him the fever was broken and the two of them should go at once to Gordon County where Grady could fully recuperate. Grady's physician agreed with Peters's prescription of fresh milk and country air in lieu of the city and newspapers. Upon arriving in Gordon County, Grady compared Peters's plantation to another continent; Atlanta seemed a million miles away. During a delightfully therapeutic week at the plantation, he wrote of country sights and sounds— the afternoon sun on the clover; at night an owl in the distance and turkeys in nearby trees; at dawn a mockingbird, quail, and a hen with chicks. Grady's breakfasts were prepared by Essex—the cook who did not know if his name signified dukes or hogs, so Grady proclaimed that he was the duke of the kitchen and his muffins tempted guests to make hogs of themselves.

Peters and his "trusted and valued agent of thirty years," Aaron Roff, took Grady on a walking tour and pointed out the finer points of various animals. The weather during the past year had been exceptionally good and every barn was overflowing with recent harvests. Peters said that after forty years, if he could have turned rainfall on and off as he did the sprinkler at his home, he could not have done better for his plantation. In years of drought or other problems, the Angoras pulled him through; he was now shipping them in ever larger numbers to Texas and New Mexico.

A dust cloud in the distance indicated that it was milking time. The cows soon came into view with "Tudora," the herd leader, first in line. As they moved through the lot and filed into separate stalls in the milking barn, Grady noted that all were Jerseys. "Alice Dunraven" walked smartly to her stall, followed by "Maude S. Helier" and "Lucy Prustey." When all thirty-eight cows were in place, Osceola and two assistants washed the udders. Then Osceola, in a white apron, took a seat beside the first cow. Grady wrote: "I just wish you could see him! With two sinewy hands and a rotary motion, the head thrown back, the foot beating time, and the milk fairly hissing into the pail, in two big streams. Three minutes to the cow, and with

---

[17]*Calhoun Times* (2 October 1879).

fine energy and abstraction, he moves from one stall to another, filling the big milk cans as he goes." Osceola could extract nearly a gallon a minute and totaled over one hundred gallons for the day's milking.

Grady's attention turned next to the plantation's butter-making process. Peters had expanded his antebellum dairy. It was now equipped with a cool, white, cement room that contained churns as well as shelves for the creaming pans. This was the domain of Rose, the dairy maid. Rose scooped the rich, yellow mantle from the pans into the churns that incorporated a new design by Peters—there were no dashers, instead the churns were hung between bars and the butter made by a swinging motion. He considered this unusual churning action superior to any already patented. The butter came quickly and each churning produced twenty pounds—"yellow as gold and fragrant as clover blossoms." Some cows produced over three pounds of butter a day, although none had been tested for record. For market, Peters divided the butter into one-pound lots wrapped in cheesecloth and each year he sold four to six thousand pounds at forty cents a pound.

Although Peters sold butter to defray the plantation's expenses, producing quality breeding stock was his principle objective. In addition to the thirty-eight Jersey milkers, Peters had a score of heifers, numerous calves, some old cows in retirement, twelve young bulls, and a few mature bulls. The herd, over one hundred in all, mostly by Signal and all registered, was divided and kept in separate fields according to classes. Peters could be seen moving from field to field all hours of the day. He carefully noted the points of each animal so that he could breed to remove weaknesses and continued to improve his herd each year regardless of sacrifice or expense. The heifers sired by his most famous bull, Signal, (nearly all were noted as butter-makers) became favorites in America, attesting to his philosophy that "the bull is half the herd."[18]

After this visit, Grady was fond of talking about his "dream farm." He used "the farm" in some of his speeches and even incorporated it into his office routine. His activities increased to such an extent that he employed a private secretary who learned to manipulate one of the first typewriters in Atlanta. When the pressure of scores of callers forced Grady to lock his of-

---

[18]Henry W. Grady, "A Rural Retreat," *Atlanta Constitution* (12 October 1884); Grady, "Forty Years in Live Stock Experiments," 38-41. Peters's plantation during the late nineteenth century was referred to as Belmont Stock Farm, Othcaloga Stock Farm, Jersey Farms, and finally Richard Peters's Stock Farm.

fice door, he left instructions to tell all visitors that he had "gone to the farm."[19]

Grady saw in Peters evidence that the South's farm problems were being solved. Peters had "the heart, the head, and the pen" for agricultural improvement, especially diversification. However, scientific farming required greater efforts than most Southerners at the time were willing to exert. The existing system of agriculture resulted in very low quality stock, a situation made worse by a general distrust by farmers of books, schools, science, knowledge, and progress. Generally, mass education was needed to fight the high rate of Southern illiteracy. Slowly, the journals, societies, agricultural departments, and new agencies led to long overdue improvements; Peters's individual efforts did much to lay the foundation for this progress. Long before the Civil War there had been "the Peters's blood of the Revolution working agriculturally in Georgia, transplanted from the land of Quaker habits and industries." Until the end of his life Peters promoted scientific agriculture. In experiments, "suffice it to say that as he has left the problem, you will rarely find one rash enough to challenge any conclusion at which he arrived."[20]

---

[19]Raymond B. Nixon, *Henry W. Grady: Spokesman of the New South* (New York: Alfred A. Knopf, 1943) 221-22, 284. Tom Watson, the future Populist, "with a fire in his eye and mutiny in his voice," gave a biting criticism of Grady's "dream farm:" "In Grady's farm life there are no poor cows. They are all fat! Their bells tinkle musically in clover scented meadows and all you've got to do is hold a pan under the udder and you catch it full of golden butter.

"In real life we find the poor old Brindle cow with wolves in her back and 'hollow horn' on her head and she always wants to back up where the wind won't play a tune on her ribs. . . ." C. Vann Woodward, *Tom Watson: Agrarian Rebel* (New York: Oxford University Press, 1963) 126-27.

[20]Georgia State Agricultural Society, *Transactions* (August 1889) 692; *Southern Cultivator* 48:3 (March 1889): 129; Range, *Century of Georgia Agriculture*, 118-35; E. Merton Coulter, *Georgia: A Short History* (Chapel Hill: University of North Carolina, 1960) 269.

CHAPTER FIFTEEN

"WORLD'S FAIR": COTTON EXPOSITION, INDUSTRY ADVOCATE

N ew South ideologists believed their region's single asset to be her abundant natural resources and they directed glowing descriptions of these natural advantages to the Northern capitalists. Southerners were urged to express their anger against the North by outproducing it in industry and agriculture. This would promote regional industrialism and concilia- tion in the guise of Southern nationalism.[1] "Consequently," wrote William I. Hair, "emotional as well as practical arguments were used on behalf of industrialization; it was pictured as a sort of nonviolent continuation of the Civil War."[2]

Although the destruction of the arsenal, railroad shops, foundries, and rolling mill had checked Atlanta's industrial expansion, the idea that in- dustry must be the handmaiden of agriculture dominated the thinking of

---

[1]Jonathan Wiener, *Social Origins of the New South: Alabama, 1860-1885* (Baton Rouge: Louisiana State University Press, 1978) 191-95, 213.

[2]William Ivy Hair, *Bourbonism and Agrarian Protest: Louisiana Politics, 1877-1900* (Baton Rouge: Louisiana State University Press, 1969) 56.

men like Peters. They had been impressed with Southern industrialist William Gregg, who predicted on the eve of the war in Atlanta at the meeting of the Manufacturing and Direct Trade Association of the Confederate States that the city would soon become "a great center of manufacturing." Peters was chiefly interested in promoting cotton factories to preclude shipping cotton to the North to be repurchased in manufactured form and during the 1870s he became a director of such a project that sputtered through the depression decade. Although a strong group of Georgians backed the venture, expectations faded when subscriptions amounted to only $100,000; the directors insisted on a $250,000 minimum capitalization.

There were complaints that the older men such as Peters, who had served well in the past but were now "old and tired" and thus responsible for the lack of subscriptions, should give way to men who were enthusiastically in favor of the factory. In the wake of this criticism, Peters, who thought the project should be delayed until economic conditions were more favorable anyway, resigned from the board of directors. The magnetic H. I. Kimball became president of the Manufacturers' Association and began work for the $250,000 subscription. The new directors quickly learned that Peters had been realistic—the depression hurt the subscription effort, cotton goods were not selling well, and Kimball was personally controversial. Although the company purchased a construction site at Marietta and Magnolia streets near the Western and Atlantic Railroad, paying co-owners Peters and George W. Adair $10,000 for the property, the project soon faltered for the second time. When subscriptions lagged, Kimball became despondent; after dissension erupted among the officers, he quit the project.

When the depression relaxed its grip, Peters believed the time was right for the factory to become a reality and participated in the final push to success. At a reorganizational meeting in June 1878, he first determined that a majority of the stock was represented, after which the stockholders declared the existing board of directors defunct and elected a new board, including Peters. The new directors met after the stockholder's meeting, ordered the subscription books reopened, and elected Edward E. Rawson, one of the original directors, president. Again, different locations were investigated, with Rawson reporting on the suitability of each. The site selected was the original tract, which placed the factory conveniently near a major railroad. After many vicissitudes, the Atlanta Cotton Factory began production the following year at Marietta and Magnolia streets and developed into an important Atlanta industry.[3]

It was clear that the industrial promise of the city and region could be fulfilled only by adequate capital investment, which meant Northern money. To create the confidence and enthusiasm for that investment, Peters and other Atlantans staged the International Cotton Exposition.[4] In August 1880, Boston economist Edward Atkinson had suggested an exposition devoted exclusively to cotton in order to publicize the value of the fiber; he spoke on the subject in Atlanta. The *Constitution* picked up the idea and promoted the exposition as an exhibit for "tools, methods, products, and processes affecting the growth and culture of cotton." The cotton planter, cotton manufacturer, and implement maker would be brought together, which in turn would advance economic union between the North and South.[5] For a city the size of Atlanta, it was an ambitious undertaking.

Peters lent his influence to the project when he commented during a press interview that the exposition was an excellent idea, but that preparations would take at least a year. He suggested that it be held in October 1881 at Oglethorpe Park in Atlanta. The Georgia Stock and Fair Association had held a series of fairs in Oglethorpe Park, and since Peters was a director of

[3]Fulton County Deed Book W; *Daily Atlanta Intelligencer* (3 March, 14 July, 11 August 1869); *Weekly Atlanta Intelligencer* (23 June 1869); *Atlanta Constitution* (5 November 1872; 16, 28 January 1873; 7 February, 29 March 1874; 5, 6 January, 25 February 1875; 8 June 1878); Franklin M. Garrett, *Atlanta and Environs: A Chronicle of Its People and Events* 2 vols. (Athens: University of Georgia Press, 1969) 1:909; Thomas H. Martin, *Atlanta and Its Builders: A Comprehensive History of the Gate City of the South* 2 vols. (Atlanta: Century Memorial Publishing Co., 1902) 2:381.

[4]David Goldfield has confirmed that during urban rebuilding of the late 1860s and 1870s, Northern capital was scarce: "Atlanta, the South's most spectacular example of urban resurrection, achieved much of its rebirth from local capital—an impressive achievement for a capital-poor region." *Cotton Fields and Skyscrapers: Southern City and Region, 1607-1980* (Baton Rouge: Louisiana State University Press, 1982) 120-21. The depression of the 1870s partly explains this lack of Northern capital. C. Vann Woodward, *Origins of the New South, 1877-1913* (Baton Rouge: Louisiana State University Press, 1964) 113.

[5]Economic union between North and South had received a boost in March 1880 when Cincinnati merchants, as part of their effort to tap Southern trade, held a grand banquet. Up from the South to be wined and dined in Cincinnati's Music Hall came apostles of the New South, including Peters. Jewell R. Alverson to Royce G. Shingleton, 3 March 1975; George R. Woolfolk, *The Cotton Regency: The Northern Merchants and Reconstruction, 1865-1880* (New York: Bookman Associates, 1958) 173.

the Western and Atlantic Railroad and president of the Atlanta Street Railroad, both of which served the park, and a vice-president of the fair association, he was not indifferent to the site. Furthermore, in addition to being attractive and accessible, it was the city's only park.[6]

When a citizen's meeting manifested sufficient interest to proceed with the project, Peters joined a group of corporators who obtained a court charter that specified $100,000 in capital stock. On 23 February 1881, in the office of the Board of Trade, he was elected to a temporary management group called the Executive Committee of the International Cotton Exposition Company. Kimball, chairman of the management group, sounded the call for action because manufacturers were already applying for space to exhibit their products. At a manager's meeting in Kimball's office two days later, Peters took a seat on a seven-member locating committee that on 1 March named Oglethorpe Park as the site. Shortly afterwards, with the approval of the city, the managers leased the park from the Georgia Stock and Fair Association, effective 1 April 1881 to 1 February 1882, with an additional two months to remove buildings from the grounds if needed.[7]

As plans developed to pay homage to cotton, Peters played a significant role in expanding the exposition beyond its original theme. The managers offered cash prizes for the best half-acre of cotton grown on the grounds, which gave fertilizer manufacturers and growers "with peculiar notions of cultivating the staple" an opportunity to test their methods. Entrants received a plot of ground at the site and Peters aided in establishing rules for the judging. But when United States Commissioner of Agriculture George B. Loring urged that other crops be grown as well, the managers faced a dilemma. Since Peters had a national reputation as a planter, he was one of those the managers asked to respond to Loring's request. Peters's belief in agricultural diversification influenced the results. In addition to growing different varieties of cotton, the managers decided to exhibit other Southern products, including tobacco, rice, sugar, hemp, jute, and silk, and all the

[6]*Atlanta City Directory* (1871); *Atlanta Constitution* (29, 31 August 1880); James M. Russell, "Atlanta, Gate City of the South, 1847-1885" (Ph.D. dissertation, Princeton University, 1971) 127-28, 135; Walter G. Cooper, *Official History of Fulton County* (Atlanta: Walter W. Brown Publishing Co., 1934) 301-304.

[7]Atlanta City Council Minute Books, 3 June 1878, 21 March 1881; *Atlanta Constitution* (24, 26 February, 1 March 1881); Wallace P. Reed, *History of Atlanta, Georgia, with Illustrations and Biographical Sketches of Some of Its Prominent Men and Pioneers* (Syracuse: D. Mason Co., 1889) 472-76.

machinery used in their culture and manufacture. The exposition was now truly a New South project.

During the second week of March 1881, the managers opened the subscription books in all the banking and business houses in the city. To demonstrate their support of the enterprise, Atlantans had to buy $35,000 of the $100,000 capital stock. Shares were $100 each. Subscriptions were to be paid in four installments of twenty-five percent each and could be called by the managers after ten days notice. Two groups canvassed the city and used as selling points the facts that visitors from the North would crowd into Atlanta, the hotels would be full, the railroads profitable—all in all, the undertaking represented "a grand enterprise and great opportunity for Atlanta." Peters, who worked the east side, was considered one of the more conservative managers, but he did not hesitate to say that the exposition would be a financial success, making investment in capital stock profitable. Cotton brokers, hotels, and railroads (notably the Western and Atlantic) naturally represented the largest subscribers, although many individuals purchased one or two shares each. The Atlanta Street Railroad represented five shares and Peters personally purchased five shares.[8]

Atlantans bought their portion of the total stock in one day and the managers were encouraged to send Kimball, the obvious choice, to promote the fair in Northern cities. In the lobby of a New York hotel, a reporter asked Kimball for the dates of the exposition. Although Peters's suggestion of October had been generally accepted, the exact dates had not been decided, but Kimball, according to his account, believed it would never do to hesitate, so he looked at a calendar and said "the exposition will open on the 5th of October and close on the 31st of December," fixing the dates for the exposition. When people in Louisville, Memphis, and New Orleans began to suggest that their city host the fair, Kimball successfully portrayed Atlanta as a rail center and heart of the Southern cotton belt. In stock purchases, New York led Northern cities with 253 shares; Cincinnati was second with 79; Boston had 63; Baltimore 48; and 43 were sold in Philadelphia.[9]

---

[8]*Atlanta Constitution* (3, 9, 10, 15, 16 March 1881); Southern Railway, "The Mill that Began as a World's Fair," *Ties* (July 1962): 11-13.

[9]*Atlanta Constitution* (10 January 1884); Reed, *History of Atlanta*, 472-76. Grady had no official position in the exposition company, but aided Kimball in New York and provided publicity for the exposition. The biggest story in the successful fund-raising campaign was that General Sherman, who had burned Atlanta, made a $2,000 subscription. Raymond B. Nixon, *Henry W. Grady: Spokesman of the New South* (New York: Alfred A. Knopf, 1943) 185.

Because of his "open-sesame" effect in raising funds and his genuine organizational ability, Kimball was named chief executive officer to attend to details under the managers with the title Director General. Joseph E. Brown received the honorary title of president. The managers organized into a permanent executive committee and, to secure harmonious and effective administration of the preparations, they created a host of sub-committees called departments: admission and protection; agriculture; audit; awards; construction; engineering and machinery; foreign; installation of exhibits; minerals and wood; publications; public comfort; and transportation. These departments, which reflect the extent of the undertaking, opened their headquarters on the grounds. Peters remained on the executive committee and was a member of the transportation department (located in the Exposition Railroad Station), which superintended the movement of goods and visitors.

After reorganization, the executive committee met each Tuesday and Friday to push the work. The committee set up telephone communications between the city and the park; decided on electric lights for the grounds and buildings; mailed thousands of publicity pamphlets; and sent an invitation to President James A. Garfield. On 30 May, they awarded the contract for the main building. To be shaped like a giant cross, each of four wings had staggered completion dates, aimed for 15 September, when the entire structure would take final form. During the spring and summer, Oglethorpe Park echoed to the sounds of hammer and saw, while numerous varieties of crops and shrubs reached for the sun. Peters persuaded his fellow Western and Atlantic lessees to construct a rail spur into the grounds and readied his street railroad by acquiring thirteen new cars and one hundred horses and mules to move thousands of visitors between Atlanta and the south gate of the park.

By July the only problem was the city's inadequate hotel accommodations. To solve the problem, Atlantans planned to house many of the visitors in private homes, which had the further advantage of allowing Northerners to observe Southern customs firsthand. The executive committee also decided to build a temporary hotel at the site. Plans called for two hundred guest rooms in a building that the committee estimated would cost $30,000; they were shocked by construction bids of up to $60,000. The matter was about to be tabled in despair when Peters asked for time to consult with J. C. Peck. The contractor said he had not made an estimate, but had looked over the plans and thought he could modify them to reduce the cost; he also believed that he would have time to build, provided the weather remained favorable. The committee gave unanimous consent to Peters's suggestion that Peck take the contract, and in forty-three days Peck built the Exposition Hotel at a cost of less than $20,000. It was located across the Western and Atlantic tracks from the park where Civil War rifle pits were still visible at nearby Fort "X," part of the Confederate defense entrenchments laid out in 1864 by L. P. Grant. Northern interests also helped alleviate the problem. From New Jersey came a large tent hotel and private encampments dotted the area near the grounds, including one built by a New York banking firm for its employees.[10]

Soon plans began to focus on opening day. On 10 September, the executive committee closed the gates to the grounds to expedite final preparations. A "Hallelujah Chorus" of over five hundred vocalists from Atlanta and neighboring towns began practice, accompanied by the 5th United States Artillery Band. The city council allowed bunting to be hung over the streets, and schools and businesses prepared to close. A citizens committee joined the executive committee to welcome visitors and cautioned Atlantans against charging high prices. A week before opening day, the executive committee toured the grounds and accepted the buildings from the contractors.

Opening day on 5 October began with a parade through Atlanta. President Garfield had been slain by an assassin's bullet, but Alfred H. Colquitt, president of the exposition (who had replaced Brown), Kimball, members of the executive committee, and an array of guests, including Senator Zebulon Vance of North Carolina and Senator Daniel W. Voorhees of Indiana, rode ceremoniously to the park. At the grounds the chorus—which had grown to nearly one thousand voices—employees in special uniforms, and speeches greeted the crowd of eight thousand that passed through the tall entrance gate. Paul Hamilton Hayne, laureate of the South, wrote "The Exposition Ode," a poem that was read following Colquitt's welcome. As the contribution of Southern literature to the occasion, it was a long poem of two hundred lines that praised the courage, energy, and perseverance of

---

[10]Atlanta City Council Minute Books, 7 October 1881; John C. Peck to Nellie P. Black, 28 June 1901, in *Richard Peters: His Ancestors and Descendants*, comp. Nellie P. Black (Atlanta: Foote and Davies, 1904) 56-58; *Atlanta Constitution* (29 March, 30 April, 7, 31 May, 2 June, 3, 24 July, 12, 24 September, 7 October 1881); David G. Chollet, "Advance and Retreat: Rage or Reason?" *Atlanta Historical Bulletin* 20:1 (Spring 1976): 57, 59.

the people of Atlanta and, by extension, the South and forecast a glorious future for the New South.

The visitors looked in wonder at the great fair. In addition to the main building, there were agricultural, carriage, art, horticultural, and railroad buildings, restaurants, and other halls. Three great steam engines drove the shafting for thousands of wheels throughout the twenty acres of exhibition space. The South was represented by more than half of the 1,113 exhibits from across the United States and seven foreign countries.[11] Exhibits included cotton manufacturing equipment, with antique and modern looms placed side by side for contrast. There were also fire extinguishers, silk goods, engraved glass, saws, sewing machines, builders' supplies, brass goods, firearms, typewriters, a soda-water apparatus, minerals, wood products, a barbed-wire manufacturing machine, art, and other exhibits, some of which had been displayed at the 1876 Philadelphia Centennial.[12]

Peters continued to work for the success of the exposition by serving on a committee to entertain guests of honor. Eight Southern governors attended on Governors' Day. General William T. Sherman and his staff were prominent visitors. Special excursions representing many large Northern and Southern cities came and went, and three Southern state legislatures attended as special groups. Interest was so great that twenty newspaper journalists from leading American dailies—the largest group of correspondents ever to visit Atlanta—enjoyed a banquet with the executive committee at the Exposition Hotel.[13]

"Thoroughly identified with the culture of fine stock," Peters won premiums against national competition. In addition to his Jerseys, he took prizes for samples of his experiments with hemp and ramie used in the manufacture of rope and bagging. He hoped ramie would replace cotton, but it

---

[11]H. I. Kimball, *International Cotton Exposition, 1881: Report of the Director General* (New York: D. Appleton and Co., 1882) 70-80, 171; Atlanta City Council Minute Books, 19 September 1881; *Atlanta Constitution* (9 September, 5, 7 October 1881); Wayne Mixon, *Southern Writers and the New South Movement, 1865-1913* (Chapel Hill: University of North Carolina Press, 1980) 15-17.

[12]*Atlanta Constitution* (16, 19 September 1881); Henry W. Grady, "Cotton and Its Kingdom," *Harper's Magazine* 63 (October 1881): 732.

[13]Nixon, *Henry W. Grady*, 185, 190.

did not catch on except to a limited extent in southern Florida.[14] One of the Angoras that Peters exhibited was the famous "Mahomet." Imported the year before along with a few ewes from the Geredeh region of Asia Minor, "Mahomet" was a prized buck that would add weight and value to American fleece. Peters had made arrangements for his importation with the aid of a contact in Boston who worked through a commercial house with a branch in Constantinople and a "confidential agent" in Angora (Ankara), probably the British vice-counsul, who had the necessary authorization from the Sultan of the Turkish empire—"the exclusive privilege of entering the Geredeh country with armed police, to secure the animals." Guards transported the animals several hundred miles from the interior in wicker baskets slung across the backs of beasts of burden. When exhibited at the exposition, "Mahomet" and his female companions "excited universal admiration."[15]

When the exposition closed on 31 December, paid attendance stood at 290,038, with another 91,520 admitted free, for an average daily attendance of 3,816. Attendance the first six weeks was disappointing, but all debts were paid after what at first appeared to be a financial disaster. Treasurer Samuel Inman's final figures to the executive committee the following spring showed a total income of approximately $263,000 and disburse-

---

[14]Jewell R. Alverson to Royce G. Shingleton, 3 March 1975; *Atlanta Constitution* (20 February 1869; 4 November 1881); *Southern Cultivator* 25:12 (December 1867): 392.

[15]*Southern Cultivator* 40:1 (January 1882): 19; James C. Bonner, "Angora Goat: A Footnote in Southern Agricultural History," *Agriculture History* 21 (January 1947): 19, 21-22; John L. Hayes, *Angora Goat: Its Origin, Culture and Products* (Cambridge: The University Press, 1882) 36-37. At the time, Peters was involved in a plan for a "pastoral bonanza" known as the Virginia Angora Company. The company consisted of 160 square miles that spilled across the borderlands of Virginia and West Virginia, a mountain region that, according to Peters, was a counterpart in soil and climate of the Angora habitat in Asia Minor. "Under certain circumstances," wrote Peters, "I might be persuaded to allow the removal of my flock" to Virginia. He went so far as to "hold off" his customers until he knew the result of the subscription effort—which apparently ran into trouble. "I should deeply regret to drop the enterprise," Peters wrote. "I honestly believe it could be made not only a paying institution to the stockholders, but will become the great U.S. center for the distribution of Angoras, both American and Asiatic." Yet shortly after the International Cotton Exposition, the company failed, partly because of a decline in the value of mohair. Peters must have imported "Mahomet" and several ewes for the mountain venture and retained possession of the goats when the undertaking did not materialize. Charter of the Virginia Angora Company, Peters Estate Collection, Atlanta Historical Society; Hayes, *Angora Goat*, 19-24, 29, 35, 38.

ments of $260,000, which left only $3,000 net profit. Yet some subscribers, particularly the institutional ones such as railroads, reaped profits from the added patronage.[16]

The International Cotton Exposition of 1881 was a sound investment in the future of the region and left no doubt that the depression had ended. It promoted self-study; it provided an opportunity to display products and compare methods; it was a lesson in regional economics and a stimulation to Southern textile manufacturing that amounted to a veritable cotton mill crusade; and it was a tremendous boost to morale. The men who undertook the enterprise at a time of reduced interest in state and local fairs gave impetus to the material reconstruction of the South and spiritual union between the sections. Peters's opinion carried a great deal of weight on the executive committee, where his quiet and pleasant words often brought order out of chaos. Arriving promptly and regularly for meetings, his cool judgment modified and carried to success some of the finest schemes of the exposition, which were considered wild when first mentioned by Kimball. The result was an early and impressive demonstration of the New South movement.

The empty exposition buildings presented an opportunity to create another cotton mill. The executive committee at first hoped to lure industry from New England, but Edward Atkinson, the originator of the exposition, opposed the idea and refused to recommend capital investment in Southern cotton mills; he thought the South should continue to grow, gin, and bale the fiber only, while the spindles should remain in the North. Therefore, the executive committee, after setting aside a proposal by Kimball to establish small industrial shops in the main building, began to view with favor an offer by Frank P. Rice and Robert H. Richards, who represented an investment syndicate of men pledging $10,000 each to buy and operate a mill. As a member of the executive committee, Peters was both a potential seller and buyer: "I will subscribe to a cotton factory with such men as Rice and Richards, and it will do more for Atlanta to get up a factory . . . than anything that can be done." Peters continued, saying that "it has been demonstrated that steam, where coal can be had for three dollars a ton, is cheaper than

---

[16]Kimball, *International Cotton Exposition*, 368-69; *Atlanta Constitution* (5, 7, October 1881; 6 January, 4 March, 24 April 1882). Nixon's figures include a $20,000 net profit. *Henry W. Grady*, 191.

water power. We have the healthiest climate in the South, and we only need to start the ball and Atlanta will have 100,000 inhabitants in less than ten years." Always the promoter, Peters was overly optimistic in his prediction of population growth.[17]

With Peters's strong backing from different vantage points, the investors closed the deal with the executive committee for the buildings, with the city (which owned the park grounds) for the site, and also purchased controlling interest in the Georgia Stock and Fair Association, which had sixteen years left on its lease of the park. On 4 March 1882 the investors, including Peters and Edward C. Peters, received a court charter for the Exposition Cotton Mills with $250,000 capital stock. The factory was to manufacture "cotton, wool, hemp, and other fibrous material into yarn, cloth, bagging, sacks, rope, and similar products, and to prepare the same for market and sale by proper labor thereon, such as bleaching, dyeing [and] printing." Since the Exposition Hotel provided convenient housing for the workers, little work was necessary to begin operations, and only one month after the charter was granted, the Exposition Cotton Mills began manufacturing cotton goods, for sale mostly in the South and China. The mill expanded rapidly and soon other buildings overshadowed the original structure. For nearly a century the mill that began as a world's fair remained a monument to the exposition and demonstrated that the cotton milling industry could succeed on a large scale in the South.[18]

---

[17]Fulton County Deed Book JJ; *The Exposition Cotton Mills, Seventieth Anniversary, 1882-1952* (Atlanta: Privately printed, 1952) n.p.; *Atlanta Constitution* (29 March 1881; 10, 11 January 1882).

[18]Atlanta City Council Minute Books, 2 January 1881; *Atlanta Constitution* (11, 15, 17, 24 January, 4, 12 March 1882). At the same time that the Exposition Cotton Mills began operation, a third cotton factory was going up in the eastern suburbs, built by the firm of Elsas and May near Oakland Cemetery and named the Fulton County Spinning Company. Other Atlanta factories during the 1880s produced glass, excelsior, soap, furniture, hardware, spices, vinegar, cottonseed oil, razors, sewing machines, gold watches, and pianos. However, this did not mean that Atlanta was becoming an industrial city. In 1890 the city's 410 industries employed 8,684 workers and its manufactured products were valued at only $13,074,037, with the lack of cheap iron and coal under freight discrimination the significant restraining factors. Nixon, *Henry W. Grady*, 282; Howard N. Rabinowitz, "Continuity and Change: Southern Urban Development, 1860-1900," *The City in Southern History: The Growth of Urban Civilization in the South*, ed. Blaine A. Brownell and David R. Goldfield (Port Washington: Kennikat Press, 1977) 109; Russell, "Atlanta," 243-44.

CHAPTER SIXTEEN

SUNSET:
HIS FINAL YEARS

During the 1880s, Peters developed his property adjacent to his Peachtree Street home. This land consisted mainly of his two Land Lots—about four hundred acres, part of which extended beyond the city limits. Observing that Peachtree Road north of Atlanta was "rugged and roundabout," even though it ran mostly through open country, he successfully petitioned Fulton County to straighten the road. The vicinity near 10th Street—called Tight Squeeze because it was difficult to get through it safely—had been inhabited by undesirable characters since the war, but upon completion of the project, which included filling a thirty-feet-deep ravine between 10th and 11th streets, the section reflected its improved status through its new name, Blooming Hill. With the road macadamized and the street railroad extended, the entire area became a pleasant suburb. Aside from postwar rebuilding, this was Atlanta's first urban renewal project.[1]

---

[1]Fulton County Commissioners of Roads and Revenues, Minute Book A, May 1881-September 1886, Fulton County Administration Building, Atlanta; *Atlanta City Directory* (1883); *Atlanta Constitution* (10 April 1883; 10 February 1886); First National Bank, *Atlanta Resurgens* (privately printed, n.d.) 35.

While improving the surroundings out Peachtree Road, Peters also developed his property to the west. Until 1882 he sold house lots mostly from Land Lot 49, but that year he turned his attention to adjoining Land Lot 80 and had some lots surveyed for sale at West Peachtree and North Avenue. A novel feature was that only alternate lots would be sold and, since each lot fronted about one hundred feet, the procedure allowed aesthetic enhancement after construction. This northern suburb was sometimes referred to as Petersburg.[2]

Peters planned the streets running through his Land Lots, petitioning the city council to have various streets extended and connected. At Mary Jane's suggestion, he adopted names for these north-south streets that were similar to those of his native Philadelphia, names that were also in keeping with the existing Peachtree Street—Myrtle, Cypress, Cherry, Juniper, and Plum. He gave those running east and west a number, beginning with Third Street because the first two, North Avenue and Ponce de Leon, had already been named.

Perhaps Peters's real estate interests explain his service as a Fulton County commissioner in 1882-1883. The group occupied the first Fulton County Courthouse, an ornate structure of red brick that stood at Pryor and Hunter (site of the present courthouse). These early commissioners were lauded as being "judicious in their purchases and avoiding extravagances," a practice that soon retired the $40,000 bond issue for the new courthouse. Two noticeable improvements occurred in the northern environs during Peters's term: the commission approved a contract with detailed specifications—perhaps a result of Peters's engineering skills—for repairs to Moore's Mill Bridge over Peachtree Creek, and another for a new bridge over Clear Creek. Partly as a result of Peters's efforts, the increase in value of his urban property more than compensated for the decline in value of his farmland.[3]

Because Peters thought of his property in terms of planned development, he was receptive when the ubiquitous Kimball advanced a land de-

---

[2]Atlanta City Council Minute Books, 5, 19 September 1881; *Atlanta Constitution* (24 July 1872; 6 May 1882); Louise Black MacDougald, "My Seventh Move," *Atlanta Historical Bulletin* 32:8 (December 1947): 35.

[3]Fulton County Commissioners, Minute Book A; *Atlanta Constitution* (5 January 1882; 15 September, 4 October 1883; 10 January 1886).

velopment scheme patterned after the Chicago suburb of Pullman, apparently the first of its kind in the South. Kimball wanted to build a suburb where "every lick struck, every clod of dirt moved, and every shrub planted, has its relation to the whole." By 1884, Atlanta had a population in excess of 50,000 and seemed ready for such an ornament. Since the highest increment occurred on land that was in the path of the population movement, Kimball and real estate auctioneer Adair carefully studied maps of Atlanta and visited several potential sites in different sections of the city before deciding on a portion of Petersburg. This "high, rolling and commanding" land, consisting basically of Peters's Land Lot 80 that extended along West Peachtree from North Avenue to Eighth Street, became Atlanta's first planned suburban subdivision.

The trio of Peters, Kimball, and Adair organized under the corporate name of the Peters Park Improvement Company. Capitalized at $300,000, the company sold a $230,000 enrollment chiefly because Peters took 1,980 shares, valued at $198,000, which he received as a result of his transfer of 198 acres to this company. A land-purchase fund (the company later purchased a few additional acres to bring the total to 216) and an improvement fund were set aside and the unsubscribed portion of the stock formed a reserve fund to be used at the discretion of the stockholders. Peters was president of the company, J. W. Culpepper was secretary-treasurer, and Kimball was the general manager.

An important meeting took place on the evening of 27 December 1884 when the stockholders of the company met in the *Constitution* office building to consider the plans of the park's designers. N. F. Barrett of New York, the company's landscape architect, began by saying that with modest expenditures the development could excel any in the United States. His plans called for a large mile-long park on the highest elevation, which would contain a central carriage course with a magnificent view. Barrett also wanted several smaller parks of one to four acres each to give the community a garden quality. Other land was reserved for houses, churches, schools, florists, a nursery, club stables, and markets. Located between Peachtree Street on the east and Marietta Street on the west—two improved streets with a streetcar line on each—the subdivision already had fine residences nearby, yet property owners near the main entrance created a fund to begin beautification of North Avenue from Peachtree Street to the main entrance at North Avenue and West Peachtree Street. The drive out Peachtree Street from the center of the city to the subdivision was already the most scenic in Atlanta, a factor that affirmed the choice of location.

No streets inside the subdivision had yet been completed, but R. M. Clayton of Atlanta, the company's civil engineer, anticipated a great deal of progress during the next few months as he worked from a stone quarry on the property. First, the sewage, gas, water, and telephone ducts had to be completed, then the streets would take shape. North-south streets would run parallel to West Peachtree and be three hundred feet apart, while east-west streets would be six hundred feet apart. Each street would consist of a central macadamized surface, with a block gutter on each side, then an area of grass, flowers, and trees, and finally a sidewalk. A total of sixty feet wide, these thoroughfares with their modern underground components would be a highlight of the project.

According to Barrett and Clayton, of the 216 total acres, 26 would be parks, 48 would be streets, and 142 would be building lots. This arrangement would provide 380 lots averaging 100-by-150 feet each. Lot improvements such as sewage installation, tree planting, grading, sodding or terracing, and erecting stone walls would be done by the company at an average cost per lot of $1,250—to be reserved from each sale and added to the improvement fund. At the end of the meeting the stockholders voiced approval of the concepts that went into Peters Park.[4] The subdivision was advertised as "the most extensive exclusively park and residence property in the world, under one ownership and management." The *Constitution* praised the project and realtors not connected with the development used proximity to the park as selling points. Competitors admitted that Peters Park, a neighborhood that for the first time in Atlanta history represented planned growth, was good for the city and quickly imitated the idea.

Soon the company completed the heaviest work of drainage and sewage, and Adair was selling lots. Priced from $3,500 to $4,500, the lots were occasionally auctioned at public sale to decide the question of location— the highest bidder would get first choice of lots, the next highest would get second choice, continuing in descending order. However, the project received a sudden jolt. On the eve of a big auction, investors withdrew their

---

[4]Fulton County Deed Book SS; *Atlanta City Directory* (1885); *Atlanta Constitution* (30 March, 28 December 1884); *Atlanta Journal* (23 January 1921); First National Bank, *Atlanta Resurgens*, 35.

support. Company stockholders informed Peters that a lingering economic recession prohibited them from paying for lots already purchased, whereupon Peters agreed to accept company stock at par in payment for the lots. Since Peters owned most of the stock based on land ownership, the return of the limited amount held by others severely curtailed the cash flow. The combination of the lots' high price and the inopportune business conditions that prevailed when the bulk of the lots were readied for sale reduced public enthusiasm for the project and Peters Park failed to become a wealthy garden suburb.[5]

Events turned in a vastly different direction when Peters became a central figure in plans then afoot to establish an engineering school in Georgia. A narrow-gauge technical institute was a natural component of industrialization and very much in accord with the New South philosophy. Grady took up the cry in the *Constitution*, calling for young Southerners trained in "hand and eye" for a particular trade. Nathaniel E. Harris, a Bibb County legislator, prodded the Georgia assembly until it passed enabling legislation for an engineering branch of the University of Georgia. With an initial appropriation of $65,000 from the legislature, the school was to be located in the city that offered the most attractive inducements. Harris, a Macon advocate, became chairman of a five-member locating commission. In the fall of 1886, the commission began meeting in the governor's office in Atlanta to choose among Athens, Atlanta, Macon, Milledgeville, and Penfield.

As the locating commission began its deliberations, Peters joined a group of citizens in Grady's office to plan the bid for Atlanta. The city council had offered $50,000 cash, plus an added inducement of $2,500 a year for twenty years, all to be raised from the sale of gas stock instead of a tax increase. The citizens group added $20,000 to the council's offer with S. M. Inman, a member of the locating committee, pledging a $5,000 donation; Peters gave $500, and $100 was pledged by his son Edward. Grady went before the commission and spoke forcefully for Atlanta. A few weeks later, after hearing from advocates of other locations, the commission accepted Atlanta's offer with "cordial and hearty support," a statement that does not reflect the bitter infighting among commission members. As a re-

---

[5]Peters Park Plat Map (1885) Atlanta Historical Society; Adair Plat Books, Atlanta Historical Society; *Atlanta Constitution* (1, 16 April 1884; 10 May, 11 June, 20 October 1885); Wallace P. Reed, *History of Atlanta, Georgia, with Illustrations and Biographical Sketches of Some of Its Prominent Men and Pioneers* (Syracuse: D. Mason Co., 1889) 478.

sult of its choice, the commission could look forward to the following funds: Georgia $65,000; city of Atlanta $50,000; and Atlanta citizens $20,000, for a total of $135,000 plus Atlanta's $2,500 annuity for twenty years. Peters was one of three men in charge of the Atlanta citizens' fund, which had to be collected immediately because the commission wanted cash. The amount actually collected was probably $15,000, but Atlanta had more than matched the original state expenditure.

The next question was where within Atlanta would the school be situated. Three offers were made to the commission—the Boulevard, Grant Park, and Peters Park. Peters offered four acres in Peters Park, which was nearest the city, but Grant Park had what was considered a natural setting, and the Boulevard appeared quite popular with many citizens. In January 1887, Grady and Hoke Smith were among those who advocated Peters Park before the commission in Inman's office. They pointed out that the park was close to manufacturing establishments on Marietta Street, and Peters sent word that he would build a street railroad line on North Avenue that would give access to both Peachtree Street and Marietta Street. Grady also stressed as important considerations the beauty of the park and, in a more practical vein, the fact that the park already had a sewage system installed.

For days the commission debated the question of an exact site. Chairman Harris was ill in bed and during his absence the others were reluctant to take action. Impatient Atlantans telephoned the *Constitution* office repeatedly for the latest news and began "propounding other conundrums too tough for the reportorial ignorance." Finally, on 27 January, by unanimous vote, the commission accepted Peters's offer and Grady expressed the belief that the citizens who had pledged the $20,000 to attract the school to Atlanta approved the Peters Park site.

Peters agreed to sell all additional land required and in February sold for $9,500 an adjoining parcel of four and three-quarter acres of prime real estate. The aggregate grounds, donated by and purchased from Peters, fronted on North Avenue and Cherry Street, two blocks from busy Marietta Street and four blocks from fashionable Peachtree Street. This plot of nearly nine acres became the nucleus of the Technological School—its name at the time. (Later, Peters's personal library added to the school's meager accumulation of books and his heirs sold three more acres and donated another lot to the institution.)

The locating commission continued as the school's trustees and Isaac Stiles Hopkins, a promoter of industrial education, was its first president.

Steady growth that included some courses offered for the first time in the South made the Georgia Institute of Technology a leading school of the region and removed a link in the chain of dependency on the North; Southerners could now learn at home how to convert Southern raw materials into finished products. It is ironic that the most enduring feature of Peters Park, although unanticipated at the outset, was Georgia Tech—a remarkable tribute to Peters, engineer and benefactor.[6]

While involved in the founding of Georgia Tech, Peters rescued from death's door plans for another exposition in Atlanta. That Southerners considered the first one a success is evidenced by the number of subsequent expositions.[7] In 1887 Atlantans were thinking of a slightly different emphasis in that they would show the nation what the South had produced since 1881 in new and improved machinery and manufactures, as well as the latest livestock and agricultural developments. This could be done through an interstate display of products from the piedmont regions of the Southern states from Virginia to Georgia. But after several meetings and considerable newspaper discussion, little had been done and the project seemed doomed. Then one day Peters, about the enter the Kimball House for a meeting on the proposed exposition, happened to see his old friend, J. C. Peck. Peters asked the contractor to oversee the construction work if the others could be persuaded to move ahead on the project. Peck agreed provided he could have a good advisory committee. Peters entered the meeting

---

[6]Fulton County Deed Book C; *Georgia Laws, 1885*; Georgia Institute of Technology Plat Map, 1894, E. B. Latham and H. B. Baylor Land Plat, Atlanta Historical Society; Atlanta City Council Minute Books, 2 August, 7 September, 19 October, 1 November 1886, 3, 22 January 1887; *Atlanta Constitution* (9 April, 1 October, 3 November 1886; 22, 26 January 1887); *Atlanta Journal* (27 June 1937); Helen K. Lyon, "Richard Peters: Atlanta Pioneer—Georgia Builder," *Atlanta Historical Bulletin* 38:10 (December 1957): 37, 39; Marion L. Brittain, *The Story of Georgia Tech* (Chapel Hill: University of North Carolina Press, 1948) 15-19; Paul W. Miller, ed., *Atlanta: Capital of the South* (New York: O. Durrell, 1949) 206-207.

[7]The International Cotton Exposition of 1881 was the first of a series of industrial and agricultural exhibits in the South that culminated in the International and Cotton States Exposition of 1895 in Atlanta. Peters, Grady, Kimball, Adair, and others had planned Atlanta's exhibits at the 1885 New Orleans exposition. Deciding against a separate building, the group chose the main building to house Atlanta manufactures with an "Atlanta Headquarters" near the entrance to display photos of each exhibit and provide printed matter describing Atlanta. *Atlanta Constitution* (16 April, 1 May 1884); Lucian L. Knight, *Reminiscences of Famous Georgians* 2 vols. (Atlanta: Franklin-Turner Co., 1908) 2:450.

and fifteen minutes later came out and called for Peck, who went in and accepted the position of construction superintendent with a three-member panel of advisors chaired by Peters. Atlanta capitalists were again ready to act on Peters's judgment.

Peters's advisory panel helped Peck draw up plans for the buildings and progress continued when a group of prominent citizens met on 19 February 1887 in Grady's office. Peters chaired the meeting and, after requesting Grady to state the purpose of the gathering, the group formed the Piedmont Fair Association. Peters then appointed a committee to develop a list of subscribers. The objective was to get fifty subscribers to pledge $500 each, with the understanding that twenty percent would soon be called in by the officers of the association. Over half the amount was raised at the meeting when all twenty-seven men present subscribed and in three days the $50,000 total was reached.

The question of location was also raised at the 19 February meeting and Joe Kingsberry, president of the Driving Park Association (formerly Gentleman's Driving Club), reflected the growing enthusiasm for the project by offering his group's 189-acre tract in northeast Atlanta near Peachtree Road (now Fourteenth Street) as the site for the exposition. The city council, seeking new fairgrounds for Atlanta, voted $15,000 to erect buildings that could later be used for annual fairs. This created a three-headed monster: the Driving Park Association owned the land, the city would own the buildings, and the Piedmont Fair Association would promote the fair. Ownership and promotion were simplified somewhat in July when the Driving Park Association and the Piedmont Fair Association merged into the Piedmont Exposition Company. The fact that several citizens, including Peters, were members of both associations quite likely facilitated the merger.[8]

The Piedmont Exposition of 1887, of shorter duration and somewhat smaller than the International Cotton Exposition of 1881, was held 10-22 October and opening day ceremonies included a speech by Governor John B. Gordon. The visit by President Grover Cleveland and his young wife highlighted the fair. The 50,000 people who crowded the grounds on 19 Oc-

---

[8]Atlanta City Council Minute Books, 21 February 1887; John C. Peck to Nellie P. Black, 28 June 1901, in *Richard Peters: His Ancestors and Descendants*, comp. Nellie P. Black (Atlanta: Foote and Davies, 1904) 56-58; *Atlanta Constitution* (19 February 1887); Reed, *History of Atlanta*, 478; William B. Williford, *Peachtree Street, Atlanta* (Athens: University of Georgia Press, 1962) 58.

tober to hear Cleveland attested to his popularity in the South. In livestock exhibits, Peters won all six premiums in the Angora category and four of the six for Essex swine. With an estimated 200,000 total attendance, boosted by a one-cent-a-mile fare to Atlanta via the Western and Atlantic and other railroads, the fair was a success.[9]

Peters continued to entertain at his home on Peachtree Street in connection with projects to promote Atlanta. He and Grady, among others, sometimes held open house for delegates attending commercial conventions in Atlanta. Such practices successfully built Atlanta's reputation as a hospitable city and promoted outside investment. Peters also celebrated family weddings in grand fashion. When his son Ralph was married in Philadelphia, Peters transported the wedding party to Atlanta in a special rail car for a reception at his home. As Chinese lanterns illuminated the evening, nearly one hundred guests, including Adair, Bullock, Brown, Hoke Smith, and other state and local officials and their ladies, enjoyed Peters's hospitality. (Peters's wedding presents sometimes consisted of land for a homesite, as was the case with his son Edward, who built Ivy Hall on Ponce de Leon Avenue.)[10]

In his modest carriage, sometimes driven by a family servant, Peters routinely visited the post office and bank, then returned to his home, business, or civic meeting. By now Atlantans had developed a habit of waiting for his judgment on suggestions that affected the prosperity of the city. Religion remained a strong force in his life.[11] His love for and care of his fam-

---

[9]*Southern Cultivator* 45:11 (November 1887): n.p.; Miller, *Atlanta*, 210-11.

[10]Mary Connally Spalding, Scrapbook, Atlanta Historical Society; *Atlanta Constitution* (8, 19 May 1885; 6 April 1888); MacDougald, "My Seventh Move," 33, 36-37; Franklin M. Garrett, "A Short History of Land Lot 49 of the Fourteenth District of Originally Henry, Now Fulton County in Georgia," *Atlanta Historical Journal* 25 (Spring 1981): 24.

[11]The membership of St. Philip's at the beginning of the 1880s was about 600, with an estimated 1,200 more under the ministration of the parish, making it the largest in the diocese. Two additions had been made to the church building, and a two-story brick rectory replaced the one burned by Federal troops. Because of the interest of his daughter Nellie in helping the poor, Peters donated a lot at Juniper and Ponce de Leon in the northern suburbs for the construction of Atlanta's first mission, the Chapel of Holy Innocents Mission School. *Atlanta City Directory* (1879); Scrapbook, Nellie P. Black Collection, University of Georgia Libraries, Athens; Louise Black MacDougald, "Holy Innocents Mission (Episcopal)," *Atlanta Historical Bulletin* 4:18 (July 1939): 166-67; Alex M. Hitz, *A History of the Cathedral of St. Philip* (Atlanta: Conger Printing Co., 1947) 15-17. When the parish revived plans for a new church building to be built beside the original St. Philip's, Bishop Beckwith, evi-

ily was always a primary concern and he maintained his usual friendly disposition and sense of humor. When Nellie was widowed after ten years of marriage, he wrote to her: "You shall not suffer from want or hunger so long as I have old clothing to spare or can catch a possum in the woods at Calhoun."[12]

Full of years and honors, Peters was as young at heart as the youngest of the Young Farmers Club of the Southern States, a club he served as advisor. Founded in Georgia with headquarters in Atlanta, the club was open to farmers younger than fifty—they were young mostly in comparison to the "Old South" types who continued to dominate the Georgia Agricultural Society. There was expectation that the younger farmers would bring diversification. Peters's example at home, where "no idle hands took advantage of wealth secured by parental activity and industry," gave weight and influence to his words of counsel to the club.[13] Grady lionized him in his later years. Once the journalist caught a view of Peters in the distance on the plantation and wrote in reverent tones of "the figure of the master of all this, erect and easy, with broad brim and duster, standing on some hill, so fixed in the sunset that he almost seemed diaphanous."[14]

---

dently displeased with the choice of location, opposed the building project. Nonetheless, construction resumed on a foundation that had been laid before the depression of the 1870s, and in October 1882 the first service was held in the second St. Philip's. Built of brick with stone trim in a modern gothic design, the building had 720 seats and could accommodate 1,000 people. St. Philip's Church Minutes, 25 June 1883; Atlanta City Council Minute Books, 17 July 1882; *Atlanta Constitution* (13 January 1878; 11 February 1879; 21 May 1880; 8 August 1882; 8 December 1883; 2 October 1885); Audria B. Gray, "History of the Cathedral of St. Philip's in the City and Diocese of Atlanta," *Atlanta Historical Bulletin* 4:1 (December 1930): 9, 11; Hitz, *History of St. Philip*, 32-44. Following Atlanta's expansion to the north, sentiment developed for a third church located in the northern suburbs. The movement was fulfilled when two lots on the corner of West Peachtree and North Avenue were donated from Peters's land for All Saints Church in memory of his work as a founder of the Episcopal Church in Atlanta. Franklin M. Garrett, *Atlanta and Environs: A Chronicle of Its People and Events* 2 vols. (Athens: University of Georgia Press, 1969) 2:442-43; Walter G. Cooper, *Official History of Fulton County* (Atlanta: Walter W. Brown Publishing Co., 1934) 565-67. Episcopalianism continued to grow and spread northward and culminated in the Cathedral of St. Philip.

[12]Richard Peters to Nellie P. Black, 14 November 1888, Black Collection; George C. Smith to Nellie P. Black, n.d., in *Richard Peters*, 53-54; Allen D. Candler and Clement A. Evans, eds., *The Cyclopedia of Georgia* 4 vols. (Atlanta: State Historical Association, 1906) 3:89-90.

[13]Farm Book, Peters Estate Collection, Atlanta Historical Society; Georgia State Agricultural Society, "Memorial," in *Richard Peters*, 143; *Southern Cultivator* 42:5 (May 1884): 155, 43:3 (March 1885): 102.

[14]*Atlanta Constitution* (12 October 1884).

Peters's reputation in his own time as a planter and livestock breeder, his modest nature, lack of significant public office, and role as a member of committees help explain his obscurity as a city builder. A younger generation of Atlantans had scant appreciation for his place in the city's history, as evidenced by the sixteen who petitioned the city council to change the name of Peters Street to West Avenue. The petitioners admitted the street showed signs of progress, but complained that the original name "brought up recollections of the old Snake Nation." The Street Committee accepted the petition and recommended that the name be changed. This prompted a lively council debate. Councilman H. C. Stockdell pointed out that the street was named for one of the most prominent men in the city: "That gentleman is still living and we ought not to change the name." The most spirited and deciding defense for retaining the name came from Councilman W. J. Garrett:

> I thought everybody knew that street was named for Col. Richard Peters, one of the oldest and most progressive citizens of Atlanta. Why, way back there when we didn't have railroads that gentleman started a stage line between Atlanta and West Point. The stages came into Atlanta on that road, and when the city was laid off the road was named Peters Street. Why, I remember how the stages used to rattle and the drivers' bugle yet. Change the name of that street? No, sir; never. The name is spotless, and Col. Peters, now in his old age, has never done anything except what would advance the interest of Atlanta. I would not vote for it if twenty-five times as many names were attached to it.[15]

The full council voted to keep the name Peters Street (to the delight of the city's press).

In January 1889, Peters, age 78, became ill and was placed under the care of his physician, W. S. Kendrick. A few weeks later, on Saturday, 3 February, Kendrick confined him to bed and the family became alarmed as Peters's condition worsened. Richard, Jr., and Ralph were called home from the North by telegraph. A concerned Kendrick called in another physician, W. S. Armstrong, for consultation. The diagnosis was "old age and inflammation." By Monday evening Kendrick sadly announced to the family that there was no hope for Peters's recovery. Death began slowly and quietly at midnight, and at 4:00 A.M. on Tuesday, 6 February, Peters died.

Charles T. Quintard, bishop of Tennessee, assisted by Bishop Beckwith, presided over Peters's funeral services the following afternoon in the second St. Philip's. Rector Bryon Holley led the St. Philip's Boys Choir.

---

[15]*Atlanta Constitution* (20 October 1884); *Atlanta Evening Capitol* (20 October 1885).

The ministers of St. Luke's of Atlanta and St. Paul's of Augusta represented their churches. As organizations, including the Georgia Agricultural Society, the Western and Atlantic lessees, and the Exposition Cotton Mills stockholders, wrote tributes and memorials to the New South champion, old friends such as Joseph E. Brown paid their last respects in what was then one of Atlanta's largest funerals. Gray-gloved pallbearers, including Henry Grady, who himself was to succumb prematurely the same year, carried Peters's draped cedar casket outside the church, where twenty rented carriages led the procession to Oakland Cemetery. Interment was in a brick-vaulted grave.[16] So it was that by sunset on that wintry day Atlanta had said farewell to Richard Peters.

---

[16]Clipping, Peters Estate Collection; Scrapbook, Black Collection; *Atlanta Constitution* (7, 8 February 1889); *Atlanta Journal* (6 February 1889). Peters specified in his will that no inventory of his property be made, but his estate records list his estimated worth (probably conservative) at $900,000, which made him one of the wealthiest men in Atlanta. Last Will and Testament of Richard Peters, 26 July 1888, Fulton County Deed Book DD; Fulton County Ordinary Court Minutes, Book F, Letters Testamentary, Book B, Fulton County Courthouse (Peters's will and a few letters testamentary are also found on microfilm in the Georgia Department of Archives and History); *Atlanta Constitution* (7 April 1889). In 1890, it was estimated that $9,000 was the average wealth of city families in America. Arthur M. Schlesinger, *The Rise of the City, 1878-1898* (New York: New Viewpoints, 1975) 77.

Peters's family sold the street railroad and focused on real estate development. On 3 February 1890, the Peters estate resolved into the Peters Land Company, with Edward C. Peters as president and the family as stockholders. Except for the Peachtree Street home, Peters's entire landed estate was included in the company: the Railroad Block building at the corner of Peachtree and Wall streets; eleven acres plus a small lot on West Peachtree Street; a large tract on Ponce de Leon extending toward Piedmont Park; much of Land Lot 49; Peters Park (most of Land Lot 80); and the plantation in Gordon County. *Atlanta Constitution* (9 April, 2 May 1889); *Atlanta Journal* (20 March, 3, 17, 22 April, 6 May, 18 June 1889); *Georgia Laws, 1884*; *Atlanta City Directory* (1890).

EPILOGUE

By the time of Peters's death, Atlanta was assured a major place in the nation's urban system.[1] The history and tradition of the South, with its distinctive black subculture and comparatively greater agricultural economy, impacted on the development of the region's cities. In the antebellum period, Atlanta's population was twenty percent black, but in 1870 it was forty-six percent. Many blacks lived in a "railroad laced area" to the west of the central business district. Other groups lived near streams, which were undesirable areas because of their susceptibility to flooding and their use as a sewage system. During the 1870s and 1880s, when New South men like Peters retained strong influence, the racial code was less severe than it eventually became. A large number of free blacks was still an anomaly; they were segregated in many ways, which was often galling, but it did allow them to develop their own businesses and institutions free from white dominance. A relatively sizable black middle class emerged, along with some outstanding black educational and religious institutions.[2]

---

[1]Most cities were built according to the gridiron plan, but Atlanta was circular during its first decades of existence. Christopher Tunnard, *The Modern American City* (Princeton: D. Van Nostrand Company, 1968) 16-17.

[2]James M. Russell, "Politics, Municipal Services, and the Working Class in Atlanta,

Southern cities spent less public funds for urban improvements because of the greater number of poor people, particularly blacks, in Southern urban centers that reduced the tax base and that, coupled with a desire to grant tax breaks to factories, resulted in relatively low city revenues. Yet tax receipts in Atlanta grew from $80,000 to $300,000 between 1866 and 1873, mainly because city property doubled in value and the value of bonds issued by the city amounted to an estimated $100,000 more than total tax revenues. This bonded indebtedness was part of a national trend to improve intraurban communication. Although Southern urban streets were among the worst in America, Atlanta's streets were in good order in comparison with others in the South. Other public services had a rough character, however, and Atlantans as well as other Southern city dwellers lived in a more violent environment than urbanites in other regions. Police were still scarce, and gas lights were selectively applied. An Atlantan complained that away from the center of town, "the scarcity of gas lights affords many convenient dark corners where almost any kind of evil deed [can] be perpetrated." Southern cities also lagged behind in the public park movement. As of 1880, Atlanta had about three acres of parkland; many Southern cities had none. Only New Orleans, with 659 acres of parks, ranked with cities of the North.[3]

The population of Southern cities, which trailed behind that of other sections by about fifty years,[4] came mainly from within the region. The

---

1865 to 1890," *Georgia Historical Quarterly* 66:4 (Winter 1982): 475-78; Howard N. Rabinowitz, "From Reconstruction to Redemption in the Urban South," *Journal of Urban History* 2:2 (February 1976): 171; Blaine A. Brownell and David R. Goldfield, "Southern Urban History," *The City in Southern History: The Growth of Urban Civilization in the South*, ed. Blaine A. Brownell and David R. Goldfield (Port Washington: Kennikat Press, 1977) 16; Howard N. Rabinowitz, *Race Relations in the Urban South, 1865-1890* (New York: Oxford University Press, 1978) 3, 101-102; Blaine A. Brownell, *The Urban Ethos in the South, 1920-1930* (Baton Rouge: Louisiana State University Press, 1975) 14. In 1889, Henry Grady charged that one of every 466 blacks in the North was in jail, whereas in the South only one of every 1,865 blacks was in prison. He concluded that prejudice ran deeper in Northern courts. Grady McWhiney, *Southerners and Other Americans* (New York: Basic Books, Inc., 1973) 158.

[3]Howard N. Rabinowitz, "Continuity and Change: Southern Urban Development, 1860-1900," *The City in Southern History*, 98, 110, 112; David R. Goldfield, *Cotton Fields and Skyscrapers: Southern Cities and Region, 1607-1980* (Baton Rouge: Louisiana State University Press, 1982) 92-93, 98.

[4]The national urban population was 15.3 percent in 1850, yet it was 1900 before Southern urban population reached a similar figure. Blaine A. Brownell, "Urbanization in the South: A Unique Experience?" *Mississippi Quarterly* 26 (Spring 1973): 106.

newcomers were mostly native Southerners from rural areas and small towns. "As early as 1868, one-half of Atlanta's population had arrived from the countryside since the end of the war," according to David Goldfield. The number of Americans born in the North or West who lived in the South during the 1870s was less than half a million. Immigrants to America also shunned the South. The "new" immigration of the 1880s, chiefly southern and eastern European Catholics and Jews, diverged greatly from the rural migrants who comprised the majority of the white urban population in the South, causing Protestant denominations to remain stronger than in Northern urban centers.[5] Rarely in any Southern city did the foreign-born exceed ten percent of the population. Southern obstacles to immigration consisted of social proscription, lawlessness, disease, and poor diet. Of the 21,780 people residing in Atlanta in 1870, 10,770 were native-born whites, 9,929 were blacks, and only 1,090 were of foreign birth—no more than five percent. Immigrants seemed to be geographically mobile within the city and also had a high degree of upward mobility, but they apparently played a relatively minor role in Atlanta during the late nineteenth century.[6]

Atlanta (as did Birmingham, Memphis, and Chattanooga) joined New Orleans and Louisville in the manufacturing ranks, but all failed to attain a size that would be considered large by Northern standards. Southern urban industry, until the infusion of Northern capital beginning in the 1880s, was nourished by Southern capital, usually in the form of an accumulation of petty savings.[7] The shortage of both capital and skilled labor in the South combined to produce more resource-oriented industries, such as Peters's

---

[5]Goldfield, *Cotton Fields and Skyscrapers*, 94, 108.

[6]Brownell, *The Urban Ethos in the South*, 7; George R. Woolfolk, *The Cotton Regency: The Northern Merchants and Reconstruction, 1865-1880* (New York: Bookman Associates, 1958) 104-105; Richard J. Hopkins, "Occupational and Geographic Mobility in Atlanta, 1870-1896," *Journal of Southern History* 34 (May 1968): 200, 213; Russell, "Politics, Municipal Services, and the Working Class in Atlanta," 468; Arthur M. Schlesinger, *The Rise of the City, 1878-1898* (New York: New Viewpoints, 1975) 21; Brownell and Goldfield, "Southern Urban History," 21. New South men wanted immigrants as factory laborers, but planters, who wanted white labor for their plantations, led the unsuccessful movement to attract immigrants. James L. Roark, *Masters Without Slaves: Southern Planters in the Civil War and Reconstruction* (New York: W. W. Norton and Company, 1977) 166-67.

[7]Brownell, "Urbanization in the South: A Unique Experience?" 111; Schlesinger, *The Rise of the City, 1878-1898*, 13-14.

flour mill, than production that was oriented toward metals, machinery, and equipment.

"D—n Atlanta," a visitor from a rival city observed. "Turn a dollar loose on Whitehall Street and every man is after it." Atlanta achieved a reputation as the most hard-working Southern city and the energy of its businessmen contributed to its rise in the urban system to a position of regional dominance. "Atlanta spirit" became a synonym for urban progress.[8] In 1870 Atlanta ranked eighth among the largest Southern cities, but by 1890 it had grown to fourth place behind New Orleans, Richmond, and Nashville. Restored to economic vitality more rapidly after the Civil War than anyone dared predict, the city was likened to the ancient Phoenix.[9]

However, these developments alone were insufficient to make Atlanta a unique urban center. One stimulus of the creation of America's influential cities was the fact that Washington, D.C., was not a commercial, financial, nor cultural center and, therefore, failed to dominate the nation as did other national capitals such as Paris, London, Rome, or Berlin. Therefore, argues Richard C. Wade, there was the regional capital, like Atlanta, Chicago, and San Francisco, that independently influenced a large hinterland.[10] Most were located at natural breaks in trade and each sought some phase that reflected its virtues: Cincinnati was "the Workshop of the Interior"; Boston, "the Center of the Whole North"; St. Louis, "the Queen City of the Mississippi Valley"; and Atlanta, first "the Gate City of the South," and then "Capital of the New South."[11]

---

[8]Goldfield, *Cotton Fields and Skyscrapers*, 85, 128. Goldfield's thesis is that the Southern city was controlled by its rural surroundings, so that the urban setting represented more of a change of scenery than a change in culture.

[9]Brownell and Goldfield, "Southern Urban History," 7; Rabinowitz, "Continuity and Change," 93. "A grim joke of the 1880s was that Atlanta businessmen would gladly sell the rest of Georgia to the devil if only he would guarantee Atlanta's prosperity." Mills Lane, ed., *The New South: Writings and Speeches of Henry Grady* (Savannah: The Beehive Press, 1971) xvii. It is probably true that most of the city's commercial-civic elite identified themselves first as Atlantans rather than as Georgians. This trait could be applied to most of the leading city boosters in the nation. Brownell, *The Urban Ethos in the South*, 64.

[10]Richard C. Wade, "Urbanization," *The Comparative Approach to American History*, ed. C. Vann Woodward (New York: Basic Books, 1968) 190-91.

[11]Blake McKelvey, *The Urbanization of America, 1860-1915* (New Brunswick: Rutgers University Press, 1963) viii, 42, 50; Woolfolk, *The Cotton Regency, 1865-1880*, 31.

A class structure similar to that of other cities developed in Atlanta. Significant changes in agriculture and trade wrought a new urban-oriented middle class in Southern cities and towns during the postbellum era. Alexander K. McClure, a Philadelphia newspaper editor and New South advocate, described the members of this class in Atlanta as "not the dawdling, pale-faced, soft-handed effeminates which were so often visible in the nurslings of the slave." He wrote that Atlanta's young men were active and intelligent, the "foremost missionaries in the new civilization in the South." McClure explained that they paid homage to the accomplishments of their fathers, but had no desire to resurrect the past. "Instead of discussing the old plantation time 'before the wah,' they talk about railroads, factories, and the tariff, the schools, the increase of crops, and the growth of wealth and trade." McClure concluded that were it not for the recent history of Reconstruction, these men would have been Republicans.[12]

Nor did Atlanta have a unique skyline. Urban horizons in America were similar because prior to 1880 very few buildings rose higher than six stories and none higher than eight. But in 1883 William L. Jenny designed Chicago's ten-story Home Insurance Building, using wrought iron for the first six floors and steel beams for the top floors. The introduction of the steel frame rendered old-fashioned the "business block" that could be seen in every city. By the 1880s, the big city seems to have come of age although its famous central silhouette had to wait for a second wave of "building tall" that swept the nation in the early twentieth century.[13]

Leadership in Atlanta also followed a familiar pattern. Echoing through the construction noise of Southern cities, W. J. Cash could hear the gallop of a Jeb Stuart, because Cash believed that Southerners were incurably romantic. Instead, the din of construction represented the booster spirit of men like Richard Peters, whose ethical and humanitarian impulses, together with wealth and influence, allowed them to make bold strokes for ur-

---

[12]Harold D. Woodman, *King Cotton and His Retainers: Financing and Marketing the Cotton Crop of the South, 1800-1925* (Lexington: University of Kentucky Press, 1968) 326, 328-29.

[13]Tunnard, *The Modern American City*, 40-43. It is widely accepted among historians that the American frontier ended in 1890, and so did the urban frontier. A few new boom towns appeared after that date, but these were exceptions. Therefore, city boosters concentrated on the unexploited potentialities of established cities, or old towns near them, rather than founding new ones. McKelvey, *The Urbanization of America*, 32.

ban advancement that had the distinctiveness of an individual city, but having a cohesion with national development as well. All this is woven not only into the pattern of the New South, but also into what we call modern America.[14]

While Atlanta flourished, agriculture languished. The early postbellum years were ones of "unprecedented disaster" in the South. The price of cotton tumbled from thirty to ten cents a pound.[15] Planters also faced piecing together their broken agricultural system amid Reconstruction politicians who continued to change the rules of the game. The result of this combination of woes was hard times in Dixie.

This disintegration of the Southern economy has caused historians to question whether or not plantations survived the Civil War. Gavin Wright, using United States census figures, found that there was a drastic decline in average farm size between 1860 and 1880; in the Deep South the reduction amounted to sixty percent.[16] Wright's research suggested that an agrarian revolution had taken place, that adverse economic forces had accomplished what the Radical Republicans had failed to do—break the plantations into little farms. In Peters's case there was some decline in size, approximately thirty-six percent. According to the 1860 census, his plantation consisted of 1,950 acres and the 1880 census revealed a reduction to 1,250 acres.

James L. Roark agreed with Wright that the census reports showed the average size of farms was halved, but maintained this was a misleading impression given by census takers who recorded rented land under the renter's name instead of the owner's. Roark concluded that the plantations themselves persisted. Peters's experience supports Roark's contention because in 1860 Peters's plantation was listed in his own name; in 1870 the name of his overseer, Aaron Roff (as "agent, manager, or owner"), appeared without mention of Peters; and in 1880 it listed Peters's son, Richard, Jr. (as the "name of the person who conducts this farm"), with no

---

[14]Frank Freidel, "Boosters, Intellectuals, and the American City," *The Historian and the City*, ed. Oscar Handlin and John Burchard (Cambridge: M.I.T. Press and Harvard University Press, 1963) 116-17; Brownell, "Urbanization in the South: A Unique Experience?" 117; Woolfolk, *The Cotton Regency*, 32-33.

[15]Henry W. Grady, "Cotton and Its Kingdom," *Harper's Weekly* 63 (October 1881): 720-21.

[16]Gavin Wright, *The Political Economy of the Cotton South: Households, Markets, and Wealth in the Nineteenth Century* (New York: W. W. Norton and Company, 1978) 166.

mention of his father. This helps confirm that, to use a phrase from Roark, Tara had not become Tobacco Road.

Apart from size, how did the antebellum elite fare in terms of the value of their land? Roark wrote: "Neither those who left nor those who stayed nor those who bought in were likely to restore to plantations the level of affluence they had known in the antebellum South." In Marengo County, Alabama, for example, the value of the average holding fell over fifty percent between 1860 and 1870, a figure quite representative of Peters's fate. The value of all Southern farms in 1880 was still thirty-three percent below the 1860 level; here Peters seems to have fared worse. The 1860 census showed his plantation valued at $40,000, $20,000 in the 1870 census, and $13,000 in the 1880 census.[17] This was a decline of almost sixty-eight percent in twenty years. It is quite clear that land values toppled after the war and the Panic of 1873 sustained the depressed market for the remainder of the decade.

Peters and other advocates of diversification understood the advantages that the South enjoyed for the cultivation of cotton. Some farms, especially the smaller ones, became so specialized in cotton that they abandoned self-sufficiency (a term many observers of the day equated with diversification).[18] Although Peters hoped to move beyond that to a diversity of income-earning activities on the farm, what he deplored most was the near exclusion of home-grown foodstuffs. The question of self-sufficiency has been investigated by Roger L. Ransom and Richard Sutch, who concluded that farms in the cotton states failed to produce enough grain to meet their food requirements: "Small family farms reported an average of only 9.7 bushels of grain per capita above the needs of the farm's work stock." An average of at least ten to fifteen bushels would have been required for each household member. Their estimates confirm what Peters saw—the great majority of farmers were purchasing supplies.

What explains this irresistible lure of cotton? As a cash crop, cotton was readily sold in an organized market, was not perishable, was easily

---

[17]*U.S. Census of 1860, 1870, 1880: Agriculture*; Roark, *Masters Without Slaves*, 171-73. Whether the antebellum owners were able to hold on to their property following the war, as Peters did, remains an unanswered question, which results in part from the confusion caused by the census reports. Perhaps many who held on to their land through the Civil War and Reconstruction lost it as a result of the depression.

[18]Wright, *Political Economy of the Cotton South*, 166, 168.

stored, had a predictable yield per acre and future price, was less risky than a food crop, and could not be eaten. All this made it excellent collateral for securing a loan to finance the farm's operation for a year.[19] Farmers borrowed from local storekeepers (usually in the form of supplies), who had borrowed from local banks, that had borrowed from Northern banks. Sometimes there was a middleman between the local bank and the storekeeper in the form of a commission merchant. The funds, therefore, went through at least three principals, each of whom exacted a percentage for the risk assumed. Grady explained that "having once mortgaged his crop for supplies to his merchant, the farmer was practically the slave to that merchant. Under the declining price of cotton his crop would barely pay his lien. He was then left dependent for the next year's supplies on his merchant, who charged him what he pleased." Interest rates were often fifty percent or more and, in a much used phrase, the small farmer was "always a year behind."[20] The lien system became more widespread than slavery had been, for it respected neither race nor class; and the economic results were perhaps more injurious to the South than slavery. This was true because the crop lien turned the South into "a vast pawn shop" and trapped the farmer in debt peonage.[21]

As these postwar developments pushed the South more deeply into cotton dependency, there was a decline in per capita outputs of most crops, including cotton, which has not been fully explained. Heretofore, many believed the decline resulted from destruction during the war, but recent scholarship attributes the decline to the refusal of the newly freed black families to work as many hours, and especially the withdrawal of black women from the field, with a resulting fall in tilled acreage. While the advent of sharecropping brought women and children back into the fields, the system also tied the workers to the land, further reducing incentives for

---

[19]Roger L. Ransom and Richard Sutch, *One Kind of Freedom: The Economic Consequences of Emancipation* (Cambridge: The University Press, 1977) 158-61.

[20]Henry W. Grady, *The New South* (New York: R. Bonner's Sons, 1890) 178; Woodman, *King Cotton and His Retainers*, 356; Wright, *Political Economy of the Cotton South*, 175.

[21]C. Vann Woodward, *Origins of the New South, 1877-1913* (Baton Rouge: Louisiana State University Press, 1964) 180; C. Vann Woodward, *Tom Watson: Agrarian Rebel* (New York: Oxford University Press, 1963) 129.

landowners "to mechanize agricultural production and modernize their techniques."[22]

Poverty in the South stemmed from the Northern-dominated economy. Because of Northern-set freight rates and the federal government's adverse Supreme Court decisions, adverse tariff policy, and restrictive "hard money" policy, Southerners failed to gain control of the Southern market for themselves. This exacerbated the lack of capital in the South, which gave impetus to the rise of the "diabolical system of credit" and cotton dependency instead of diversification.[23] With capital, Southerners could raise their own provisions and breed their own stock. The cotton crop would triple in value if produced as finished goods and cotton factories would offer not only an alternative to sharecropping but also promote urbanization, which in turn would increase the market for food crops and livestock.[24]

The emphasis on cotton manufactures in the 1880s quickly broadened to include a newness in many phases of Southern life following the Civil War that in turn implied that there had been an Old South before the war. But did the Civil War cause a breakdown of one civilization and the beginning of another, or was the war merely an interruption of Southern progress? From the time that Henry Grady wrote "the New South is simply the Old South under new conditions,"[25] writers have grappled with the question of Southern continuity. "Nearly every major work of the southern literary renaissance of the twentieth century," explained George B. Tindall, "has been built around the conflict between southern tradition and modernity."[26]

---

[22]Wright, *The Political Economy of the Cotton South*, 101, 120, 158, 160, 184; Jonathan Wiener, *Social Origins of the New South: Alabama, 1860-1885* (Baton Rouge: Louisiana State University Press, 1978) 14, 108. Ronald L. F. Davis, *Good and Faithful Labor: From Slavery to Sharecropping in the Natchez District, 1860-1890* (Westport: Greenwood Press, 1982), challenges the view that planters originated the sharecropping system. Instead, according to Davis, the freedman desired the system and forced the landlords to acquiesce because sharecropping was a means of avoiding gang labor and a step toward economic independence.

[23]Woolfolk, *The Cotton Regency*, 94, 195.

[24]Grady, "Cotton and Its Kingdom," 723-32; Raymond B. Nixon, *Henry W. Grady: Spokesman of the New South* (New York: Alfred A. Knopf, 1943) 180-81.

[25]Scrapbook, Henry W. Grady Collection, Emory University, Atlanta.

[26]George B. Tindall, *The Persistent Tradition in New South Politics* (Baton Rouge: Louisiana State University Press, 1975) 17.

Not surprisingly, in spite of the admonition by English historian Marcus Cunliffe that American historians have an "excessive propensity for discovering watersheds,"[27] they are among the writers who have given the issue considerable attention.

The most emphatic advocate of the continuity school of thought was Robert S. Cotterill. He pointed out that in 1860 the South had 188 cotton mills with an annual output of $14,000,000, so that after the war Southerners resumed rather than began manufacturing. By the 1880s the region was not suddenly industrial, but suddenly articulate. To Cotterill then, the beginning was not in manufacturing but in "a rash of publicity." The only important change from the Old South, as he saw it, was the widespread use of sharecropping instead of slave labor and the exchange of the country store for the factorage system, but he made clear that both sharecropping and the country store had been antebellum institutions.[28] Wilbur J. Cash believed that "the extent of the change and of the break between the old South that was and the South of our time has been vastly exaggerated."[29] Cash remains highly influential among the continuitarians. David Goldfield also supported the continuity, or progressive, view. He maintained that Cash was "correct concerning the persistence of southern culture and the identity between Progress and Tradition."[30]

During the last twenty years or so, several writers have refuted the evolutionary interpretation of Southern history and have instead emphasized

---

[27]Ibid., 2. The fire that destroyed the Kimball House in 1883, rather than the burning of Atlanta in 1864 by Sherman, is perhaps a more appropriate watershed between the Old South and the New. "As if to clear the stage drastically of old scenery," wrote one historian, "the old Kimball House burned to the ground." Concurrently, leading representatives of the antebellum South bowed off the stage—Herschel V. Johnson in 1880, Alexander H. Stephens in 1883, and Robert Toombs, crippled by cataracts and strong drink after 1883, declined into decrepitude and followed them two years later. Woodward, *Tom Watson: Agrarian Rebel*, 113.

[28]Robert S. Cotterill, "The Old South to the New," *Journal of Southern History* 15 (February 1949): 3-6. Cotterill pointed out that sharecropping, as old as agriculture itself, is mentioned in Genesis. Jacob tended the flocks of his Uncle Laban on shares. Ibid., 7. As to the postwar country store, Harold D. Woodman agrees with Cotterill that the institution "was heavily freighted with the remnants of the antebellum South." Woodman, *King Cotton and His Retainers*, 296.

[29]Wilbur Cash, *Mind of the South* (New York: Alfred A. Knopf, 1970) x.

[30]Goldfield, *Cotton Fields and Skyscrapers*, 197.

discontinuity—to them the Civil War was a disruption instead of an interruption. This deviation is attributed in large measure to C. Vann Woodward. Yet Woodward would cheerfully concede the presence of both continuity and change. He observed that the Old South was "one of the most significant inventions of the New South" and that "when the New South was personified by the cartoonist it was significantly in the garb of the antebellum planter."[31] James Roark saw some postwar behavior as simply an extention of prewar practices, but concluded that "emancipation had caused a basic transformation."[32] Harold D. Woodman saw a new business class after the war. It was built "on the ruins of slavery and the plantation system . . . and its members, although only rarely industrialists, had much in common with the business classes in the North."[33]

It is clear from these arguments that historians have been baffled by the origins of the New South. Sheldon Hackney, while suggesting that a biographical approach should shed light on the ambiguity, chronicled his despair in ever resolving the question: "Who knows? Perhaps one day we will get that rock to the top of the hill." Then he added, but "I doubt it."[34] The career of Richard Peters is a lever for moving that rock upward. His antebellum roots and his outlining the path for Southerners as voiced by Grady make Peters's life a strong statement in support of continuity.

---

[31]Woodward, *Origins of the New South*, 154-55, 161. Ironically, Grady himself played a major role in inventing the Old South, according to Woodward. This resulted in large measure from glorification of the Lost Cause. In 1886 Grady resurrected Jefferson Davis from his Gulf Coast exile as a means of electing General John B. Gordon governor of Georgia. Ibid., 155. When Davis spoke in Atlanta, Grady planted war widows and orphans in the crowd, along with nearly a thousand former soldiers (some of them maimed) with Confederate flags. The climax of the event occurred when General James Longstreet, clad in Confederate uniform and on horseback, galloped to the speaker's platform and, before the ecstatic audience, embraced Davis. Gordon was elected in 1886 and renominated without opposition two years later. Grady was a highly effective campaign manager, but in a deeper sense he must have realized that no people can be great who turn away from the memory of their heroes. Lane, *The New South*, xx, 108; Nixon, *Henry W. Grady*, 226-27, 313.

[32]Roark, *Masters Without Slaves*, 179, 205.

[33]Woodman, *King Cotton and His Retainers*, 333.

[34]Sheldon Hackney, "Origins of the New South in Retrospect," *Journal of Southern History* 38:2 (May 1972): 201, 216.

BIBLIOGRAPHIC NOTE

The only previous work on Richard Peters is a small and rare genealogical volume entitled *Richard Peters: His Ancestors and Descendants* (Atlanta: Foote and Davies, 1904) compiled by his daughter Nellie Peters Black. The book contains Peters's brief and incomplete memoirs that he dictated in the summer of 1887 to Nellie; he unfortunately tired of the experience when he reached the Civil War period and his memoirs terminate at that point. Nellie explains: "The recital ended here, a far-away look came over the dear face and it seemed unfair to tease him to say more." Before publishing the volume, she asked a few men who had known Peters to comment on his life and the results enrich Peters's own account. Various other materials relating to Peters are included, as well as sections on family members. In spite of the severe time limitations in Peters's memoirs, along with a few minor errors, this publication is the best single source.

The Peters Estate Collection in the Atlanta Historical Society dates from 1848 to 1897 and contains business correspondence, legal documents, account books, record books, livestock breeding records, and publications, all relating chiefly to Peters's plantation. The Nellie Peters Black Collection in the University of Georgia Libraries, Athens, covers the period 1875-1920 and contains some 12,600 items, much of it useful in reconstructing Peters as an individual. Since there is material on Peters in the Peters Estate Collection at the Atlanta Historical Society and in the Black Collection at the

University of Georgia Libraries, what might be termed the Peters "papers" are divided between the two depositories.

Other sources on Peters maintained by the Atlanta Historical Society include the Martha Lumpkin Compton Scrapbook (produced by the woman for whom Marthasville was named), which has clippings that deal with Peters's activities soon after he arrived in Marthasville. The Lemuel Pratt Grant Papers contain a few letters from Peters on the subject of stagecoach operations. The Atlanta Assessor's returns reveal some idea of Peters's worth at different stages of his career. The William L. Calhoun Collection and the James R. Crew Collection are among the better sources for the wartime period. The *City Directory* for each year, covering mostly the post-bellum years, lists residents, occupations, members of various business organizations, and gives useful prefatorial material. The Atlanta City Council Minute Books are not complete for the antebellum period, but the volumes of the postwar years clearly reveal Peters's role in setting Atlanta on the road to recovery after the Civil War. The Adair Plat Books, prepared by the city's premier real estate dealer to inform the public of lots for sale, contain maps of some of Peters's urban land. The Western and Atlantic Railroad Company Minute Books are the most valuable sources dealing with the first lease of the state's railroad; the Atlanta Historical Society's holdings cover the twenty-year period of the lease. Accordingly, Peters's association with the Western and Atlantic is well documented.

Records of Atlanta's first government—the commission appointed by the state legislature—are not extant and some confusion exists regarding the date of the naming of Atlanta. The date often given in secondary sources is 1847, but that was the year the legislature upgraded the town to city status and altered the form of government from commission to mayor-council. The correct date for the name change is 1845 as given in *Acts and Resolutions of the General Assembly of the State of Georgia*, compiled by William H. Hotchkiss (Savannah: J. M. Cooper, 1845).

The Fulton County Deed Books are retained in the Fulton County Courthouse. Fairly complete and indexed, they provide information on many of Peters's land holdings in Atlanta. The Fulton County Commissioners of Roads and Revenues Minute Books, covering the brief period when Peters was a commissioner, are located in the Fulton County Administration Building. The Georgia Department of Archives and History has some helpful material, especially the United States Census Reports, which give details concerning the size and value of Peters's plantation, as well as livestock on hand and crop production figures.

The Henry Woodfin Grady Papers, 1828-1971, Emory University Library, Atlanta, contain approximately 395 items. The main section of the collection consists of general correspondence—primarily letters from Grady to members of his immediate family. Other documents in the main collection include legal papers of the Grady family; manuscripts of Grady's speeches; news clippings; reprints of Grady's New South speech (reconstructed subsequent to the event since Grady spoke from a few scribbled notes); and miscellaneous material. The collection also contains twelve scrapbooks of news clippings relative to Grady's activities and writings as well as the manuscript of Raymond B. Nixon's biography *Henry W. Grady: Spokesman of the New South* (New York: Alfred A. Knopf, 1943). Nixon was the first to have access to Grady's private papers and his is the only full-length, documented account of the New South journalist's brilliant but tragically short life.

Newspapers are a major source that provide a chronicle of events on a daily basis and offer a valuable key for unlocking the secrets of Peters's life in the postbellum period. Atlanta newspapers of the antebellum period have been only sporadically preserved, but solid Atlanta newspaper coverage is available from the point that Peters's memoirs terminate. The first daily paper published in Atlanta was the *Daily Atlanta Intelligencer* (1851-1871), owned by Judge Jared I. Whitaker. The paper was industry-oriented and an important mouthpiece of the Democratic party in Georgia. When the bluejackets swarmed down from North Georgia in 1864, the headquarters staff of the *Intelligencer* fled to Macon and, to insure mobility, set up publication in a box car. It was the only Atlanta paper to survive the Civil War. Atlanta's other principal antebellum newspaper was the *Gate City Guardian* (1859-1864). Renamed the *Southern Confederacy* in 1861, the paper was "rabidly secessionist" under its "fire-eater" owner Dr. James B. Hambleton. The *New Era* (1865-1871) was the chief Republican organ during Reconstruction, especially after 1870 when its owner, Dr. Samuel Bard, abruptly sold it to a group of Radicals. The *Atlanta Constitution* (1868-present) was founded by Carey W. Styles to fight Republican rule during Reconstruction. (Styles had visited President Andrew Johnson in Washington and the president had suggested that *Constitution* would be an excellent name for a newspaper seeking to restore constitutional government in the South.) Although it had a Democratic orientation, Grady's influence caused it to become a strong supporter of the New South. In addition to the latest word on New South themes, Grady brought to the *Constitution* circulation-building devices such as an annual drawing for Christmas presents. In 1888 the paper had nearly 123,000 subscribers. Most of the newspapers used in this study can be found in the Atlanta Historical Society or in the Emory University Library.

The most comprehensive source for Peters's experiments in agriculture is the *Southern Cultivator*, an almost complete set of which is located in the Atlanta Public Library. Started in Augusta in 1843, the enduring monthly journal (most Southern journals ran less than three years) had 10,000 subscribers during the antebellum period. According to its editors, the *Southern Cultivator* was a "Practical and Scientific Journal, for the Plantation, the Garden and the Family Circle, and is devoted to the Improvement of Southern Agriculture, Horticulture, Vine Growing, Stock Breeding, Mechanical Inventions, and Household Economy." It was the only Southern farm journal to survive the war. In 1865, publication was moved to Athens, and after 1879, it was headquartered in Atlanta. The publishers often solved circulation problems by taking over rivals as well as becoming the voice of the Grange, Alliance, Young Farmers Club, Georgia Agricultural Society, or the State Department of Agriculture. When the politics of a group became a liability, the journal severed connections and concentrated on its role of disseminating agricultural information. Its progressive orientation appealed to Peters and he was identified with it as both an advertiser and a contributor—including reprints of articles that first appeared in periodicals such as the *Georgia Grange* and *County Gentleman*. In 1888, when the journal claimed 100,000 readers, he is listed among its "brilliant corps of writers." Peters was "gratified at the increasing and permanent popularity of our monthly," where he realized that the accounts of his agricultural experiments would live in history.

In addition to Peters's own writing, visitors to his plantation often published their own accounts. Henry Grady, for example, wrote several such pieces, the most useful of which is "Forty Years All Told Spent in Live Stock Experiments in Georgia." The story first appeared in the *Atlanta Constitution* (1883) and realized instant popularity. It was published in pamphlet form (Black Collection) and is numbered among the selections in the Peters genealogical volume.

Because the documentation on Peters is scattered, few writers have realized his important role in Southern history. Yet several historians have called for further inquiry into a number of categories that together suggest a biography of Peters is long overdue. Paul M. Gaston has pointed out in "The New South," *Writing Southern History: Essays in Historiography in Honor of Fletcher M. Green*, ed. Arthur S. Link and Rembert W. Patrick (Baton Rouge: Louisiana State University Press, 1965) that biographies of a few significant Southern figures have been published, but "important men still await biographies" (332). Harold D. Woodman, *King Cotton and His Retainers: Financing and Marketing the Cotton Crop of the South, 1800-1925* (Lexington: University of Kentucky Press, 1968), wrote that "emphasis on the continuity of institutions is a necessary corrective in an area which has been traditionally divided at the Civil War" and noted that further studies are needed to bridge the Civil War years (374). Sheldon Hackney agreed. In "Origins of the New South in Retrospect," *Journal of Southern History* 38:2 (May 1972), Hackney stated: "A comparison of the social origins and affiliations of the elites of the 1880s and the 1850s should tell us something about the transformation of the South in the era of the Civil War and lead us on to fruitful refinements of the question of continuity" (201-202). Blaine A. Brownell and David R. Goldfield in "Southern Urban History," *The City in Southern History: The Growth of Urban Civilization in the South*, ed. Brownell and Goldfield (Port Washington: Kennikat Press, 1977) maintained that the role of urban leadership is an especially significant area for investigation in the urban South (5). However, it was James C. Bonner in "Plantation and Farm," *Writing Southern History*, ed. Link and Patrick, who, in calling for more books on agricultural leaders, wrote specifically that there is a great need for a full-length biography of Richard Peters (172).

INDEX

B
Peters Shingleton, Royce.

CENTRAL LIBRARY

Shingleton, Royce.
    Richard Peters : champion of the new
South / Royce Shingleton. -- Macon, GA
: Mercer University Press, c1985.
    xiv, 258 p. : ill. ; 24 cm.
    Bibliography: p. [245]-249.
    Includes index.
    ISBN 0-86554-126-4 (alk. paper)

    1. Peters, Richard, 1810-1889.
2. Businessmen--Southern States--
Biography. 3. Politicians--Southern
States--Biography. 4. Southern States
--Economic conditions. I. Title

R00131 92337

GA   29 JAN 86   11344173   GAPAxc   84-22701